Workshop Manual

FOR

COMMANDO

MODELS 850 & 750: INTERSTATE
                            ROADSTER
                            HI RIDER
                            INTERPOL
                            FASTBACK
                            "SS"
                            'S' TYPE
                            FASTBACK L.R.

FROM 1970

NOTE: European Type 850 MK1A variations covered in separate supplement.

Part No. 065146

ACKNOWLEDGEMENT

We would like to take the opportunity to extend our appreciation to Norton Motorcycle Company for the publications included in this compilation. It is important to remember that the company was founded in 1898 and helped pave the way for the motorcycles we enjoy today. We are pleased to offer this reprint as a service to all Norton motorcycle owners and collectors worldwide, and we extend our thanks to the Norton Motorcycle Company for their contribution to the British motorcycle industry.

INTRODUCTION

Welcome to the world of digital publishing ~ the book you now hold in your hand was printed using the latest state of the art digital technology. The advent of print-on-demand has forever changed the publishing process, never has information been so accessible and it is our hope that this book serves your informational needs for years to come. If this is your first exposure to digital publishing, we hope that you are pleased with the results. Many more titles of interest to the classic automobile and motorcycle enthusiast, collector and restorer are available via our website at www.VelocePress.com. We hope that you find this title as interesting as we do.

NOTE FROM THE PUBLISHER

The information presented is true and complete to the best of our knowledge. All recommendations are made without any guarantees on the part of the author or the publisher, who also disclaim all liability incurred with the use of this information.

TRADEMARKS

We recognize that some words, model names and designations, for example, mentioned herein are the property of the trademark holder. We use them for identification purposes only. This is not an official publication.

INFORMATION ON THE USE OF THIS PUBLICATION

This manual is an invaluable resource for those interested in performing their own maintenance. However, in today's information age we are constantly subject to changes in common practice, new technology, availability of improved materials and increased awareness of chemical toxicity. As such, it is advised that the user consult with an experienced professional prior to undertaking any procedure described herein. While every care has been taken to ensure correctness of information, it is obviously not possible to guarantee complete freedom from errors or omissions or to accept liability arising from such errors or omissions. Therefore, any individual that uses the information contained within, or elects to perform or participate in do-it-yourself repairs or modifications acknowledges that there is a risk factor involved and that the publisher or its associates cannot be held responsible for personal injury or property damage resulting from the use of the information or the outcome of such procedures.

WARNING!

One final word of advice, this publication is intended to be used as a reference guide, and when in doubt the reader should consult with a qualified technician.

FOREWORD

The purpose of this manual is to provide the necessary technical instructions to enable distributor and dealer staff, and also enthusiastic private owners, to carry out all routine maintenance, running repairs and major overhaul operations.

Separate sections of the manual cover major areas and, where necessary, cross references are used to facilitate step by step dismantling and re-assembly. The manual is well provided with line illustrations for clarity and care has been taken to ensure that each illustration fulfils a useful purpose rather than merely increasing manual content.

Where special service tools are necessary, they are referred to by part number in the text. An illustrated service tools catalogue will be made available at a later stage. This catalogue will be separate for ease of up-dating, but will be suitably sized and pierced for inclusion with this binder.

For each year from 1971, the fully illustrated parts list and Rider's Manual are available and will further assist service operations.

To ensure repair to the same standards as used for a new Commando, it is essential to use only genuine Norton spares available through the normal spares supply system. The main distributors for the various markets of the world are given below:

EUROPE: Norton Villiers Europe Limited,
North Way,
Walworth, Andover,
Hampshire.
Telephone: Andover (0264) 61414

U.S.A. **West of Mississippi River:**
Norton Villiers Corporation,
6765 Paramount Boulevard,
North Long Beach,
California 90805.
Telephone: (213) 531-7138.

East of Mississippi River:
Berliner Motor Corporation,
Railroad Street and Plant Road,
Hasbrouck Heights,
New Jersey 07604.
Telephone: (201) 288-9696.

CANADA:	**Quebec, the Maritime Provinces and Central Western Canada:** Norton Villiers Canada Limited, 9001 Salley Street, La Salle, Province of Quebec. Telephone: (514) 363–7066.
	Ontario: Firth Motorcycle Limited, 1857-9 Danforth Avenue, Toronto, Ontario. Telephone: 465–1195.
	British Columbia: British Motorcycles Limited, 4250 Fraser Street, Vancouver 10, British Columbia. Telephone: 876–0520.
AUSTRALASIA, NEW ZEALAND, FAR EAST:	Norton Villiers Australia Pty. Ltd., 25 Moxon Road, Punchbowl, New South Wales, 2196. Telephone: Punchbowl 02–700731.
BRAZIL:	Silvimex, Importadorae Exportadora Ltda., Rua Voluntarios da Patria 69, Rio de Janeiro, G.B. Telephone: 266–5971.
SOUTH AFRICA:	Jack's Motors (Pty.) Ltd. 115 Main Street, Johannesburg. Telephone: Johannesburg 217.021.

CONTENTS

INDEX	OVERLEAF	Page 2
TECHNICAL DATA	SECTION A	Page 7
CONVERSION TABLES	SECTION B	Page 21
ENGINE/PRIMARY DRIVE	SECTION C	Page 29
GEARBOX	SECTION D	Page 69
CARBURETOR	SECTION E	Page 77
FRAME AND ANCILLARIES	SECTION F	Page 83
FORKS/STEERING HEAD BEARINGS	SECTION G	Page 107
BRAKES, WHEELS AND TYRES	SECTION H	Page 119
ELECTRICAL	SECTION J	Page 143
ROUTINE MAINTENANCE	SECTION K	Page 161

Each section is laid out generally in order of disassembly and assembly; however, use the following index to locate any particular subject.

ENGINE

Engine "Top End"

	Section
Removing Cylinder Head	C1
Servicing Cylinder Head	C2–C8, C10
Refitting Cylinder Head	C9
Removing Cylinder and Pistons	C11
Servicing Cylinder and Pistons	C12
Refitting Pistons and Cylinder	C33

Engine "Bottom End"

Removing Crankcase Assembly from Frame	C15
Dismantling the Crankcase	C16
Crankcase Overhaul	C17
Reassembly of Crankshaft to Crankcases	C29
Reassembly of Crankcase Assembly to Frame	C32
Removing Connecting Rods	C18
Refitting Connecting Rods	C28
Crankshaft Servicing	C19, C20, C27

Engine Accessory Systems

Lubrication	C21
Oil Pump	C24, C25
Servicing other Lubrication Components	C22, C23

Timing

Timing Cover	C26, C31
Assembly of Timing Side of Engine	C30
Tachometer	C36

Ignition (Also see "Electrical", Section J)

Ignition Timing	C38
Auto Advance and Contact Breaker	C39, C40

Engine Complete

Removing and Refitting Engine Complete	C37

PRIMARY TRANSMISSION

Removing Primary Chaincase	C13
Dismantling Primary Transmission and Clutch	C14
Assembling Primary Transmission	C34
Clutch Operating Assembly	C35
Chains	C41

GEARBOX

Description..	D1
Gearbox Dismantling	D2–D5
Inspection of Gearbox Parts	D6
Assembly of Gearbox	D9, D10, D12
Servicing Gearbox Outer Cover	D11
Changing Countershaft Sprocket	D8
Removing Gearbox from Motorcycle	D7

CARBURETOR AND AIR FILTER

Description..	E1
Removal and Disassembly of Carburetors	E2, E3
Examination and Reassembly	E4, E5
Carburetor Adjustment	E7, E9
Fuel Taps	E6
Air Filter	E10

FRAME

Removal and Refitting of Power Unit Complete	F1, F4
Frame Checking Dimensions	F3
Servicing Suspension Units (Shocks)	F5, F7
Servicing Swinging Arm..	F8
Removing and Replacing Fuel Tank	F9
Removing and Replacing Oil Tank	F10
Accessory and Side Covers	F11
Servicing Isolastic Mounting Assembly	F2, F12–F17
Rear Fender	F18
Exhaust Systems	F19

FORKS

Description..	G1, G2
Removing and Dismantling Forks	G3, G4
Servicing Steering Head Bearings	G6, G7
Refitting Front Forks	G8

BRAKES WHEELS AND TIRES

Removing and Dismantling Rear Wheel	H1, H3, H4
Reassembling and Refitting Rear Wheel	H2, H5
Servicing Disc Front Wheel	H6, H7
Servicing Drum Front Wheel	H8, H9
Rear Brake Adjustment	H11
Front Brake Adjustment (Drum Only)	H10
Drum Brake Overhaul	H12
Norton-Lockheed Disc Brake	H13
Tires	H14

ELECTRICAL

Description	J1
Charging System	J2
Alternator	J3
Rectifier	J4
Zener Diode	J5
Battery and Fuse	J6, J7
Warning Light and Assimilator	J8
Ignition Switch (Pre-1971)	J9
,, ,, (1971 and later Models)	J10
Coils, Capacitors (Condensers), Ballast Resistor	J11, J12, J13
Contact Breaker and Auto Advance	J12
Spark Plugs	J14
Lighting System	J15
Head and Tail Lamps	J16, J17, J18
Handlebar Switch Clusters	J19
Power Take-off Socket	J20
Flashing Direction Indicators	J21
Alternating Horn Set (Police)	J22
Horn Adjustment	J23
Electrolytic Capacitor	J24
Making a 1 Ohm Test Resistor	J25
Wiring Diagrams	J25

ROUTINE MAINTENANCE

Breaking in	K1
Routine Maintenance-Introduction	K2
Maintenance Table	K3
Engine, Gearbox and Primary Oil Service	K4–K9
Swing Arm Pivot Lubrication	K10
Front Fork Oil Changing	K11
Checking Hydraulic Brake Fluid Level	K12
Checking Battery Electrolyte Level	K13
Spark Plugs	K14
Tire Pressure	K15
Adjusting Cam Timing Chain	K16

GLOSSARY OF PART NAMES AND ALTERNATIVES

ENGINE

Gudgeon Pin	Piston pin. Small-end pin. Wrist pin.
Inlet Valve	Intake valve.
Piston Oil Control Ring	Piston scraper ring.
Induction Manifold	Inlet manifold. Intake manifold.
Oil Sump	Oil pan. Oil reservoir. Sump tray.
Muffler	Silencer. Expansion box.
Gasket	Joint. Sealing washer.
Engine	Motor.
Banjo Bolt	Pipe union bolt.
Crankcase Drain Plug	Sump plug.
Garter Type Seal	Spring pressure seal.
Mute	Sound deadener.
Oil Filter Gauze	Gauze strainer.

CLUTCH

Clutch Lining	Friction plate.
Primary Chaincase	Oil bath. Transmission case.
Clutch Operating Arm	Clutch thrust mechanism.
Clutch Sprocket	Clutch drum. Clutch housing.

GEARBOX

Gearbox	Transmission.
Gear Lever	Change speed lever. Gearshift lever.
Selector Fork	Change speed fork. Shift fork.
Countershaft	High sleeve gear. Output gear.
Countershaft Sprocket	Final drive sprocket. Gearbox sprocket.
Kickstarter	Starter pedal.

FRAME

Frame Rails	Frame tubes.
Oil Tank	Oil reservoir.
Battery Tray	Battery carrier.
Crankcase Shield	Sump shield. Skid plate. Bash plate. Rock guard.
Accessory Cover	L.H. side cover.
Grab Rail	Sissy bar. Passenger handhold.
Footrest	Footpeg.
Passenger Footrest	Pillion footrest. Buddy peg.
Prop. Stand	Side stand. Jiffy stand.
Frame	Chassis.
Swinging Arm	Swinging fork. Pivoting fork.
Suspension Unit	Rear shock absorber. Shock.

FORK

Front Fork	Telescopic fork. "Roadholder" fork. Front suspension.
Main Tube	Stanchion.
Fork Slider	Bottom member. Sliding member.

FUEL

Throttle Stop Adjuster Screw	Idle speed adjuster
Pilot Air Screw	Idling screw. Volume control screw. Idle mixture screw.
Pilot Jet	Slow running jet. Idling jet.
Fuel Line	Petrol pipe. Gas line.
Fuel Tap	Petrol tap. Gas cock. Pet cock.
Air Cleaner	Air filter. Air box. Air silencer.
Fuel Tank	Petrol tank. Gas tank.
Petrol	Gasoline.
Paraffin	Kerosene.

ELECTRICAL

A.C. Generator	Alternator.
Alternator	Rotor and stator.
Capacitor	Condenser.
Lens	Glass.
Direction Indicators	Flashing indicators. Turn signals. Flashers
Rear Lamp	Tail lamp. Stop/tail lamp.
Headlamp Rim	Headlamp bezel. Headlamp surround.
H.T. Lead	High tension lead. Plug lead.
Assimilator	Simulator, Actuator. Control unit.
Contact Breaker	Points. Breaker.

WHEELS AND BRAKES

Axle	Spindle.
Security Bolt	Tire lock.
Brake Expander	Brake cam.
Master Cylinder	Main cylinder. Reservoir.
Brake Lining	Brake facing.

INSTRUMENTS

Odometer	Mileage recorder.
Speedometer Gearbox	Speedometer drive box.
Tachometer	Rev. counter. Engine speed indicator.

Technical Data   A

Technical Data

Technical Data

SECTION A

TECHNICAL DATA

FRAME, ENGINE MOUNTINGS AND REAR SUSPENSION UNITS

Steering head bearing type: Double sealed ball (2 off single row sealed ball)
Front engine mounting:
    Spacer length: 2·573/2·553 in. (65·3/64·8 mm)
    Bonded bush thickness: $\frac{5}{8}$ in. tapering to 0·510 in. (15·87 mm tapering to 12·95 mm)
    Bonded bush quantity: 2
    Buffer thickness: $\frac{1}{2}$ in. (12·70 mm)
    Buffer outside diameter: $1\frac{11}{16}$ in. (42·8 mm)
    Buffer quantity: 2
    Bolt size: 7·13 in. $\frac{1}{2}$ in. x 20 UNF
    Ideal free play: 0·010 in. (·254 mm)
    Shim thicknesses available: ·005 in., ·010 in., ·020 in., ·030 in. (·127 mm, ·254 mm, ·508 mm, ·762 mm)

Rear engine mounting
    Spacer length: 1·560 in./1·550 in. (39·6/39·37 mm)
    Bonded bush thickness: $\frac{1}{2}$ in. tapering to 0·410 in. (12·70 mm tapering to 10·4 mm)
    Bonded bush quantity: 3
    Buffer thickness: $\frac{1}{2}$ in. (12·70 mm)
    Buffer outside diameter: $1\frac{5}{16}$ in. (33·3 mm)
    Buffer quantity: 2
    Stud thread size: $\frac{1}{2}$ in. x 20 UNF 2A
    Stud length: 13·00 in. (330·2 mm)
    Ideal free play: 0·010 in. (·254 mm)
    Shim thicknesses available: ·005 in., ·010 in., ·020 in., ·030 in. (·127 mm, ·254 mm, ·508 mm, ·762 mm)
    Bolt torque setting: 300 in./lb. (3·456 kg./mtr.)

Rear suspension units
    Type – Girling: Spring/oil damped
    Total length 13 inches between centres.
    Spring fitted length: 8·4 in. (213·36 mm)
    Spring colour code: Red/Yellow/Red (chrome spring)
    Spring rate: 126 lb. per inch
    Sping free length: 8·75 in. (222·25 mm)

SPEEDOMETER GEARING

Using Dunlop 4·10 in. x 19 in. rear tyre
    Rolling radius: 12·57 in. (319·3 mm)
    Revs./mile: 806
    Gearbox ratio: 15/12   1:1·25

Technical Data

WHEELS AND BRAKES

Front wheel
    Rim size: WM2 – 19
    Spokes – Drum brake wheel: Inside LH – 90° head. 8 SWG swaged, ·375 in. (9·5 mm) head
                                  Outside – 90° head. 8 SWG swaged, ·531 in. (13·45 mm) head
    Spokes – Disc brake wheel: Inner L.H. – 90° head 9 SWG ·270 (6·9 mm) head
                                  Outer L.H. – 90° head 9 SWG ·270 (6·9 mm) head (80°bend)
                                  Right hand – 90° head 8 SWG ·290 (7·35 mm) head
    Wheel bearing L.H.: 17 mm x 40 mm x 12 mm
    Wheel bearing R.H.: NM 17721
    Bearing housing I.D.: 1·5732 in./1·5740 in. (39·95 mm/39·97 mm)
    Spindle (bearing/dia.): 0·6675/0·6670 in. (18·554/18·542 mm)
    Tyre size: 4·10X19
    Tyre pressure: 26 lbs./psi (1·83 kg/sq. cm.). Refer "Tyre Pressures" section for permissible
        variation
    Tyre diameter (Dunlop): 26·46 in. (672 mm)
    Sectional width (Dunlop): 4 in. (101·6 mm)

Front brake (drum)
    Type: Internal expanding two leading shoe
    Drum dia.: 8 in. (203·2 mm)
    Lining area – total 2 Shoes: 18·69 sq. in./474·776 sq. mms

Front brake (disc)
    Type: Disc – hydraulically operated
    Pad type: Steel backed, moulded and bonded friction material
    Pad friction area diam.: 1·65 in. (41·9 mm)
    Pad new thickness (Pad and backing together): ·38/·37 in. (9·652/9·398 mm)
    Pad minimum thickness ·0625 in. (1·5875 mm)
    Disc diameter: 10·70 in. (271·7 mm)
    Disc width at friction area: 0·260/0·250 in. (6·604/6·35 mm)
    Brake fluid type: Lockheed series 329 Hydraulic Fluid for disc brakes.
            (Complies with U.S. Safety Standard 116).

Rear wheel
    Rim size: WM2 – 19
    Spokes: Rear outer: 6·093 in. long: 8/10 SWG: 90° head: offset length ·531 in. (13·45 mm
              Rear inner: 6·093 in. long: 8/10 SWG: 90° head: offset length ·375 in. (9·5 mm)
    Wheel bearings 1971 on: Ball journal 17 mm x 40 mm x 12 mm
    Sprocket bearing: NM.17721: post 1971
    Hub bearing housing I.D.: 1·5732/1·5740 in. (39·95 mm/39·97 mm)
    Tyre size: 4·10 x 19 in.
    Tyre pressure: 26 lbs/psi (1·83 kg/sq. cm.). Refer "Tyre Pressure" section for permissible
        variation
    Tyre diameter (Dunlop): 26·46 in. (672·084 mm)
    Tyre sectional width (Dunlop): 4 in. (101·6 mm)

Technical Data

Rear brake
    Internal drum dia.: 7·007/6·997 in. (177·8 mm)
    Lining area – total 2 Shoes: 13·6 sq. in./345·44 sq. mm.

Front forks
    Type: Telescopic, hydraulically damped, internal springs
    Main tube O.D.: 1·3590/1·3575 in. (34·29 mm/34·467 mm)
    Top bush fitted I.D.: 1·3595/1·3605 in. (34·53/34·48 mm)
    Bottom bush O.D.: 1·4980/1·4990 in. (38·05 mm/38·075 mm)
    Fork slider I.D.: 1·4995/1·5010 in. (38·087/38·125 mm)
    Spring – No. of coils: $75\frac{1}{2}$ approx.
        Free length: 18·687 in. (474·65 mm)
        Rate: 36·5 lb./in. Red paint marked
    Steering crown lug and stem
        Stem diam. at bearing areas: ·9840/·9836in. (24·97/24·96 mm)
        Pre 1971 – Head race adjuster nut size: 1·3125/1·3005 in. across flats (33·33/33·03 mm)
        Fork tube top nut hexagon size: 1·3125/1·3005 in. (33·33/33·03 mm)
        Head bearing spacer length: 5·06 in. (128·5 mm)
    Fork leg capacity: 150 cc (5 fl. oz.) each leg
    Total fork movement: 6 in. (15·24 cm)

ELECTRICAL
    System voltage: 12 volt – Positive earth
    Alternator type: RM 21
    Rectifier type: 2 DS 506
    Zener diode type: Z D 715
    Battery type: Norton Villiers 063244; Yuasa 12N9-4B; PUZ5A Lucas
    Battery rating: 10 AH at 10 hour rate
    Coil type: 17M6
    Ballast resistor type: 3 BR
    Contact breaker type: 6CA (10CA later models)
    Warning light assimilator type: 3 AW
    Fuse rating: 35 amp ($17\frac{1}{2}$ amp continuous rated)
    Direction indicator flasher unit type: 8 FL

    Bulbs:
        Headlight: Type 370 – 12 volt – 45/40 watt
        Tail light/stop light: Type 380 – 12 volt – 21/6 watt, transverse offset pin
        Parking light: Type 989 – 12 volt – 6 watt, coil, miniature bayonet cap
        Direction indicator lights: Type 382 - 12 volt - 21 watt
        Warning lights type: Type 281 – 12 volt – 2·0 watt, coil, sub-miniature

Technical Data

ENGINE

Specification:	750	850
Capacity:	745 cc (45 cu. in.)	828 cc (50·5 cu. in.)
Bore:	2·875 in. (73 mm)	3·030 in. (77 mm)
Stroke:	3·503 in. (89 mm)	3·503 in. (89 mm)
Max. Torque:	48 lb./ft. at 5000 r.p.m. (Standard)	56 lb./ft. at 5000 r.p.m.
	49 lb./ft. at 6000 r.p.m. (Combat)	
Compression Ratio:	9 : 1 (Standard)	$8\frac{1}{2}$: 1
	10 : 1 (Combat)	

Crankshaft
  Material: EN16
  Big end journal diameter: 1·7505/1·7500 in. (44·462/44·450 mm)
  Crankcheek bolts: EN 16 S
  Balance factor: 52% Dry
  Permissible end Float: 0·005–0·015 in. (·1270–·3810 mm)

	Pre 1972	1972 Onward
Main bearings:		
Drive side:	Single Lipped Roller	Special Roller (Single Lipped)
Timing side:	Single Row Ball	Special Roller (Single Lipped)

All 30 mm x 72 mm x 19 mm

Connecting rods
  Material: Aluminium alloy BS.L83 or 2L65 or L77
  Length between centres: 5·877/5·873 in. (149·275/147·535 mm)
  Big end eye I.D.: (Less shells cap bolted on) 1·8950/1·8955 in. (48·133/48·145 mm)
  Width at big end eye: 1·010/1·008 in. (25·65/25·60 mm)
  Rod side clearance: ·013 – ·016 (·330/·406 mm)
  Rod end clearance: Less than ·001 (·0254 mm)

Pistons
  Material: BS.1490 – LM..13WP
  Wrist pin boss I.D.: ·6869/·6867 in. (17·447/17·442 mm)
  Diameter – bottom of skirt: 2·8713/2·8703 in. (72·931/72·906 mm) (750) std. bore
    3·028/3·0271 in. (76·888/76·913 mm) (850) std. bore

Piston rings
  Type: Top chrome compression. Second compression.
    Taper. "S.E." oil control. Earlier models
  Top ring fitted gap: ·010 – ·012 in. (·254/·305 mm)
  Middle ring (taper) fitted gap: ·008 – ·012 in. (·203/·305 mm)

Wrist pins (Gudgeon pins)
  Length: 2·438/2·423 in. (61·925 mm/61·544 mm) 750
    2·559/2·544 in. (65 mm/64·619 mm) 850
  Diameter: 0·6869/0·6867 in. (17·447 mm/17·442 mm)

Technical Data

Cylinder block

    Material: Cast iron
    Finished size: Grade A 2·8746/2·8750 in. ⎫ 750   3·0315/3·0320 in. ⎫ 850
                   Grade B 2·8750/2·8754 in. ⎭   3·0320/3·0325 in. ⎭

Cylinder head	Standard	Combat
Material:	RR 53 B	RR 53 B
Valve seat angle:	45°	45°
Inlet port nominal dia.:	1⅛ in. (28·573 mm)	1⅛ in. – 1¼ in. (28·575 – 31·75 mm)
Ex. port nominal dia.:	1¼ in. (31·76 mm)	1¼ in. (31·75 mm)
Ex. ring thread size:	1·997 in. x 14 T.P.I.	1·997 in. x 14 T.P.I.

Camshaft	Standard	Combat
Material:	EN 32 B	EN 32 B
Maximum lift – inlet	0·332 in. (8·389 mm)	·390 in. (9·906 mm)
exhaust:	0·322 in. (8·389 mm)	·346 in. (8·788 mm)
Base circle dia.:	·885 in. (22·479 mm)	·906 in. (23·012 mm)
Bearing journal dia.:	·8735 in. (22·187 mm)	·8735 in. (22·187 mm)

Camshaft bushes	Pre 1972	1972 Onward
Fitted I.D. (Left bush):	·8750 in. (22·225 mm)	·8750 in. (22·225 mm)
Fitted I.D. (Right bush):	·8750 in. (22·225 mm)	·8750 in. (22·225 mm)

Tappets

    Material: Cast iron Grade 14 – stellite tipped

Push rods

    Material: Heat treated Dural tube "B" or "S"
    Inlet – assembled length: 8·166/8·130 in. (207·416/206·466 mm)
    Exhaust-assembled length: 7·321/7·285 in. (186·053/185·039 mm)

Rockers

    Material: EN33
    Rocker ratio – inlet: 1·13:1
    Rocker ratio – exhaust: 1·13:1
    Bore diameter: 0·4998/0·5003 in. (12·694/12·708 mm)
    Adjuster thread size: $\frac{9}{32}$ in. x 26 TPI. Whit Form

Technical Data

Rocker shaft

    Diameter: ·4988/·4985 in. (12·694/12·669 mm)

Valve (tappet) Clearances (engine cold)

    Inlet: ·006 in. (0·15 mm) (Commando 850 and 750); ·008 in. (0·2 mm) (Combat)

    Exhaust: ·008 in. (0,2 mm) (Commando, 850 and 750); 0·010 in. (0·25 mm) (Combat)

Valve Lift	Standard	Combat
	Inlet: ·375 in. (9·525 mm) Exhaust: ·375 in. (9·525 mm)	Inlet: ·441 in. (11·21 mm) Exhaust: ·391 in. (9·931 mm)

Valve duration: (excluding ramps)	Standard	Combat
	152°	164°

Valves

    Material: Inlet – EN52 – Chrome plated stem

             Ex. – KE965 – Chrome plated stem

    Inlet – head dia.: 1·490 in. (37·846 mm)

        stem dia. (plated area): 0·3115/0·3105 in. (7·912/7·886)

    Exhaust – head dia.: 1·302 in (33·0708 mm)

        stem dia.: 0·3115/0·3105 in. (7·912/7·886 mm)

Valve guides

    Inside dia.: 0·3145/0·3135 in. (7·988/7·962 mm)

    Outside dia.: 0·5015/0·50 in. (12·738/12·725 mm) 750

                 0·6265/0·6260 in. (15·90/15·88 mm) 850

    Heat resisting washer material: Tuffnol grade ASP

    Heat resisting washer thickness: 0·062 in. (1·574 mm)

	Std Inlet	Combat Inlet	Exhaust
Valve springs Inner – free length: 1·482 in. (37·642 mm) Fitted length	1·197 in. (30·40 mm)	1·259 in. (31·98 mm)	1·222 in. (31·04 mm)
Outer – free length: 1·618 in. (41·097 mm) Fitted length	1·259 in. (31·98 mm)	1·32 1in. (33·55 mm)	1·284 in. (32·61 mm)

Technical Data

A

Valve timing (measured at ·013 in. (·3302 mm) cam lift)

	Standard 750 and 850	Combat
Inlet opens BTDC	50°	59°
Inlet closes ABDC	74°	89°
Exhaust opens BBDC	82°	88°
Exhaust closes ATDC	42°	60°

Intermediate timing gear
    Bush material: Phosphor bronze
    Bush finished dia.: 0·5627/0·5620 in. (14·292/14·274 mm)

Intermediate gear shaft dia.: 0·5615/0·5610 in. (14·262/14 249 mm)

Camshaft chain
    Size: ·375 in. x ·225. Single row (Endless)
    No. of links: 38
    Ideal adjustment: $\frac{3}{16}$ in. (4·8 mm) up and down on top run of chain

Ignition timing
    Fully advanced position: 28° BTDC

Contact breaker
    Points gap: ·014/·016 in. (·35/·4 mm)
    Centre bolt thread size: $\frac{1}{4}$ in. x 26 T.P.I.

Spark plug
    Type: Champion N7Y (was N6Y)
    Gap: ·023/·028 in. (·59–·72 mm)

Carburetor Standard Commando 750
    Type: Twin concentric float Amal 930 30 mm

	1970	1971	1972
Main jet:	220 with early megaphone mufflers 180 with restricted megaphone 210 with modified megaphone	220	220 (210 with mute)
Needle jet:	·107	·106	·106
Needle position:	Middle	Middle	Middle (Top with mute)
Throttle valve:	3	3	3

Technical Data

Carburetor – Combat
    Type: Twin concentric float Amal 932 32 mm
    Main jet: 230 (220 with mute)
    Needle jet: ·106
    Needle position: Middle (Top with mute)
    Throttle valve: 3

Carburetor – 850
    Type: Twin concentric float Amal 932 32 mm
    Main jet: 260
    Needle jet: ·106
    Needle position: Top
    Throttle valve: $3\frac{1}{2}$
    Needle: 928/104
    Choke (spray) tube: 928/107

Air filter
    Element type: Pleated design impregnated paper

TORQUE SETTINGS
    Cylinder head nuts and bolts ($\frac{3}{8}$ in.): 360 in./lb. 30 ft./lb. (4·15 Kg/m)
    Cylinder head bolts ($\frac{5}{16}$ in.): 240 in./lb. 20 ft./lb. (2·75 Kg/m)
    Cylinder base nuts ($\frac{3}{8}$ in.): 300 in./lb. 25 ft./lb. (3·45 Kg/m)
    Cylinder base nuts ($\frac{5}{16}$ in.): 240 in./lb. 20 ft./lb. (2·75 Kg/m)
    Cylinder through bolt (850): 360 in./lb. 30 ft./lb. (4·15 Kg/m)
    Connecting rod nuts: 300 in./lb. 25 ft./lb. (3·45 Kg/m)
    Rocker spindle cover plate bolt: 100 in./lb. 8 ft./lb. (1·11 Kg/m)
    Crankshaft nuts: 300 in./lb. 25 ft./lb. (3·45 Kg/m)
    Cam chain tensioner nuts: 180 in./lb. 15 ft./lb. (2·07 Kg/m)
    Oil pump stud nuts: 180 in./lb. 15 ft./lb. (2·07 Kg/m)
    Rocker feed banjo bolts: 180 in./lb. 15 ft./lb. (2·07 Kg/m)
    Engine mount bolts: 300 in./lb. 25 ft./lb. (3·45 Kg/m)
    Rotor nut: 960 in./lb. 80 ft./lb. (11·06 Kg/m)
    Alternator stud nuts: 180 in./lb. 15 ft./lg. (2·07 Kg/m)
    Clutch-to-mainshaft nut: 840 in./lb. 70 ft./lb. (9·68 Kg/m)
    Mainshaft nut: 480 in./lb. 40/50 ft./lb. (5·50 Kg/m)
    Countershaft sprocket nut: 960 in./lb. 80 ft./lb. (11·06 Kg/m)
    Gearbox inner cover nuts: 144 in./lb. 12 ft./lb. (1·66 Kg/m)
    Top gearbox fixing bolts: 660 in./lb. 55 ft./lb. (7·60 Kg/m)
    Rear suspension unit nuts: 360 in./lb. 30 ft./lb. (4·15 Kg/m)
    Main isolastic unit bolts: 300 in./lb. 25 ft./lb. (3·45 Kg/m)
    Fork tube top chrome nuts: 360 in./lb. 30 ft./lb. (4·15 Kg/m)
    Fork tube lower yoke pinch bolts: 360 in./lb. 30 ft./lb. (4·15 Kg/m)
    Steering head main nut (1971 – later): 360 in./lb. 30 ft./lb. (4·15 Kg/m)
    Disc brake caliper-to-fork leg bolts: 360 in./lb. 30 ft./lb. (4·15 Kg/m)
    Disc brake caliper end plug: 312 in./lb. 26 ft./lb. (3·60 Kg/m)
    Discs-to-hub nuts: 240 in./lb. 20 ft./lb. (2·75 Kg/m)
    Drum brake cam fixing nuts: 360 in./lb. 30 ft./lb. (4·15 Kg/m)
    Sidestand nut (1972 – later): 600 in./lb. 50 ft./lb. (6·91 Kg/m)
    Zener diode nut: 24 in./lb. 2 ft./lb. (·28 Kg/m)
    Coil mounting bracket nuts: 10 in./lb. 1 ft./lb. (·14 Kg/m)
    Oil-pressure release valve: 300 in./lb. 25 ft./lb. (3·75 Kg/m)

Technical Data

GEARBOX

Ball journal bearings:
    Mainshaft (Clutch end) Ball journal $1\frac{1}{4}$ in. x $2\frac{1}{2}$ in. x $\frac{5}{8}$ in.
    Mainshaft (K/S end): Ball journal $\frac{5}{8}$ in. x $1\frac{9}{16}$ x $\frac{7}{16}$ in.
    Layshaft (Clutch end): Ball journal 17 mm x 40 mm x 12 mm

Reductions
    4th (HIGH) : 1 :1
    3rd : 1·21 :1
    2nd : 1·70 :1
    1st (LOW) : 2·56 :1

Theoretical road speeds using various countershaft (gearbox) sprockets
  Table assumes standard sprockets: Engine 26T
                                Clutch 57T
                                Rear 42T

	Sprocket Teeth	19	20	21	22	23
	Overall Gear Ratio	4·84	4·60	4·38	4·18	3·99
Engine RPM	6000	92	97	102	106	112
	6500	99	105	110	115	121
	7000	107	113	119	124	130

Overall Ratios

	With 19T Gearbox Sprocket	With 21T Gearbox Sprocket	With 22T Gearbox Sprocket
4th (HIGH) :	4·84 : 1	4·38 : 1	4·18 : 1
3rd :	5·90 : 1	5·30 : 1	5·10 : 1
2nd :	8·25 : 1	7·45 : 1	6·84 : 1
1st (Low) :	12·40 : 1	11·20 : 1	10·71 : 1

No. of teeth on pinions
    Layshaft: 4th 14t
    Layshaft: 3rd 20t
    Layshaft: 2nd 24t
    Layshaft: 1st 28t
    Mainshaft: 4th 23t
    Mainshaft: 3rd 21t
    Mainshaft: 2nd 18t
    Mainshaft: 1st 14t

Technical Data

Gearbox
    High gear bush O.D.: 0·9060/0·9053 in. (23·012/22·995 mm)
    High gear bush I.D.: 0·8145/0·8140 in. (20·688/20·675 mm)
    High gear bush fitted I.D.: 0·8133/·8120 in. (20·657/20·625 mm)
    Layshaft bush I.D.: 1·126 in./1·124 in. (28·60/28·549 mm)
    Mainshaft second gear bush fitted I.D.: 0·8125/0·8115 in. (20·637/20·608 mm)
    Layshaft third gear bush fitted I.D.: 0·8125/0·81 in. (20·637/20·57 mm)
    Layshaft first gear bush fitted I.D.: 0·6885/0·6875 in. (17·488/17·462 mm)
    Footchange spindle bush, K/S case fitted I.D.: 0·6290/0·6285 in. (15·976/15·964 mm)
    Camplate/Quadrant bush fitted I.D.: 0·5005/0·4995 in. (12·713/12·687 mm)
    K/S spindle bush fitted I.D.: 0·675/0·673 in. (17·145/17·094 mm)
    Gearbox sprocket: 19T or 21T Standard (Alternative sprockets available – see table above)

Camplate plunger spring
    Free length: 1·500 in. (38·1 mm)
    Spring rate: 21 lbs./in.

Selector spindle diameter: 0·3740/0·3735 in. (9·499/9·486 mm)
    Selector fork bore: 0·3755/0·3745 in. (8·537/9·525 mm)

Primary Transmission and Rear Chain
    Engine sprocket no. of teeth: 26
    Primary chain details 92 pitches: ·375 in. x ·250 in. Triple row
    Rear chain details: 99 pitches: 0·400 in. x 0·380 in. simple type
    Clutch chainwheel no. of teeth: 57
    Clutch pushrod – length: 9·813/9·803 in. (249·250/248·996 mm)
    Clutch pushrod – diameter: 0·237/0·232 in. (5·984/5·857 mm)
    Clutch operating ball diameter: $\frac{1}{2}$ in. (12·70 mm)
    Clutch operating body lock ring thread size: $1\frac{5}{8}$ in. x 20 TPI
    Clutch type: Multi plate, diaphragm spring
    Clutch friction plate no. off: 4 – fibre clutch; 5 – metal clutch
    Clutch friction plate thickness: ·148/·142 in. (3·759/3·607 mm)
    Clutch friction plate material: DON 112, fibre clutch – sintered bronze, metal clutch
    Clutch centre bearing specification: Deep grove ball bearing – one dot
                                              OD 62 mm, ID 35 mm, Width 14 mm
                                              Corner rad 1·5 mm
    Clutch adjuster dia. and thread: $\frac{1}{2}$ in. x 20 UNF 2A
    Clutch adjuster length: 0·904 in. x 0·894 in. (22·962/22·708 mm)

CAPACITIES

    Fastback fuel tank capacity: $3\frac{1}{4}$ Imp. galls (15 litres)
    L.R. Fastback fuel tank capacity: 4 galls. (18 litres)
    Roadster fuel tank capacity: GRP $2\frac{1}{4}$ Imp. galls (10 litres): Steel $2\frac{1}{2}$ Imp. galls (11 litres)
    S.S. Hi-rider fuel tank capacity: 2 Imp. galls (9 litres)
    Interstate fuel tank capacity: GRP $5\frac{1}{4}$ Imp. galls. (24 litres): Steel $5\frac{1}{2}$ Imp galls. (25 litres)
    Interpol fuel tank capacity: No radio: 4 Imp. galls. (18 litres)
                                Radio insert: $3\frac{1}{2}$ Imp. galls. (16 litres)
    Oil tank: 5 Imp./6 U.S. pints, 2·8 litres
    Gearbox: 0·75 Imp./0·9 U.S. pints, 0·42 litres
    Front forks: 150 cc (5 fl. oz.) each leg
    Primary chaincase: 200 cc (7 fl. oz.)

Technical Data

MISCELLANEOUS DATA

Height: Fastback etc. – 40·75 (103·5 cm)

       Hi-Rider only – 50¼ in. (127·6 cm)

Length: 87·5 in. (222 cm)

Wheelbase: 56·75 in. (144 cm)

Total weight (with oil and 1 gal. fuel):

    Roadster 422 lb. (191·440 Kg)   (Dry): 395·4 lb. (179·3 Kg)

    Interstate 436 lb. (197·749 Kg)   (Dry): 410 lb. (186·1 Kg)

Weight on front tyre (dry): 179·7 lb. (84·37 Kg).({Weights for Roadster and Interstate model similar

Weight on rear tyre (dry): 215·7 lb. (97·5 Kg)

(For motorcycle equipped with 4·10 in. x 19 in. tyres front and rear)

Ground clearance: 6 in. (15 cm)

Width: 26 in. (66 cm)

Front brake drum diameter: 7·95 in. (20·32 cm)

Rear brake drum diameter: 7 in. (17·78 cm)

Total braking area (front): 18·69 sq. in. (120 sq. cm.)

Total braking area (rear): 13·60 sq. in. (88 sq. cm.) drum brake

Overall length of exhaust system (from flange at exhaust port end of pipe to tip of muffler: 60 in. (152·4 cm)

Exhaust system maximum diameter: 3·5 in. (8·92 cm)

Maximum theoretical road speed: 112·6 m.p.h. (181·111 K.p.h.) Standard 750 engine
                122 m.p.h. (196·336 K.p.h.) 850 engine

Road speed at 1000 r.p.m. in gears (19t sprocket)

    Bottom: 6·28 m.p.h. (10·106 K.p.h.)

    Second: 9·46 m.p.h. (15·220 Kph)

    Third: 13·18 m.p.h. (21·211 Kph)

    Top: 16·09 m.p.h. (25·894 Kph)

Total movement of front forks: 6 in. (15·2 cm)

Turning circle (full circle): 17 ft. 10 in. (518·16 cm)

Gross vehicle rating: 859 lb. (389·6 Kg)

Centre of gravity: 19¾ in. (501·65 mm) above ground unladen

Seat height (nominal): 33 – 34 in. (838·2 – 863·6 mm) dependent on model

Technical Data

SPECIAL WORKSHOP TOOLS

060941   Engine sprocket (clutch hub and cam sprocket) puller

060949   Auto advance unit lock washer (for static timing)

060999   Clutch diaphragm spring tool

061015   Clutch lock tool (locks clutch body with plates removed)

064298   Rocker spindle and auto advance slide hammer

ET2003   Crankshaft timing pinion extractor

063964   Valve guide screw-type extractor and inserter

063965   Peg spanner (wrench) for wheel bearings and disc caliper

064292   Contact breaker seal and crankshaft-to-timing cover seal drift set

063968   Exhaust lockring "C" spanner

063969   Valve seat cutting tool complete

063970   Roller bearing race extractor

063971   Front Isolastic bush insertion tool complete

060942   Steering head adjustment spanner (Pre 1971)

061359   Contact breaker oil seal guide

NM12093 $\frac{7}{8}$ in. box spanner

064622   Strap wrench

Note: A separate illustrated tool list will be available shortly.

NOTES

Conversion Tables   B

Conversion Tables

Conversion Tables B

THREADS

U.N.E.F.

Dia.	No of thds.
1/4 in.	32
5/16 in.	32
3/8 in.	32
7/16 in.	28
1/2 in.	28
9/16 in.	24
5/8 in.	24
11/16 in.	24
3/4 in.	20
13/16 in.	20
7/8 in.	20
15/16 in.	20
1 in.	20
1-1/16 in.	18
1-1/8 in.	18
1-3/16 in.	18
1-1/4 in.	18
1-5/16 in.	18
1-3/8 in.	18
1-7/16 in.	18
1-1/2 in.	18
1-9/16 ins.	18
1-5/8 in.	18
1-11/16 in.	18

U.N.F.

Dia.	No. of thds.
1/4 in.	28
5/16 in.	24
3/8 in.	24
7/16 in.	20
1/2 in.	20
9/16 in.	18
5/8 in.	18
3/4 in.	16
7/8 in.	14
1 in.	12
1-1/8 in.	12
1-1/4 in.	12
1-3/8 in.	12
1-1/2 in.	12

U.N.C.

Dia.	No. of thds.
1/4 in.	20
5/16 in.	18
3/8 in.	16
7/16 in.	14
1/2 in.	13
9/16 in.	12
5/8 in.	11
3/4 in.	10
7/8 in.	9
1 in.	8
1-1/8 in.	7
1-1/4 in.	7
1-3/3 in.	6
1-1/2 in.	6
1-3/4 in.	5
2 in.	4-1/2

B.A.

No.	Dia. of bolt	Thds. per inch
0	·2362	25·4
1	·2087	28·2
2	·1850	31·4
3	·1614	34·8
4	·1417	38·5
5	·1260	43·0
6	·1102	47·9
7	·0984	52·9
8	·0866	59·1
9	·0748	65·1
10	·0669	72·6
11	·0591	81·9
12	·0511	90·9
13	·0472	102·0
14	·0394	109·9
15	·0354	120·5
16	·0311	133·3

B.S.W.

Dia. of bolt (inch)	Threads per inch
1/4	20
5/16	18
3/8	16
7/16	14
1/2	12
9/16	12
5/8	11
11/16	11
3/4	10
13/16	10
7/8	9
15/16	9
1	8

B.S.F.

Dia. of bolt (inch)	Threads per inch
7/32	28
1/4	26
9/32	26
5/16	22
3/8	20
7/16	18
1/2	16
9/16	16
5/8	14
11/16	14
3/4	12
13/16	12
7/8	11
1	10
1-1/8	9
1-1/4	9
1-3/8	8
1-1/2	8
1-5/8	8

Conversion Tables   B

WIRE GAUGES

No. of Gauge	Imperial Standard Wire Gauge	
	Inches	Millimetres
1	·300	7·620
2	·276	7·010
3	·252	6·400
4	·232	5·892
5	·212	5·384
6	·192	4·676
7	·176	4·470
8	·160	4·064
9	·144	3·657
10	·128	3·251
11	·116	2·946
12	·104	2·641
13	·092	2·336
14	·080	2·032
15	·072	1·828
16	·064	1·625
17	·056	1·422
18	·048	1·219
19	·040	1·016
20	·036	·914
21	·032	·812
22	·028	·711
23	·024	·609
24	·022	·558
25	·020	·508
26	·018	·457
27	·0164	·416
28	·0148	·375
29	·0136	·345
30	·0124	·314

No. of Gauge	Brown and Sharpe's American Wire Gauge	
	Inches	Millimetres
1	·289	7·348
2	·258	6·543
3	·229	5·827
4	·204	5·189
5	·182	4·621
6	·162	4·115
7	·144	3·664
8	·128	3·263
9	·114	2·906
10	·102	2·588
11	·091	2·304
12	·081	2·052
13	·072	1·827
14	·064	1·627
15	·057	1·449
16	·051	1·290
17	·045	1·149
18	·040	1·009
19	·035	·911
20	·032	·811
21	·028	·722
22	·025	·643
23	·023	·573
24	·020	·511
25	·018	·454
26	·016	·404
27	·014	·360
28	·012	·321
29	·011	·235
30	·010	·254

DRILL SIZES (INCHES)

Number	Size	Number	Size	Letter	Size
1	·2280	27	·1440	A	·234
2	·2210	28	·1405	B	·238
3	·2130	29	·1360	C	·242
4	·2090	30	·1285	D	·246
5	·2055	31	·1200	E	·250
6	·2040	32	·1160	F	·257
7	·2010	33	·1130	G	·261
8	·1990	34	·1110	H	·266
9	·1960	35	·1100	I	·272
10	·1935	36	·1065	J	·277
11	·1910	37	·1040	K	·281
12	·1890	38	·1015	L	·290
13	·1850	39	·0995	M	·295
14	·1820	40	·0980	N	·302
15	·1800	41	·0960	O	·316
16	·1770	42	·0935	P	·323
17	·1730	43	·0890	Q	·332
18	·1695	44	·0860	R	·339
19	·1660	45	·0820	S	·348
20	·1610	46	·0810	T	·358
21	·1590	47	·0785	U	·368
22	·1570	48	·0760	V	·377
23	·1540	49	·0730	W	·386
24	·1520	50	·0700	X	·397
25	·1495	51	·0670	Y	·404
26	·1470	52	·0635	Z	·413

Conversion Tables   B

PINTS (IMPERIAL) TO LITRES

	0	1	2	3	4	5	6	7	8
	—	·568	1·136	1·705	2·273	2·841	3·841	3·978	4·546
¼	·142	·710	1·279	1·846	2·415	2·983	3·552	4·120	4·688
½	·284	·852	1·420	1·989	2·557	3·125	3·125	4·262	4·830
¾	·426	·994	1·563	2·131	2·699	3·267	3·836	4·404	4·972

GALLONS (IMPERIAL) TO LITRES

	0	1	2	3	4	5	6	7	8	9	
—		4·546	9·092	13·638	18·184	22·730	27·276	31·822	36·368	40·914	—
10	45·460	50·005	54·551	59·097	63·643	63·189	72·735	77·281	81·827	86·373	10
20	90·919	95·465	100·011	104·557	109·103	113·649	118·195	122·741	127·287	131·833	20
30	136·379	140·924	145·470	150·016	154·562	159·108	163·645	168·200	172·746	177·292	30
40	181·838	186·384	190·930	195·476	200·022	204·568	209·114	213·660	218·206	222·752	40
50	227·298	231·843	236·389	240·935	245·481	250·027	254·473	259·119	263·605	268·211	50
60	272·757	277·303	281·849	286·395	290·941	295·487	300·033	304·579	309·125	313·671	60
70	318·217	322·762	327·308	331·854	336·400	340·946	345·492	350·038	354·584	359·130	70
80	363·676	368·222	372·768	377·314	381·860	386·406	390·952	395·498	400·044	404·590	80
90	409·136	413·681	418·227	422·773	427·319	431·865	436·411	440·957	445·503	450·049	90

MILES TO KILOMETRES

	0	1	2	3	4	5	6	7	8	9	
—		1·609	3·219	4·828	6·437	8·047	9·656	11·265	12·875	14·484	—
10	16·093	17·703	19·312	20·922	22·531	24·140	25·750	27·359	28·968	30·578	10
20	32·187	33·796	35·406	37·015	38·624	40·234	41·843	43·452	45·062	46·671	20
30	48·280	49·890	51·499	53·108	54·718	56·327	57·936	59·546	61·155	62·765	30
40	64·374	65·983	67·593	69·202	70·811	72·421	74·030	75·639	77·249	78·858	40
50	80·467	82·077	83·686	85·295	86·905	88·514	90·123	91·733	93·342	94·951	50
60	96·561	98·170	99·780	101·389	102·998	104·608	106·217	107·826	109·436	111·045	60
70	112·654	114·264	115·873	117·482	119·092	120·701	122·310	123·920	125·529	127·138	70
80	128·748	130·357	131·967	133·576	135·185	136·795	138·404	140·013	141·623	143·232	80
90	144·841	146·451	148·060	149·669	151·279	152·888	154·497	156·107	157·716	159·325	90

MILES PER GALLON (IMPERIAL) TO LITRES PER 100 KILOMETRES

10	28·25	15	18·83	20	14·12	25	11·30	30	9·42	35	8·07	40	7·06	50	5·65	60	4·71	70	4·04
10½	26·90	15½	18·22	20½	13·78	25½	11·08	30½	9·26	35½	7·96	41	6·89	51	5·54	61	4·63	71	3·98
11	25·68	16	17·66	21	13·45	26	10·87	31	9·11	36	7·85	42	6·73	52	5·43	62	4·55	72	3·92
11½	24·56	16½	17·12	21½	13·14	26½	10·66	31½	8·97	36½	7·74	43	6·57	53	5·33	63	4·48	73	3·87
12	23·54	17	16·61	22	12·84	27	10·46	32	8·83	37	7·63	44	6·42	54	5·23	64	4·41	74	3·82
12½	22·60	17½	16·14	22½	12·55	27½	10·27	32½	8·69	37½	7·53	45	6·28	55	5·13	65	4·35	75	3·77
13	21·73	18	15·69	23	12·28	28	10·09	33	8·56	38	7·43	46	6·14	56	5·04	66	4·28	76	3·72
13½	20·92	18½	15·27	23½	12·02	28½	9·91	33½	8·43	38½	7·34	47	6·01	57	4·96	67	4·22	77	3·67
14	20·18	19	14·87	24	11·77	29	9·74	34	8·31	39	7·24	48	5·89	58	4·87	68	4·16	78	3·62
14½	19·48	19½	14·49	24½	11·53	29½	9·58	34½	8·19	39½	7·15	49	5·77	59	4·79	69	4·10	79	3·57

Conversion Tables

POUNDS PER SQUARE INCH TO KILOGRAMS PER SQUARE CENTIMETRE

	0	1	2	3	4	5	6	7	8	9	
—		0·070	0·141	0·211	0·281	0·352	0·422	0·492	0·562	0·633	—
10	0·703	0·773	0·844	0·914	0·984	1·055	1·125	1·195	1·266	1·336	10
20	1·406	1·476	1·547	1·617	1·687	1·758	1·828	1·898	1·969	2·039	20
30	2·109	2·179	2·250	2·320	2·390	2·461	2·531	2·601	2·672	2·742	30
40	2·812	2·883	2·953	3·023	3·093	3·164	3·234	3·304	3·375	3·445	40
50	3·515	3·586	3·656	3·726	3·797	3·867	3·937	4·007	4·078	4·148	50
60	4·218	4·289	4·359	4·429	4·500	4·570	4·640	4·711	4·781	4·851	60
70	4·921	4·992	5·062	5·132	5·203	5·273	5·343	5·414	5·484	5·554	70
80	5·624	5·695	5·765	5·835	5·906	5·976	6·046	6·117	6·187	6·257	80
90	6·328	6·398	6·468	6·538	6·609	6·679	6·749	6·820	6·890	6·960	90

POUNDS TO KILOGRAMS

	0	1	2	3	4	5	6	7	8	9	
—		0·454	0·907	1·361	1·814	2·268	2·722	3·175	3·629	4·082	—
10	4·536	4·990	5·443	5·987	6·350	6·804	7·257	7·711	8·165	8·618	10
20	9·072	9·525	9·079	10·433	10·886	11·340	11·793	12·247	12·701	13·154	20
30	13·608	14·061	14·515	14·968	15·422	15·876	16·329	16·783	17·237	17·690	30
40	18·144	18·597	19·051	19·504	19·953	20·412	20·865	21·319	21·772	22·226	40
50	22·680	23·133	23·587	24·040	24·494	24·948	25·401	25·855	26·308	26·762	50
60	27·216	27·669	28·123	28·576	29·030	29·484	29·937	30·391	30·844	31·298	60
70	31·751	32·205	32·659	33·112	33·566	34·019	34·473	34·927	35·380	35·834	70
80	36·287	36·741	37·195	37·648	38·102	38·855	39·009	39·463	39·916	40·370	80
90	40·823	41·277	41·731	42·184	42·638	43·091	43·545	43·998	44·452	44·906	90

FOOT POUNDS TO KILOGRAMETRES

	0	1	2	3	4	5	6	7	8	9	
—		0·138	0·277	0·415	0·553	0·691	0·830	0·968	1·106	1·244	—
10	1·383	1·521	1·659	1·797	1·936	2·074	2·212	2·350	2·489	2·627	10
20	2·765	2·903	3·042	3·180	3·318	3·456	3·595	3·733	3·871	4·009	20
30	4·148	4·286	4·424	4·562	4·701	4·839	4·977	5·116	5·254	5·392	30
40	5·530	5·668	5·807	5·945	6·083	6·221	6·360	6·498	6·636	6·774	40
50	6·913	7·051	7·189	7·328	7·466	7·604	7·742	7·881	8·019	8·157	50
60	8·295	8·434	8·572	8·710	8·848	8·987	9·125	9·263	9·401	9·540	60
70	9·678	9·816	9·954	10·093	10·231	10·369	10·507	10·646	10·784	10·922	70
80	11·060	11·199	11·337	11·475	11·613	11·752	11·890	12·028	12·166	12·305	80
90	12·443	12·581	12·719	12·858	12·996	13·134	13·272	13·411	13·549	13·687	90

Conversion Tables   B

MILLIMETRES TO INCHES

mm.	0	10	20	30	40	50	60	70	80	90
0		·39370	·78740	1·18110	1·57480	1·96851	2·36221	2·75591	3·14961	3·5433
1	·03937	·43307	·82677	1·22047	1·61417	2·00788	2·40158	2·79528	3·18891	3·5826
2	·07874	·47244	·86614	1·25984	1·65354	2·04725	2·44095	2·83465	3·22835	3·6220
3	·11811	·51181	·90551	1·29921	1·69291	2·08662	2·48032	2·87402	3·26772	3·6614
4	·15748	·55118	·94488	1·33858	1·73228	2·12599	2·51969	2·91339	3·30709	3·7007
5	·19685	·59055	·98425	1·37795	1·77165	2·16536	2·55906	2·95276	3·34646	3·7401
6	·23622	·62992	1·02362	1·41732	1·81103	2·20473	2·59843	2·99213	3·38583	3·7795
7	·27559	·66929	1·06299	1·45669	1·85040	2·24410	2·63780	3·03150	3·42520	3·8189
8	·31496	·70866	1·10236	1·49606	1·88977	2·28347	2·67717	3·07087	3·46457	3·8582
9	·35433	·74803	1·14173	1·53543	1·92914	2·32284	2·71654	3·11024	3·50394	3·8976

MILLIMETRES TO INCHES (DECIMALS OF)

1/1000	
mm.	inches
0·001	·000039
0·002	·000079
0·003	·000118
0·004	·000157
0·005	·000197
0·006	·000236
0·007	·000276
0·008	·000315
0·009	·000354

1/100	
mm.	inches
0·01	·00039
0·02	·00079
0·03	·00118
0·04	·00157
0·05	·00197
0·06	·00236
0·07	·00276
0·08	·00315
0·09	·00354

1/10	
mm.	inches
0·1	·00394
0·2	·00787
0·3	·01181
0·4	·01575
0·5	·01969
0·6	·02362
0·7	·02756
0·8	·03150
0·9	·03543

INCHES TO MILLIMETRES (DECIMALS OF)

Inches	0	10	20	30	40
0		254·0	508·0	762·0	1016·0
1	25·4	279·4	533·4	787·4	1041·4
2	50·8	304·8	558·8	812·8	1066·8
3	76·2	330·2	584·2	838·2	1092·2
4	101·6	355·6	609·6	863·6	1117·6
5	127·0	381·0	635·0	889·0	1143·0
6	152·4	406·4	660·4	914·4	1168·4
7	177·3	431·8	685·8	939·8	1193·8
8	203·2	457·2	711·2	965·2	1219·2
9	228·6	482·6	736·6	990·6	1244·6

1/1000	
inches	mm.
·001	·0254
·002	·0508
·003	·0762
·004	·1016
·005	·1270
·006	·1524
·007	·1778
·008	·2032
·009	·2286

1/100	
inches	mm.
·01	·254
·02	·508
·03	·762
·04	1·016
·05	1·270
·06	1·524
·07	1·778
·08	2·032
·09	2·286

1/10	
inches	mm.
·1	2·54
·2	5·08
·3	7·62
·4	10·16
·5	12·70
·6	15·24
·7	17·79
·8	20·32
·9	22·86

FRACTIONS TO DECIMALS — DECIMALS OF INCH TO MILLIMETRE

Fractions			Decimals	mm.
		1/64	·015625	·3969
	1/32		·03125	·7937
		3/64	·046875	1·1906
1/16			·0625	1·5875
		5/64	·078125	1·9844
	3/32		·09375	2·3812
		7/64	·109375	2·7781
1/8			·125	3·1750
		9/64	·140625	3·5719
	5/32		·15625	3·9687
		11/64	·171875	4·3656
3/16			·1875	4·7625
		13/64	·203125	5·1594
	7/32		·21875	5·5562
		15/64	·234375	5·9531
1/4			·25	6·3500
		17/64	·265625	6·7469
	9/32		·28125	7·1437
		19/64	·296875	7·5406
5/16			·3125	7·9375
		21/64	·328125	8·3344
	11/32		·34375	8·7312
		23/64	·359375	9·1281
3/8			·375	9·5250
		25/64	·390625	9·9219
	13/32		·40625	10·3187
		27/64	·421875	10·7156
7/16			·4375	11·1125
		29/64	·453125	11·5094
	15/32		·46875	11·9062
		31/64	·484375	12·3031
1/2			·5	12·700

Fractions			Decimals	mm.
		33/64	·515625	13·0969
	17/32		·53125	13·4937
		35/64	·546675	13·8906
9/16			·5625	14·2875
		37/64	·578125	14·6844
	19/32		·59375	15·0812
		39/64	·609375	15·4781
5/8			·625	15·875
		41/64	·640625	16·2719
	21/32		·65685	16·6687
		43/64	·671875	17·0656
11/16			·6375	17·4625
		45/64	·703125	17·8594
	23/32		·71875	18·2562
		47/64	·734375	18·6531
3/4			·75	19·05
		49/64	·765625	19·4469
	25/32		·78125	19·8437
		51/64	·796875	20·2406
13/16			·8125	20·6375
		53/64	·828125	21·0344
	27/32		·84375	21·4312
		55/64	·859375	21·8281
7/8			·875	22·225
		57/64	·890625	22·6219
	29/32		·90625	23·0187
		59/64	·921875	23·4156
15/16			·9375	23·8125
		61/64	·953125	24·2094
	31/32		·96875	24·6062
		63/64	·984375	25·0031
1				25·4

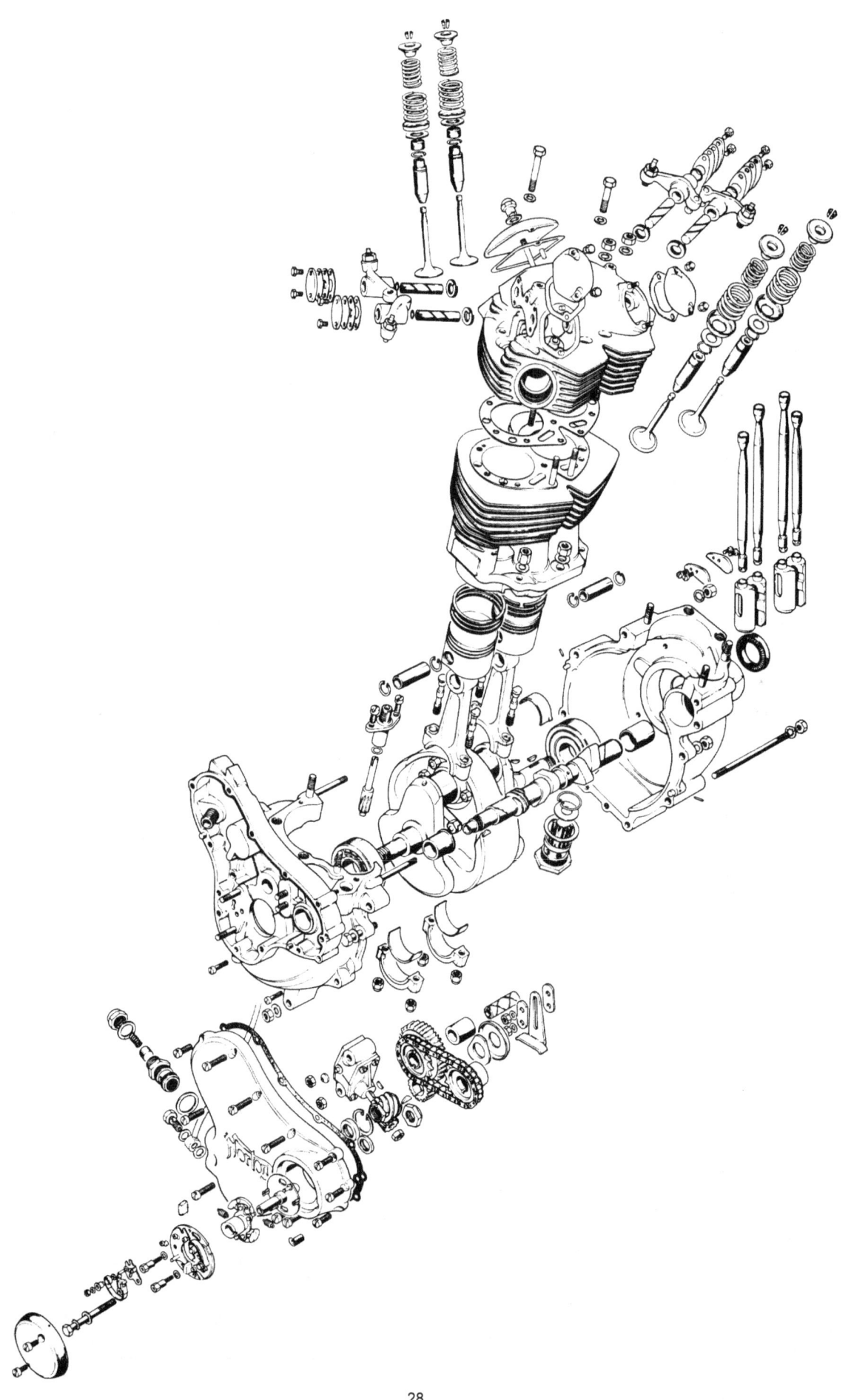

Engine/Primary Transmission C

Engine and Primary Transmission

Engine/Primary Drive C

ENGINE/PRIMARY DRIVE

SECTION C

The engine/gearbox/primary transmission can be removed from the main frame as an assembly, bolted up in the engine plates as in Section F1. Alternately, either the engine or gearbox can be removed from the frame as complete assemblies after dismantling the primary transmission. For engine removal see Section C15 and for gearbox removal see Section D7. Unless it is specifically required to remove the engine complete, the simplest method is to dismantle to crankcase level for removal as in Section C11.

SECTION C1

REMOVING CYLINDER HEAD

Commence dismantling by removing surrounding parts as follows:

1. Release the two large knurled knobs and lift clear the seat — on Fastback models lift straight up — on other models lift up and rearwards. Remove the fuse from the battery negative lead.

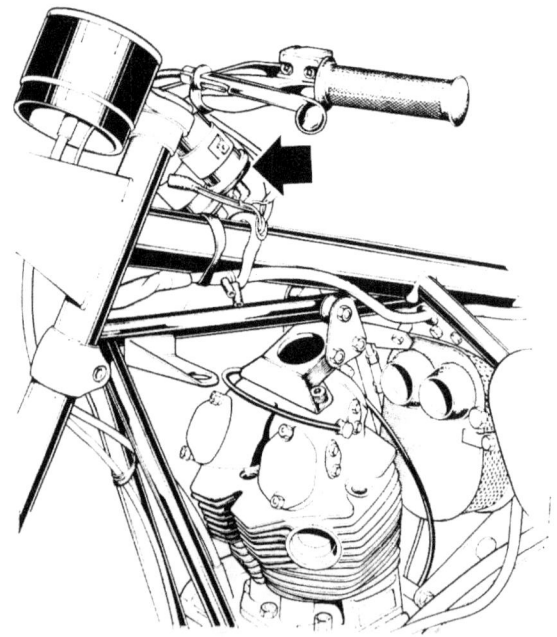

Fig. C1 Coil Cluster lifted clear of cylinder head

2. Remove the fuel tank (see Section F9).

3. Remove the exhaust system (see Section F19).

4. Remove the carburetors with spacers (see Section E2.

5. Lift off the spark plug caps and remove the coil cluster complete from the frame. On 1970 models it is secured by 2 x ¼ in. bolts and nuts and on 1971/72 models either by 4 x ¼ in. bolts with separate nuts and washers with the bolts passing uphill or by 4 set screws with washers screwing into captive nuts on the underside of the bracket. The more complicated 1971/72 cluster is best tied up to the handlebar with wire or string to keep it clear for work on the cylinder. (See *Fig.* C1)

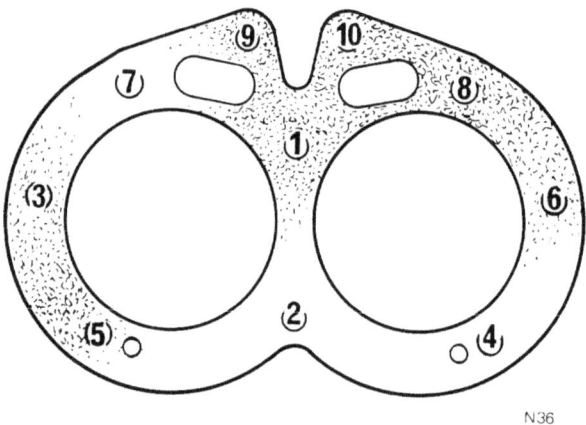

TIGHTENING SEQUENCE

Fig. C2 Cylinder head; order of slackening and tightening

6. Dismantle the cylinder head steady. Remove the nuts from the rubber mountings first, for otherwise the mountings will tend to revolve in the frame.

7. Remove the three $\frac{7}{32}$ in. A.F. socket headed screws securing the head steady to the cylinder head.

It is not necessary to remove the rocker covers at this stage since they may be removed with the cylinder head. During removal of the head securing bolts and nuts, leave the front centre bolt (shown in *Fig.* C2) till last.

Engine/Primary Drive C

Fig. C3 Tilting cylinder head with pushrods held into cylinder head.

Technique at this stage is to lift the cylinder head and recess the pushrods into the head as far as possible so that the head can be slid out between the cylinder barrel and frame tubes. Do this as follows:

13 Lift the cylinder head from either side of the motorcycle, support with one hand and slide the pushrods as far as possible into the cylinder head. *Fig.* C3 shows the cylinder head tilted to the rear to facilitate the operation.

14 Withdraw the cylinder head.

The cylinder head gasket may adhere either to the cylinder or cylinder head. The gasket should be removed and protected from damage since, if remaining in undamaged condition, it may be put into further service.

SECTION C2

REMOVAL OF ROCKERS

In order to gain access to the inlet valve guides, the inlet rockers and spindles may have to be removed as follows:

8 Remove the rocker feed pipe banjo unions from both sides of the rocker boxes and collect the copper washers from both sides of the banjos. Leave the rocker feed pipe connected to the timing case.

9 Remove both sparking plugs.

10 Remove the cylinder head securing bolts and nuts (excepting the front centre bolt), in opposite order as shown in Fig. C2.

11 To achieve the minimum valve lift position and allow maximum space for removing the cylinder head, turn the engine by revolving the rear wheel with top gear engaged until the pistons are as near as possible to top dead centre.

12 Remove the cylinder head front centre bolt and the head should lift slightly against valve spring pressure.

1 Remove the two set screws retaining each rocker spindle cover plate (see *Fig.* C4).

2 Collect the cover plate, retaining plate and gaskets as a set. In all probability these items will adhere to one another and need not be disturbed.

3 Use service tool 064298 to extract the rocker spindles as shown in *Fig.* C5. Heat the cylinder head gently to ease removal and avoid damage to head or spindles. Ensure the shaft of the slide hammer is threaded well into the rocker spindles then slide the weight back against the nut sharply several times and the spindle will be drawn out.

Engine/Primary Drive   C

4   Lift out the rockers and collect the plain and double spring thrust washers. On each rocker the plain thrust washer is outboard of the rocker and the double spring washer inboard (see *Fig.* C4).

SECTION C3

VALVE REMOVAL AND REASSEMBLY

The valves need to be removed during decarbonising (as described in Section C4) or when changing valve springs or inlet guide to stem seals. Removal of the cylinder head (Section C1) and inlet rocker cover stud is necessary to gain access to the valves.

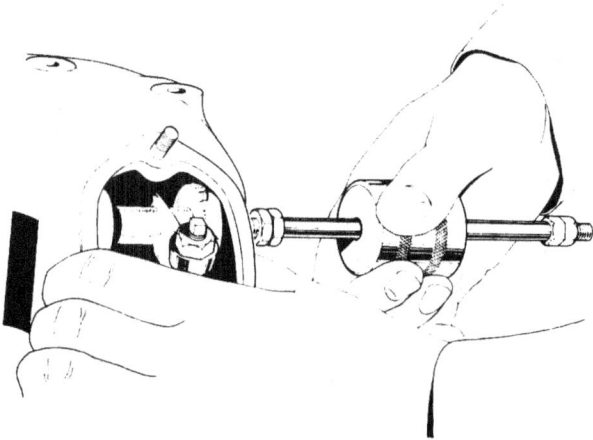

Fig. C5   Extracting rocker spindles using slide hammer 064298

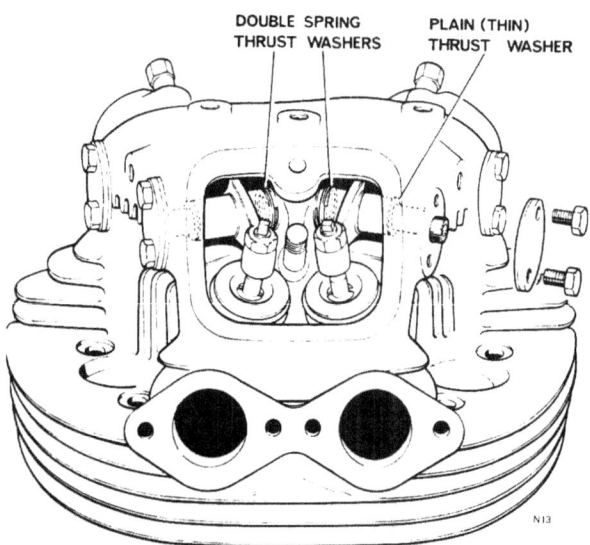

Fig. C4   Rocker thrust washers and securing plates.

Proceed as follows:

1   Using a suitable overhead valve spring compressor, (proprietary spring compressors are readily available) place the fixed jaw against the valve head and the movable jaw against the valve collar. Tighten down the movable jaw to compress the valve spring and remove the split collets. Collet removal may be facilitated by the use of a small screwdriver or long nose pliers.

2   Release the pressure from the compressor and collect the valve, springs, collars and where necessary, the inlet guide seals.

3   As each valve is removed, mark it in some way so that it can be replaced in the original position.

4   Examine the valves for burning or damage and grind in the cleaned up or new valves as described in Section C7. The seats should not need to be recut unless new valve guides have been fitted.

5   Check the valve springs for collapse. This can most easily be done by comparison with new springs or by checking free length to the dimension given in Technical Data.

6   Clean all parts very thoroughly in gasoline (petrol) and allow to dry.

7   Ensure that heat insulators are fitted between the exhaust valve spring seat and cylinder head on all engines and that insulators are also fitted at the inlet positions on pre 1972 cylinder heads.

Engine/Primary Drive   C

8   On all engines fitted with guides having a locating groove adjacent to the inlet valve guide shoulder, ensure that the inlet guide to stem seals are fitted and located correctly.

9   With the valve spring seat in position, loose assemble the valve (with lightly lubricated stem) inner and outer valve spring and top valve collar.

10   Using the valve spring compressor, compress the collar and springs and insert the split valve cotters.

11   When the collets are firmly in position in the valve stem groove, remove the compressor. The cylinder head is now ready to refit.

SECTION C4

DECARBONISING

After the motorcycle has been in use for some time, carbon deposits accumulate within the combustion chamber and exhaust ports and also the valves cease to seal completely due to wear and a certain amount of burning on the valve seatings. These conditions result in a lack of compression and an increase in the compression ratio, giving symptoms of a gradual loss of power, poor compression and difficult starting. To remedy these conditions, it is necessary to remove the carbon deposits and grind the valves to their seatings to obtain a gas-tight seal. To do so, remove the cylinder head (Section C1) and remove the valves (Section C3).

Unless a carbon dispersant vat is available, the carbon must be scraped from the combustion chambers, exhaust ports and piston crowns. Since the cylinder head and pistons are produced from an aluminium alloy material which is scratched easily, the carbon must only be removed by a soft metal or hard wood scraper which will not damage the surface. A steel scraper or screwdriver blade must not be used. *DO NOT* remove the thin ring of carbon round the top of each cylinder bore and leave also a ring of carbon around the edge of each piston crown. Removal of this carbon will tend to increase the oil consumption.

The valve stems and heads should be scraped clear of carbon but take care not to scratch the facings. Examine the facings for deep pitting which would render the valves unfit for re-use.

When all parts are perfectly clean and in good condition grind in the valves and reassemble.

SECTION C5

VALVE GUIDE RENEWAL

The cast iron valve guides are a tight interference fit in the cylinder head and can be removed and refitted only after heating the cylinder head to a temperature of 150° to 200°C. A special Service Tool 063964 is available for removing and refitting the valve guides. Proceed as follows:

1   Place the tool adaptor marked "Remover" hollow end down over the valve guide.

2   Place the cranked and threaded stem through the valve guide from the hemisphere.

3   Hold the cranked stem to prevent it turning and screw on the handle (see *Fig.* C6). As the handle is tightened the guide and cranked stem will be pulled through into the remover body.

Caution: If guides seem difficult to remove, ensure head is heated evenly. Do not force guides in or out of their bores.

New valve guides are available in oversizes of $+\cdot002$ in., $+\cdot005$ in., $+\cdot010$ in. and $+\cdot015$ in. for the long-stroke 750 and $+\cdot002$ in. and $\cdot010$ in for the 850 engine. The

Engine/Primary Drive   C

valve guide to cylinder head interference should be ·0015 in. — ·0025 in. and if there is ovality and oversize guides are to be fitted the valve guide bores in the head must be reamed to suit. As a matter of course use the improved inlet guides with valve guide-to-stem seals during re-assembly.

Fit new valve guides as follows:

4 Place the new guide in line with the bore in the cylinder and place the adaptor marked "Replacer" from Service Tool 063964 over the guide.

5 Place the replacer stem through the cylinder head and bore of the valve guide and locate the abutment to the valve seat.

6 Fit the handle and turn to pull the guide fully home into the head. If necessary the abutment can be prevented from turning by the use of a suitable key in the socket provided. Be careful not to crush the circlips on 850 guides, just pull down tightly enough to seat.

7 Recut the valve seats at the points where new guides have been fitted. This operation is described in Section C6.

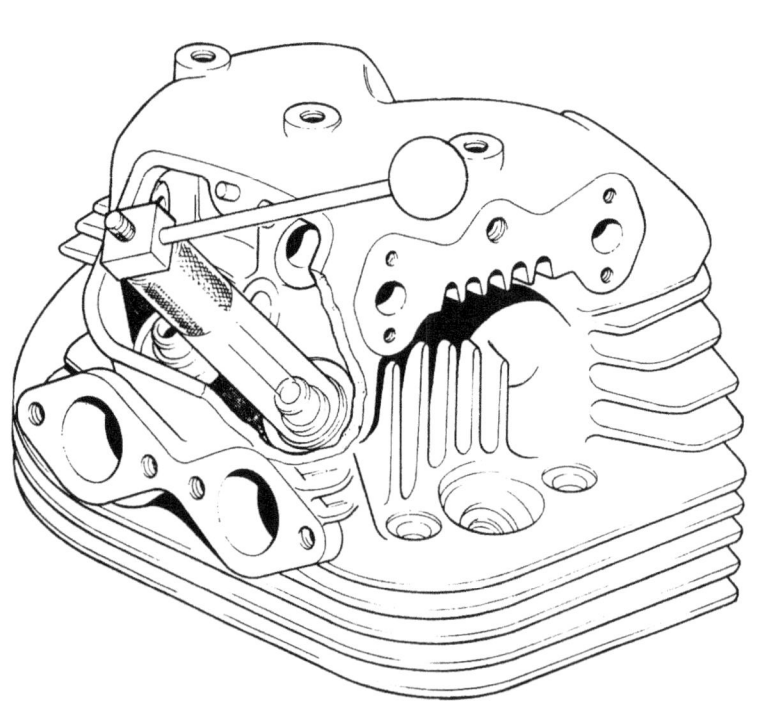
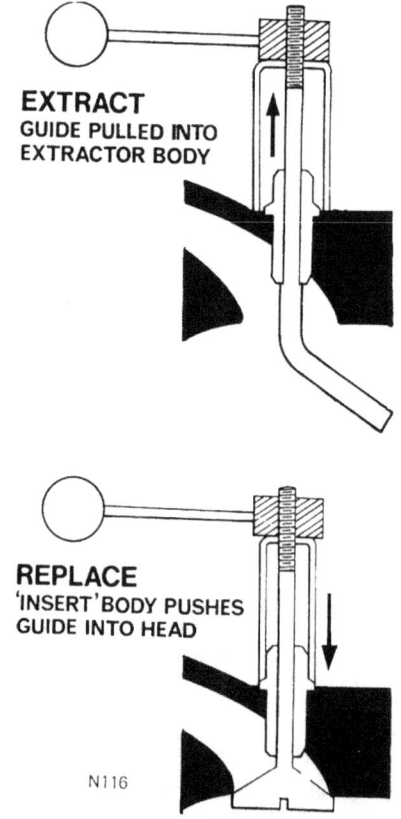

Fig. C6   Using valve guide tool 063964 to remove a valve guide

Engine/Primary Transmission C

SECTION C6

RESEATING THE VALVES

After renewal of valve guides (as in Section C5) or where the valve seats are in badly pitted condition, it is necessary to recut the valve seats. During decarbonising or after recutting the valve seats, the valves must be reground.

Cutting the valve seats — Valve seat cutters, a suitable arbor and pilot are available under the following Part Number: 063969

    Arbor and pilot.
    Valve seat cutter (45°).
    Blending cutter.

Before commencing to cut the seats we stress that the essence of cutting valve seats satisfactorily is to remove the minimum of metal and to use the cutters in such a way as to prevent possible "chatter" in the cutting pattern. Proceed as follows:

1. Assemble the cutter and pilot to the arbor.

2. Enter the pilot into the valve guide from inside the combustion chamber hemisphere.

3. Applying sufficient pressure on the arbor to give a clean cut without "chatter", take the first 120° cut.

4. Repeat the operation, 120° at a time until the seats are cleaned up free of any pitting.

5. Wash with gasoline (petrol) and blow clear any displaced material.

6. Cut the other valve seats which are affected by pitting.

7. Use a good quality fine grade grinding compound and smear a little compound all round the valve facing.

8. Drop the valve into position and using a backward and forwards rotary motion by holding either the valve head or valve stem with a suitable grinding tool, lap the valve facing to the seat.

9. Lift the valve off the seat and rotate the head 180°.

10. Repeat the lapping and rotating operations until there is a uniform dull grey bedding-in pattern on both surfaces.

11. Wash the affected areas free of grinding compound, then assemble the valves and springs to the head as in Section C3.

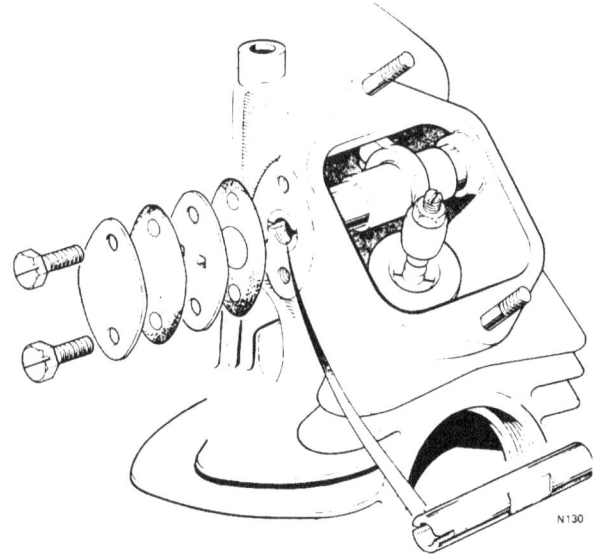

Fig. C7 Aligning rocker spindle

12. Test the seating of the valves by supporting the cylinder head with valves assembled, hemispheres upwards. Pour gasoline or kerosene (petrol or paraffin) into each inlet port and allow 20 seconds to elapse. If the liquid has not passed the seatings into the combustion chambers in this time, the lapping operation has been successful. Repeat the operation at the exhaust valves.

SECTION C7

Grinding-in the valves — Examine the valve heads for cleanliness and the valve stems for cleanliness, excessive wear or pronounced scuffing. Excessive wear or scuffing would necessitate renewal of a valve. If the valve head facings are pitted, they can be cleaned up on a valve facing machine though excessive removal of material is not recommended since it would affect the performance of the valve.

Grind the valve facings to the seats as follows:

Engine/Primary Transmission C

SECTION C8

REFITTING ROCKERS

The rocker spindles must be positioned correctly to allow satisfactory lubrication. It is recommended that the cylinder head be heated to 150°–200°C. prior to offering the rocker spindles, to facilitate entry and alignment. Assembly is as follows:

1. Heat the cylinder head gently.

2. Engage a rocker spindle into the cylinder head with flat facing rearwards on the inlet side and forwards on the exhaust and tap it through very gently with a soft drift until it protudes approximately $\frac{1}{16}$ in. (1·59 mm) through the outer boss into the rocker cavity.

3. Fit the plain washer then the rocker in position.

4. Drive the rocker spindle part way through the rocker and fit the double spring washer between the other end of the rocker and the boss in the rocker box.

5. Centralise the spring washer and drive the spindle through until it protrudes no more than $\frac{3}{8}$ in. (9·52 mm).

6. Align the rocker spindle as shown in *Fig. C7*.

   Note: Flat on spindle faces away from centre of head, towards rocker cover.

7. Drive the spindle home taking care that the rocker spindle does not turn during this operation. The spindle should be flush or fractionally below the joint facing on the rocker box.

SECTION C9

REFITTING CYLINDER HEAD

The cylinder head should be cleaned, inspected and overhauled as described in previous sections, and the valves and rockers assembled. As with dismantling, the cylinder head and pushrods should be offered as a set. The operation is described fully below:

1. Place the cylinder head gasket in position on top of the cylinder.

2. Turn the engine until the pistons are at top dead centre so that there is minimum valve lift and on assembly one pair of pushrods is fractionally higher than the other.

3. Place the pushrods in the pushrod tunnels in the cylinder head with the inlet pushrods (that is the longer pair) inboard and the shorter exhaust ones, outboard.
   The cupped end of each pushrod is uppermost.

4. Take the cylinder head firmly in one hand and feed the pushrods as far into the cylinder head as possible, holding them with the other hand. See *Fig. C3*.

5. Place the cylinder head over the cylinder, forward end downwards and allow the pushrods to drop down the cylinder barrel pushrod tunnels.
   Note that the pushrods cannot do other than locate on the cam followers at the lower end.

6. Starting with the pair of pushrods which are slightly higher, engage the tops of the pushrods to the rocker ball ends as the cylinder head is lowered. Use an implement such as a thin screwdriver through the exhaust rocker box to guide the pushrods into position as shown in *Fig. C8*. Having engaged the first pair of pushrods engage the second pair in a similar manner.

The cylinder head is ready to be secured. The tightening sequence is shown in *Fig. C2*.

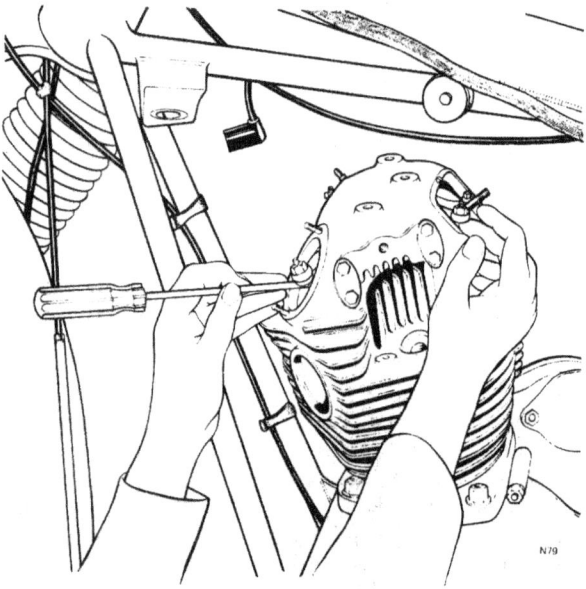

Fig. C8 Guiding pushrods into engagement with the rockers

Engine/Primary Transmission C

7 Fit and tighten down the short cylinder head bolt with its washer – this bolt should be inserted down through the cylinder head fins to the centre front position. The cylinder head should be pulled down to the gasket against valve spring pressure using this bolt.

8 Check that all four pushrods are correctly engaged to the ball ends of the rocker arms.

9 If pushrod engagement is correct, fit the four bolts with washers on either side of the sparking plugs, followed by a long sleeve nut under each exhaust port and a short nut under the inlet ports, (these are without washers) and 2 $\frac{5}{16}$ in. nuts and washers on the studs (no's 9 and 10 in *Fig.* C2) which seal the joint by the pushrod tunnel. There are no washers on the nuts fitted from beneath the cylinder head.

10 Finally tighten the cylinder head bolts and nuts in the order shown in *Fig.* C2. The torque settings are:
Cylinder head bolts and nuts $\frac{3}{8}$ in: 30 lbs./ft. (3·68 Kg/m).
Cylinder head bolts $\frac{5}{16}$ in.: 20 lbs./ft. (2·75 Kg/m)

11 Adjust the rocker clearances as described in Section C10.

12 Using new sealing gaskets only if the originals are unfit for further use, refit the inlet and exhaust rocker covers and secure with the blind nuts. There is a washer only at the inlet rocker cover nut.

13 Refit the carburettors with spacers as described in Section E5, and refit the sparking plugs to avoid washers being dropped into the engine during the next operation.

14 Refit the cylinder head steady as a reversal of the dismantling procedure.

15 Reconnect the rocker feed pipe banjos at the cylinder head using copper washers at each side of the banjos. Take care that the plastic part of the rocker pipe is clear of the rocker boxes, cylinder head and head steady.

16 Refit the coil cluster to the frame as a reversal of the dismantling procedure and connect the spark plug caps.

17 Reconnect the low tension leads from the contact breaker to the main harness. These leads are coloured white/black and yellow/black and should be connected colour to colour. The standard assembly procedure is white/black to right cylinder and yellow/black to left cylinder.

18 Refit the exhaust system (Section F19).

19 Refit the fuel tank (Section F9) and connect the fuel lines.

20 Refit the seat and secure with the knurled side nuts.

21 Refit the fuse.

SECTION C10

ROCKER CLEARANCES

It is essential for the correct valve to rocker clearances to be maintained to prevent excessively noisy operation and subsequent wear or conversely to prevent insufficient clearances, a loss of compression and burning of the valves and seats. After checking clearances at the time of the first free service, the clearances should be checked and corrected as necessary at 2500 mile (4000 Km) intervals. To provide sufficient room at the rocker boxes for satisfactory checking, the fuel tank should be removed as in Section F9.
The correct rocker clearances are as below, checked with the engine cold:

Standard Commando Engine (750 and 850)	Inlet	0·006 in. (0·15 mm)
	Exhaust	0·008 in. (0·2 mm)
Combat Engine	Inlet	0·008 in. (0·2 mm)
	Exhaust	0·010 in. (0·25 mm)

Engine/Primary Transmission C

Proceed to check rocker clearances as below:

1. Remove the two exhaust and one inlet rocker covers.
2. To facilitate rotating the engine, remove both sparking plugs.

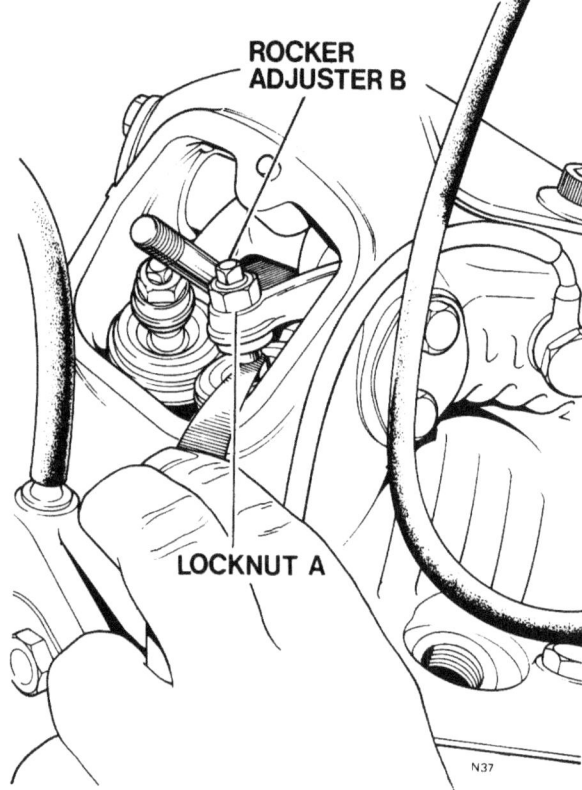

Fig. C9   Checking valve clearances

3. Rotate the engine, either by the kickstart or by turning the rear wheel forwards with fourth gear engaged, until the left side inlet valve is fully open.
4. Using the correct feeler gauge (see table above for thickness) check the rocker clearance of the right side inlet valve. *Fig.* C9 shows the point where the feeler gauge is inserted.
5. If the clearance is correct i.e. the feeler gauge *just* nips, proceed to check the next valve as in (7). If gauge will not enter or if it does not nip, adjust as in (6).
6. Referring to *Fig.* C9, slacken the adjuster locknut (A) and screw out the adjuster (B) two turns. Place the feeler gauge between the adjuster and end of the valve stem and screw the adjuster in until it *just* nips the feeler gauge. Tighten the locknut and withdraw the gauge which should not be gripped tightly but should slide relatively easily from the gap. This clearance is now correct.

7. Rotate the engine until the right side inlet valve is fully open and adjust the left side inlet valve in a similar manner.
8. Adjust the right side and left side exhaust valves in the same sequence but using a feeler gauge in accordance with the table of clearances.

SECTION C11

REMOVING CYLINDER AND PISTONS

Remove the cylinder head as detailed in Section C1. The cylinder is then removed as follows:

1. For the 850, remove the four through-bolts and release the five cylinder base nuts. The 750 engine has nine base nuts that should be removed. It will be necessary to raise the cylinder so that the nuts will clear the fins. All nuts have washers except the front centre one. Be very careful that all nuts and washers are removed before the cylinder is lifted off.

At this stage the engine may be decarbonized as in Section C4 or the cylinder, pistons and piston rings given attention.

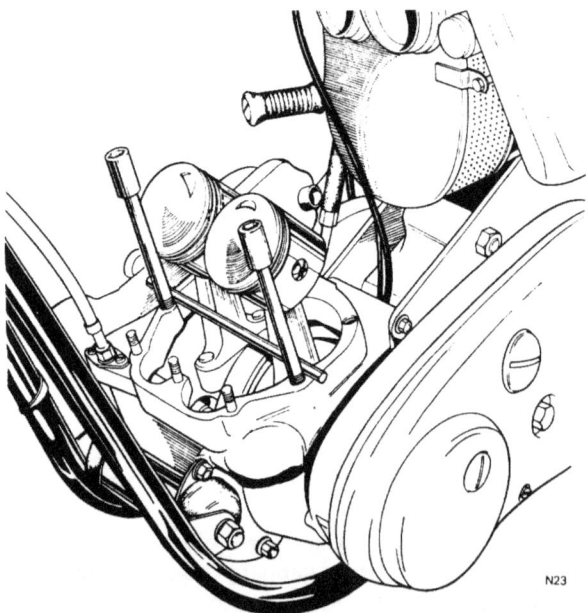

Fig. C10   Support connecting rods to prevent damage against crankcases

Engine/Primary Transmission C

2. Commence lifting the cylinder off the base studs and prepare to support the connecting rods as the cylinder is lifted clear of the pistons. In *Fig.* C10 a suitable implement has been inserted between the refitted cylinder through bolts (or studs other than on 850 models) to prevent the connecting rods and pistons falling against the crankcase mouth. Any damage to the connecting rods could result in failure of the rods at a later stage of use.

3. Place a piece of clean non-fluffy cloth over the crankcase mouth to prevent foreign matter entering the crankcase mouth.

4. Remove one circlip from each wrist pin (gudgeon pin).

5. Before removing the piston, support the body (*Fig.* C11) shows the piston body being supported by a second operative) and push out the first wrist (gudgeon) pin, then the second, using a suitable sized implement such as an aluminium drift.

SECTION C12

CYLINDER REBORING AND OVERSIZE PISTONS

After considerable mileages, or on engines where air filtering has been inefficient or oil changes neglected, wear may be expected on the cylinder bores or pistons. The maximum degree of wear may be expected to occur at the top front and rear areas of the cylinder bores. Similarly, the maximum wear will take place on the front and rear faces of the pistons. Measure the cylinder bore diameter front and rear within $\frac{1}{2}$ in. (12·70 mm) of the top of each bore and again front and rear at a point in the bore below the piston ring swept area. If the bores are in acceptable condition, the difference between the measurements should not exceed 0·005 in. (·1270 mm).

An alternative (but less accurate) method of measurement is to place one compression ring in the bore, approximately $\frac{1}{2}$ in. (12·70 mm) from the top and measure the ring gap with feeler gauges. Place the ring lower in the bore below the piston ring swept area and again measure the gap. Subtract the second reading from the first and divide by three to arrive at the diameter wear. The amount of wear should not exceed 0·005 in. (·1270 mm).

Excessive wear will necessitate reboring and the fitting of oversize pistons which are available in oversizes of + 0·010 in. + 0·020 in. (and + 0·030 and + 0·040 in. for the long-stroke 750 only). Bore measurements are listed below:

750

STANDARD:	2·875 in. (73·025 mm)
+·010 in. oversize	2·885 in. (73·279 mm)
+·020 in. oversize	2·895 in. (73·533 mm)
+·030 in. oversize	2·905 in. (73·787 mm)
+·040 in. oversize	2·915 in. (74·041 mm)

850

STANDARD:	3·032 in. (77·013 mm)
+·010 in. oversize	3·042 in. (77·267 mm)
+·020 in. oversize	3·052 in. (77·521 mm)

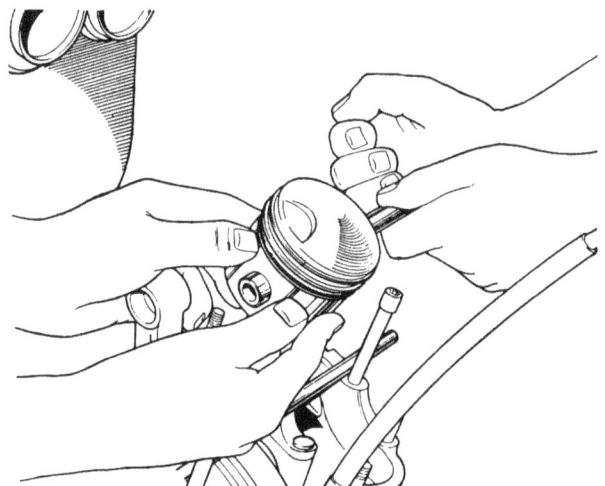

Fig. C11 Supporting piston body whilst pushing out gudgeon pin

Engine/Primary Transmission C

SECTION C13

REMOVING PRIMARY CHAINCASE

To remove the engine or gearbox from the mounting plates or from the frame it is necessary to dismantle the primary transmission completely but the engine/gearbox transmission assembly can be removed from the frame as a single unit.

Dismantle the outer primary chaincase as follows:

1. Remove the three nuts and plain washers securing the left hand foot rest complete with brake pedal and stop switch. It is unnecessary to disconnect either the stop lamp leads or the rear brake cable and the pedal assembly may be allowed to hang down clear of the primary chaincase.

2. Place a sufficiently large drain tray beneath the chaincase to receive all the chaincase lubricant. There is no drain plug to the chaincase thus as the chaincase joint is parted, the chaincase will drain very quickly.

3. Remove the centre sleeve nut which secures the outer chaincase and by rocking the chaincase slightly to clear the locating dowels top and bottom, lift the outer chaincase clear.

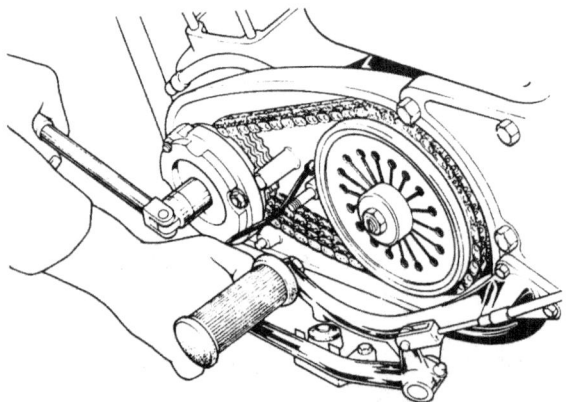

Fig. C12 Removing rotor nut whilst applying rear brake to prevent movement

SECTION C14

DISMANTLING PRIMARY TRANSMISSION AND CLUTCH

Whilst removing either the clutch or the engine sprocket, the transmission should be prevented from turning by placing the rear brake pedal and left hand foot rest assembly loosely in position and applying the rear brake fully. Proceed with dismantling as follows:

1. Using a suitable sized socket wrench $\frac{1}{2}$ in. Whit. on the alternator rotor nut, remove the rotor nut as shown in *Fig.* C12.

2. As the rotor nut is removed, collect the fan disc washer from behind.

3. Remove the alternator stator. This is secured by three nuts and plain washers. As the stator is removed, it may be left hanging on the stator lead whilst the two snap connector terminals are disconnected beneath the air box.

4. At this stage remove the alternator rotor which is keyed to the engine crankshaft. If the rotor should prove to be extremely tight on the engine crankshaft, slight pressure may be applied from behind equally, using two flat section tyre levers. Remove the rotor key, packing collar and shims from the engine shaft.

5. Remove the three stator spacers from the stator mounting studs on the chaincase.

6. Slacken the clutch push rod adjuster nut and remove the adjuster and nut altogether.

7. In order to dismantle the clutch, a compressor tool part number 060999 is needed for the diaphragm spring of the clutch. The tool is shown in use in *Fig.* C13. Note that the tool has been screwed into the adjuster hole in the spring centre. The centre bolt must be lightly tightened and must be at least $\frac{1}{4}$ in. engaged into the diaphragm spring centre. Now place a spanner on the withdrawal nut as shown in *Fig.* C13. Turning clockwise will tighten the withdrawal nut until pressure has been released from the diaphragm spring and the spring is completely free to rotate.

Engine/Primary Transmission C

8   When the spring is compressed and free to rotate and using a screwdriver blade as shown in *Fig.* C14, lift the first end of the diaphragm spring clear of the circlip groove in the housing and commence to peel the circlip away from the groove.

9   The compressor tool and diaphragm spring should now be lifted clear as a pair.
It is not necessary to remove the tool from the diaphragm spring. If it is desired to remove the tool from the diaphragm spring, support the centre bolt to prevent it turning and slacken off the withdrawal nut to relieve all spring pressure. If this is not done there is a grave risk of the spring being released suddenly from the tool with possible injury.

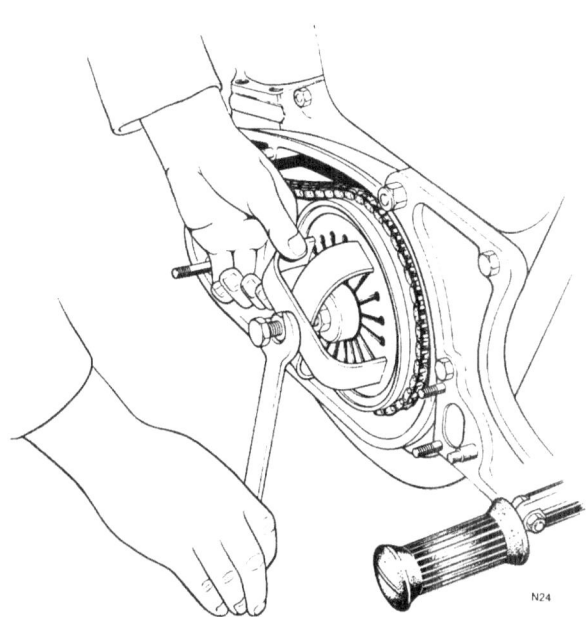

Fig. C13   Diaphragm spring compressor tool 060999 in use

10 Fit clutch tool 061015 over hub and remove the clutch centre nut and washer (and tab washer fitted on later models. Note that the tab washer can be fitted to advantage on all Commando). Alternatively the clutch can be held by fitting the rear brake pedal loosely into position and applied while the nut is slackened.

11 Prepare to remove the engine sprocket, primary chain and remainder of the clutch as a set. This necessitates the use of engine sprocket puller part number 064297 assembled to the sprocket and engine crankshaft as shown in *Fig.* C15. It is essential that the side bolts are screwed into the sprocket at least $\frac{1}{2}$ in. prior to tightening of the centre bolt for extraction purposes for otherwise the thread may be stripped. Now tighten the centre bolt of the puller against the crankshaft and shock the side of the sprocket using a soft metal drift and hammer, whereupon the taper joint between the sprocket and shaft should be broken.

12 For convenience, remove the engine sprocket puller from the sprocket and lift away the remainder of the clutch, the engine sprocket and primary chain as a set as shown in *Fig.* C16, feeding the stator between the runs of the primary chain.

13 It will be noted that clutch and engine sprocket alignment has been ensured by the use of a collar and spacers over the gearbox mainshaft and these items should be collected and stored carefully for use during re-assembly. Note that if the crankshaft, engine sprocket, mainshaft or clutch have been renewed, re-alignment may be necessary.

14 In order to remove the inner primary chaincase the three set screws with tab washers should be removed. Before attempting removal, tap the tabs clear of the set screw heads, remove the set screws then the tab washers and lift clear the inner primary chaincase. The chaincase may be removed with or without the stator, whichever is desired. The stator is secured to the chaincase at this stage only by the main cable passing through the grommet in the back of the chaincase.

Engine/Primary Transmission C

15 Collect the spacer washer or washers used on the centre stud. Note that if a sufficient quantity of oil has drained into the crankcase prior to stripping, oil will tend to run from the chaincase securing holes in the crankcase, thus it is recommended that the bolts be replaced finger tight in the lower holes.

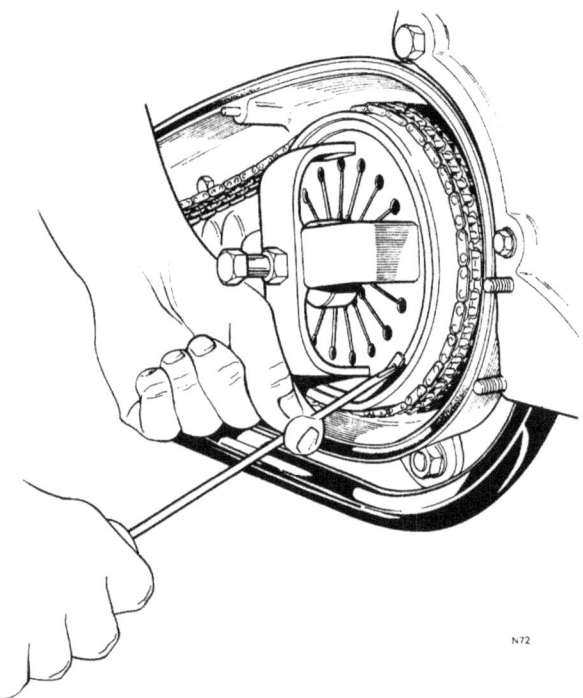

Fig. C14   Using a screwdriver blade to peel circlip away from housing

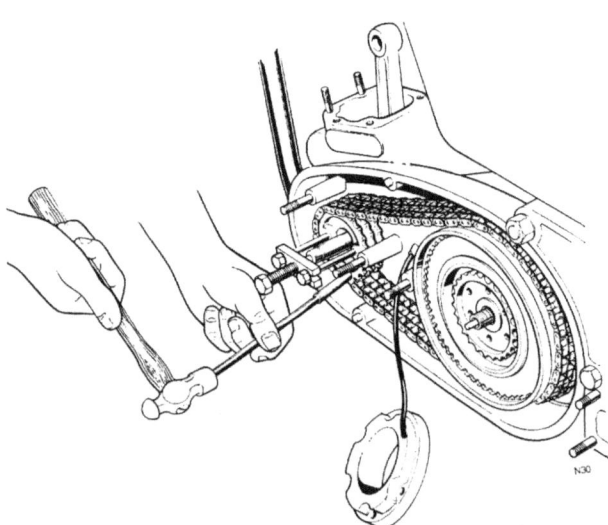

Fig. C15   Use of engine sprocket puller 064297

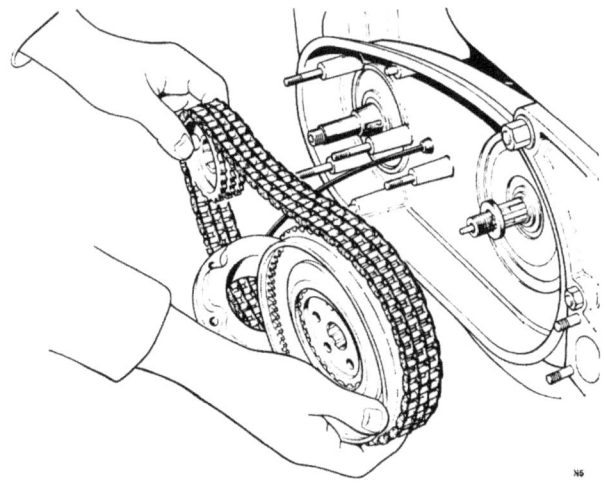

Fig. C16   Removing engine sprocket clutch and primary chain as a set

SECTION C15

REMOVING CRANKCASE ASSEMBLY FROM FRAME

Removal of the crankcase assembly from the frame is most easily achieved by removing the remaining ancillary equipment then taking out the front mounting complete and draining all remaining oil from the crankcase.

The full routine is as follows:

1 Disconnect the tachometer cable at the front of crankcase.

2 Remove the rocker feed pipe from the back of the crankcases and collect the copper washers.

3 Remove the gear indicator and set screw.
   Remove also the gear pedal which is secured by one bolt.

4 Push the crankcase breather pipe clear of the oil tank.

5 Place a large capacity drain tray beneath the crankcases.

6 Remove the oil pipe junction block from the rear of the crankcase.

Engine/Primary Transmission C

7. Slacken the large hexagon sump filter on the bottom of the crankcases. This filter requires the use of a $\frac{7}{8}$ in. Whit. (or $1\frac{1}{2}$ in. AF) spanner. Service tool NM 12093 is suitable. (A smaller drain plug was fitted to 1972 and '73 750's only. Similar instructions apply.)

8. Remove the large diameter centre bolt of the front mounting from the timing side. This will necessitate aligning the flats on the bolt head to clear the timing case. To facilitate removal of the front mountings from between the frame down tube brackets, slide back the gaiter at the left hand side so that the spacer, end cap and shims can be withdrawn. Remove the two nuts from the timing side of the engine mounting studs, then pull out the studs complete with remaining nuts from the drive side. The front mounting can then be pulled free away from the crankcases.

9. Remove the bottom rear crankcase-to-engine-plate bolt and the bottom centre stud. Extract the bottom stud by lifting the crankcase assembly slightly so that the stud clears the frame rails.

10. The sump filter can now be removed completely and the engine lifted vertically to enable the crankcase to be drained. *Fig.* C17 shows the crankcases supported by a bar from below whilst the sump filter is removed with the fingers after slackening at an earlier stage.

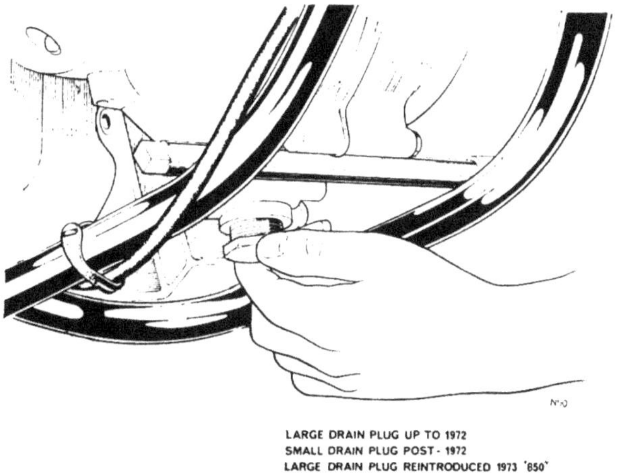

11. Remove the top rear engine to engine plate nut, supporting the weight of the crankcase as the stud is pulled out.

12. The crankcase assembly is now free to be removed from the mounting plates as shown in *Fig.* C18. Further dismantling of the engine can proceed more conveniently on the bench after removal.

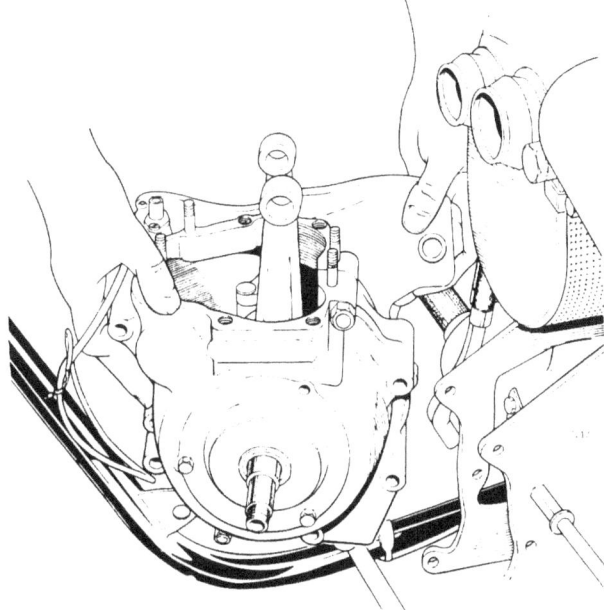

Fig. C18 *Removal of the crankcase assembly from mounting plates*

SECTION C16

DISMANTLING THE CRANKCASES

The majority of the work on the crankcases can be carried out best with the crankcase mounted in a plain jaw vice as shown in *Fig.* C19.

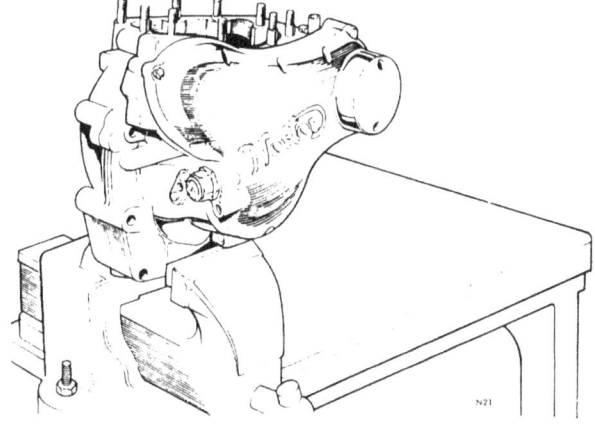

LARGE DRAIN PLUG UP TO 1972
SMALL DRAIN PLUG POST - 1972
LARGE DRAIN PLUG REINTRODUCED 1973 '850'

Fig. C17 *Showing crankcases supported by a bar to remove sump filter*

Fig. C19 *Showing crankcases mounted in a plain jaw vice for ease of handling*

Engine/Primary Transmission C

The basic order of dismantling is to remove the timing cover and dismantle the camshaft chain and sprockets, then the oil pump. At this stage the crankcases should be removed from the vice to be parted for removal of the crankshaft. The full routine is described below:

1. If the remaining crankcase bottom bolt is still fitted, this should be removed to allow the crankcase to be mounted securely in a vice.

2. Remove the two contact breaker cover screws and lift away the C.B. cover.

3. Remove the contact breaker cam centre bolt, serrated washer and plain washer.

4. Using service tool 064298 as shown in *Fig. C20*, screw the shaft into the contact breaker cam then slide the weight back sharply several times until the cam is lifted off the camshaft taper. It is unnecessary to remove the contact breaker plate from the timing cover at this stage unless so desired.

5. Remove the timing cover screws and part the joint between the timing cover and crankcase by a careful tap from behind the pressure release valve body using a hide hammer.

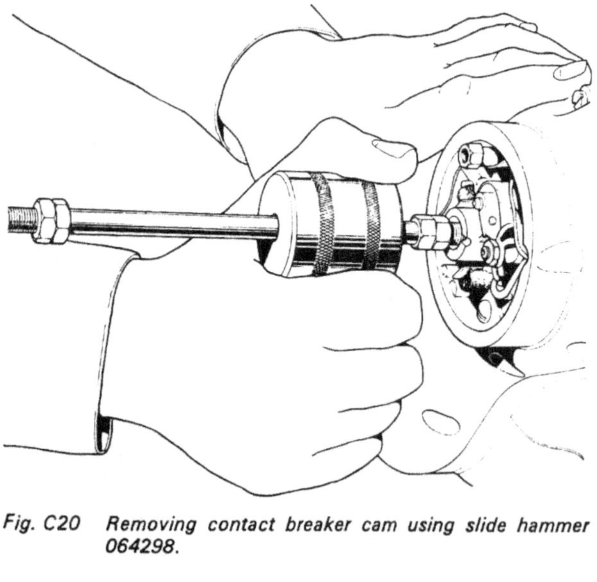

6. Lift the timing cover away, withdrawing the contact breaker lead from the timing case. It may be necessary to turn one of the snap connector bullets backwards so that the lead feeds through the case, one snap connector bullet at a time.

7. Remove the two nuts securing the oil pump. The oil pump may be quite tight on its studs and in these circumstances it is advantageous to turn the oil pump drive wheel nut so that the oil pump will pull itself away along the worm drive. This operation is shown in *Fig. C21*.

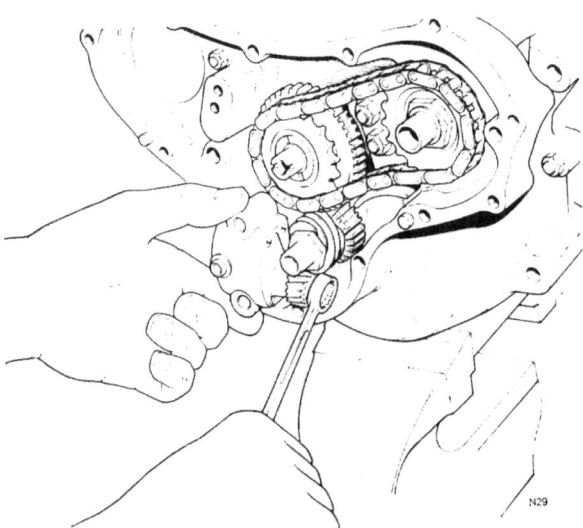

Fig. C21 Using a spanner to turn the oil pump drive wheel nut and remove the pump

8. Remove the oil pump driving worm from the crankshaft with its integral left hand threaded nut. To achieve this it is necessary to stop the crankshaft turning in the cases either by passing a round bar through the small ends and supporting on clean wooden blocks across the crankcase mouth or by placing a suitable bar into the deepest balance hole and allowing the bar to abut against the crankcase mouth in a similar manner to that shown in *Fig. C22*.

Special Note: There is a risk of breaking the oil shroud portion of the crankcase over the camshaft if the bar is allowed to abut to this.

Fig. C20 Removing contact breaker cam using slide hammer 064298.

Engine/Primary Transmission C

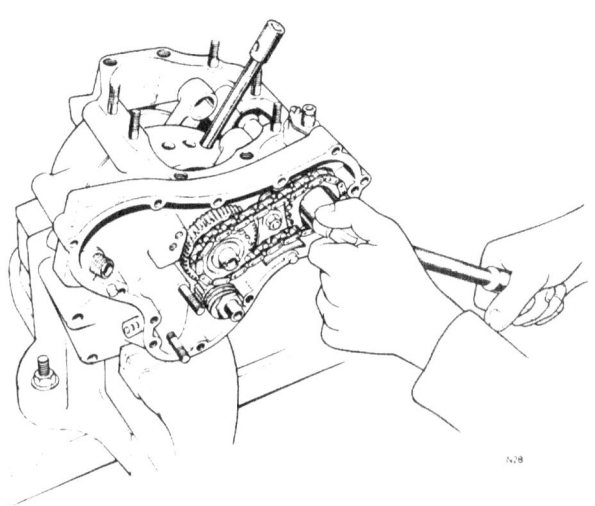

Fig. C22 Preventing flywheel turning by use of a bar lodged in a flywheel balance hole

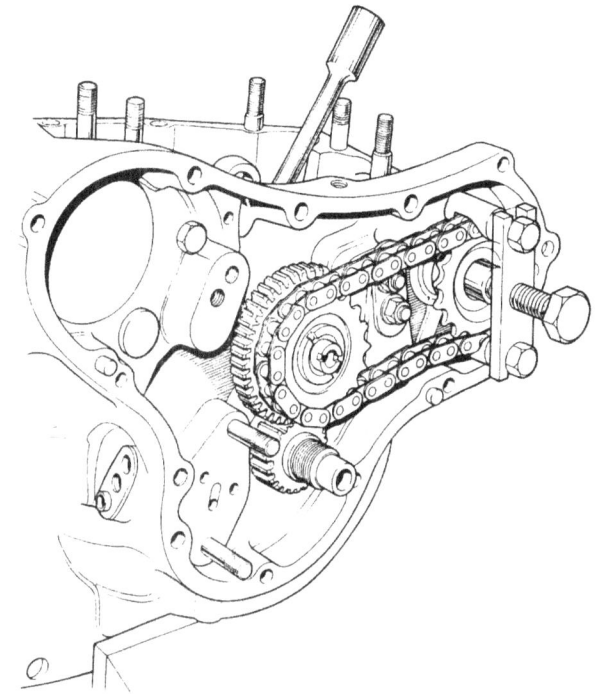

Fig. C23 Releasing a tight camshaft using sprocket service tool 064297

9   With the flywheel still prevented from turning, remove the nut securing the camshaft sprocket. Under no circumstances must anything but firm steady pressure be applied to unscrew the camshaft sprocket nut — normal right hand thread — unless a dummy cut away timing cover is fitted and secured with screws at extreme front rear and bottom. If a hammer or mallet is used without such a cover to support the end of the intermediate gear spindle, there is risk of the latter being pulled out of the crankcase.
The size of the sprocket nut is $\frac{9}{16}$ in. Whitworth.

10 Lift the sprocket, idler gear, and timing chain away as a set. If the camshaft sprocket should prove to be tight on the camshaft, it may be removed by using the special jaws supplied with the 064297 engine sprocket extractor.

Do not remove camshaft key from camshaft except for replacement.

11 Providing the timing cover joint gasket is not damaged during dismantling, there is no reason why it should be removed from the crankcase facing as it will be perfectly suitable for re-use.

12 Using Service Tool ET.2003 as shown in *Fig.* C24, extract the crankshaft pinion. It should be noted that the jaws of the service tool locate to the spaces provided in the pinion backing washer.

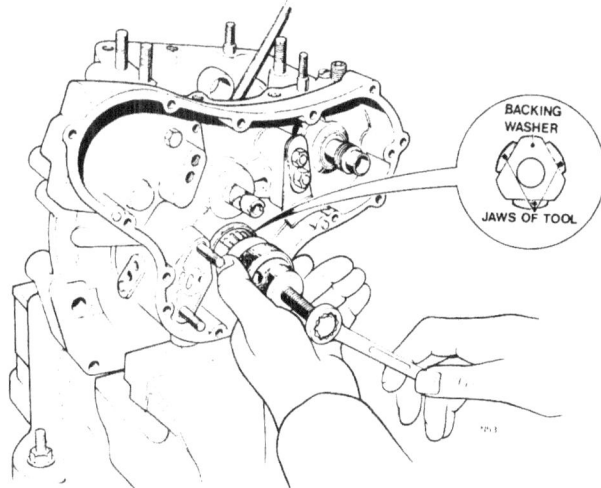

Fig. C24 Extracting crankshaft pinion using tool ET 2003

Engine/Primary Transmission C

13 Lift away the pinion key which is of the Woodruff type. Remove also the backing washer.

14 Remove the oil sealing disc which is lipped. This disc tends to cling to the main bearing due to the presence of oil and the use of two small magnets or some other means is recommended to lift the disc clear.

15 If desired, the timing chain tensioner, clamping plates, nuts and fan disc washers can be removed from the crankcase at this stage.

16 Dismount the crankcases from the vice so that they may be parted and the crankshaft assembly extracted.

17 Remove the crankcase breather pipe complete with elbow by slackening the locking nut at the crankcase or on 850 models by sliding the pipe off the crankcase breather stub. On 750 models after engine number 200000 remove the breather and breather pipe as an assembly, after removing the locking wire, or flattening the tab washer and taking out the two securing bolts.

18 Remove the two studs, one bolt and two set screws, holding the crankcases together. Unless the additional bottom stud has been removed to mount the crankcases in a vice, the stud should be removed at this stage.

19 Part the crankcases, releasing the crankcase joint by the use of bar of wood against the drive side crankcase as shown in *Fig.* C25.

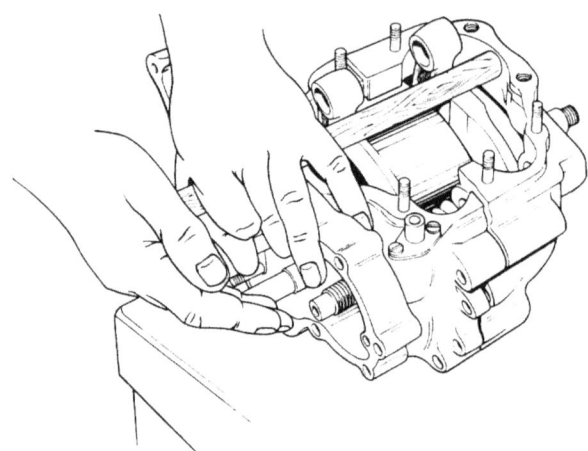

Fig. C25 Parting the crankcases using a wood block against the inner drive side

20 On Commando engines before engine number 200000, the rotary engine breather disc and spring should be collected from the drive side cam bush as the drive side crankcase is lifted away.

21 Withdraw the camshaft from the timing crankcase and collect the chamfered thrust washer. Note that on engines between engine number 200000 and 300000 there is an additional flat thrust washer that must be collected.

22 Part the timing side crankcase from the crankshaft. This practice is preferred to removal of the crankshaft from the crankcase. Removal is accomplished without striking the end of the crankshaft by the use of a tubular drift driven against the crankshaft shoulder. *Fig.* C26 illustrates a suitable tube fitted over the crankshaft, the tube standing on the bench and a hammer driving a lump of soft wood against the crankcase facing, permitting this to be jarred free of the crankshaft. If removal should prove difficult by this means, the crankcase in the area surrounding the main bearing should be heated by a soft flame and the same removal procedure followed so that the main bearing and crankshaft together are displaced from the crankcase. The bearing can then be removed at a later stage. On engines after number 200000 a roller timing side bearing is used and on such units there should be no difficulty in crankshaft removal.

Engine/Primary Transmission C

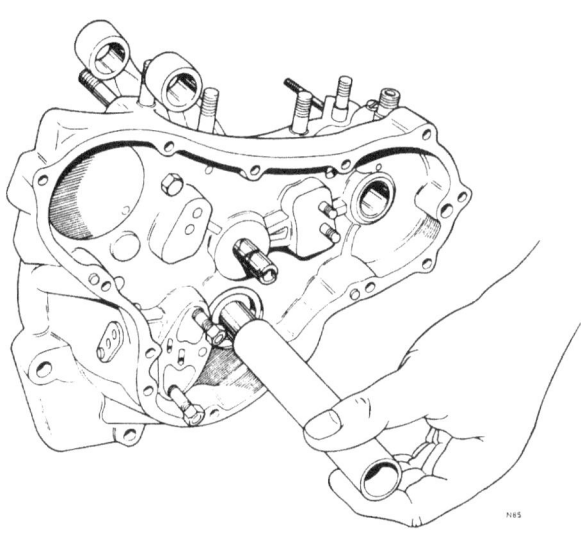

Fig. C26 Showing suitable tube to abutt to crankshaft shoulder yet pass through crankcase

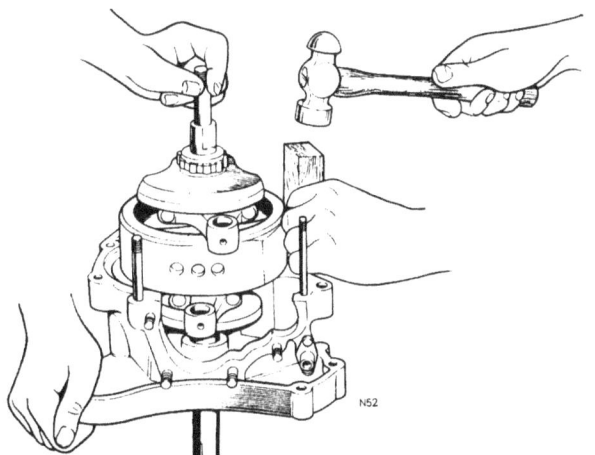

Fig. C27 Supporting the crankcase shoulder on a tube whilst separating the crankcase from the crankshaft

SECTION C17

CRANKCASE OVERHAUL

The following text covers the renewal of main bearings only. In our experience the camshaft bushes have an extremely long life and renewal cannot be accomplished without extensive machining facilities. To remove the main bearings, it is necessary to heat the area surrounding each main bearing with a soft flame such as a gasoline or kerosene (petrol or paraffin) blow lamp or butane or propane. Once the cases have been heated, in the case of a timing side crankcase equipped with the ball type of main bearing, use a suitable soft drift against the inner race of the main bearing and the bearing can be drifted out. In the case of a timing side crankcase equipped with the roller type of main bearing, heat the area of the crankcase surrounding the main bearing and by bumping the joint facing of the cankcase hard against a flat wooden surface, the main bearing outer race should be dislodged. In the case of drive side crankcases, the complete crankcase will need to be appreciably hotter since the only method of removing the main bearing outer race will be to bump the crankcase sharply against a flat wooden surface.

To refit the main bearings, the cases must be similarly heated and the main bearings, whether of the ball or roller variety should drop, completely freely, into their housings. The main bearings must be fully home into the housings both at the drive side and timing side cases.

SECTION C18

REMOVING CONNECTING RODS

Remove the connecting rods by releasing the two self locking nuts when it should be possible to pull the connecting rod away from the cap by hand pressure. The bearing shells remain in position at this stage but if they are to be re-used, they must be protected from dirt and possible damage. It is vitally important that at no stage are the connecting rod end caps interchanged between rods and it is equally important that the end caps should not be reversed on their own connecting rods.

A scribe marking is used on the connecting rod and end cap to show the correct direction of fitting. The locating tabs on both of the bearing shells fit to the same side of each connecting rod.

Engine/Primary Transmission C

SECTION C19

DISMANTLING THE CRANKSHAFT

It is to be expected that the crankshaft assembly which is now to be stripped will contain approximately one teacup full of oil and provision should be made for collecting this oil in a suitable receptacle.

Before parting the crank cheeks from the flywheel, it is recommended that the flywheel be marked e.g. "T.S." for timing side so that it is not reversed during re-assembly. Proceed as follows:

1. Slacken the fixed nuts on the timing side securing the crank cheek to the flywheel, noting that the nuts have been centre punched during assembly and may be expected to be extremely tight.

2. Jar the crank cheeks free from the flywheel using a hammer and soft drift. The drive side crankshaft will come away complete with the two studs, tab washer and nuts which can now be removed if desired.

Dependent upon mileage there is likely to be a considerable build up of sludge and foreign matter in both the crank cheeks and the recess in the flywheel. This foreign matter must be cleaned out most thoroughly.

Tool No. 063970 is available to remove roller bearing races from the crankshaft, as shown in *Fig.* C28.

SECTION C20

CRANKSHAFT INSPECTION AND REGRINDING

Wash each crank cheek in clean petrol and blow dry with an air line. Examine the big end journals for scoring and remove light score marks by the use of smooth emery tape. If there is excessive scoring or ovality and it exceeds 0·0015 in. (·0381 mm) on the big end journals, regrinding is necessary.

The regrind sizes are shown overleaf. The revised big end journal sizes necessitate the use of connecting rod shell bearings of the correct undersize. The steel backed big end shells are finished to provide the correct diametrical clearance and must not, under any circumstances, be scraped. Shell bearings are available in undersizes of minus 0·010 in., minus 0·020 in., minus 0·030 in. and minus 0·040 in.

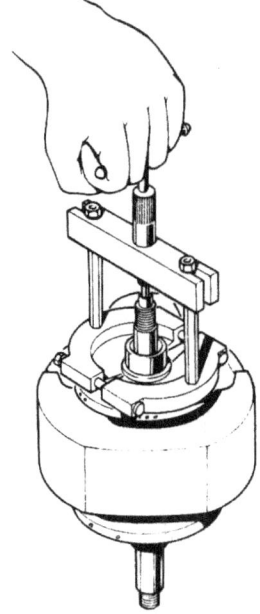

Fig. C28   Removing roller bearing inner race using extractor 063970.

SECTION C21

ENGINE LUBRICATION SYSTEM

The Commando lubrication system as shown in *Fig.* C29 is of the dry sump type, oil contained in the separate oil tank being fed through a wire strainer by gravity and by suction through the feed side of the gear type oil pump to the crankshaft. The oil pump delivers lubricant under pressure to the oil pressure relief valve and a bleed off the main feed supplies lubricant to the rocker gear. The main oil supply is delivered through the end of the crankshaft, (which is sealed by a garter type seal in the timing cover) to both big ends and escapes between the big end shells and crank journals to lubricate the cylinder walls, main bearings, camshaft and cam followers by splash. Oil collects in the crankcase sump, the inlet rocker box draining through a drill way in the cylinder barrel, and the exhaust rocker box draining through a drill way into the push rod tunnel and providing additional lubrication whilst returning to the crankcase between the cam followers to the camshaft.

The return side of the oil pump draws oil from the sump via the sump filter (or collecting area in later crankcases) and returns it through the full flow oil filter to the oil tank. A bleed from the oil tank return pipe at the tank lubricates the rear chain via a regulator comprising a plastic tube and felt insert.

Engine/Primary Transmission C

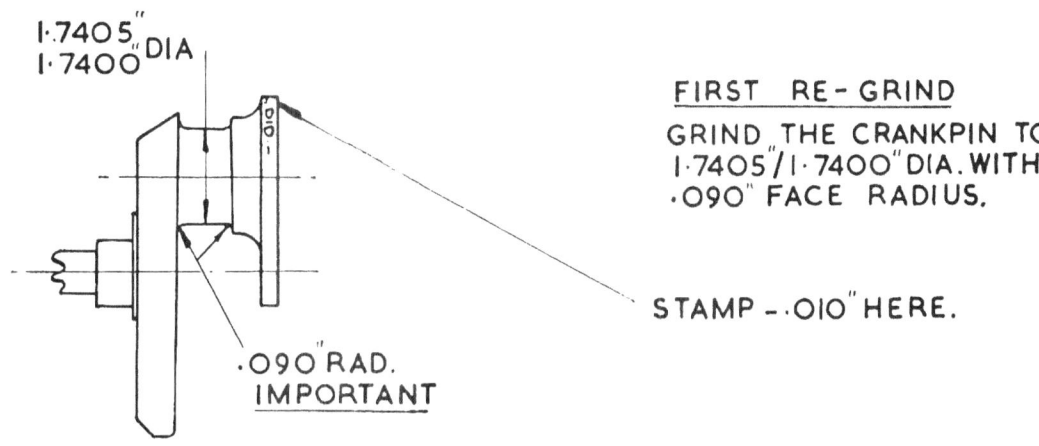

FIRST RE-GRIND

GRIND THE CRANKPIN TO 1·7405"/1·7400" DIA. WITH ·090" FACE RADIUS.

STAMP -·010" HERE.

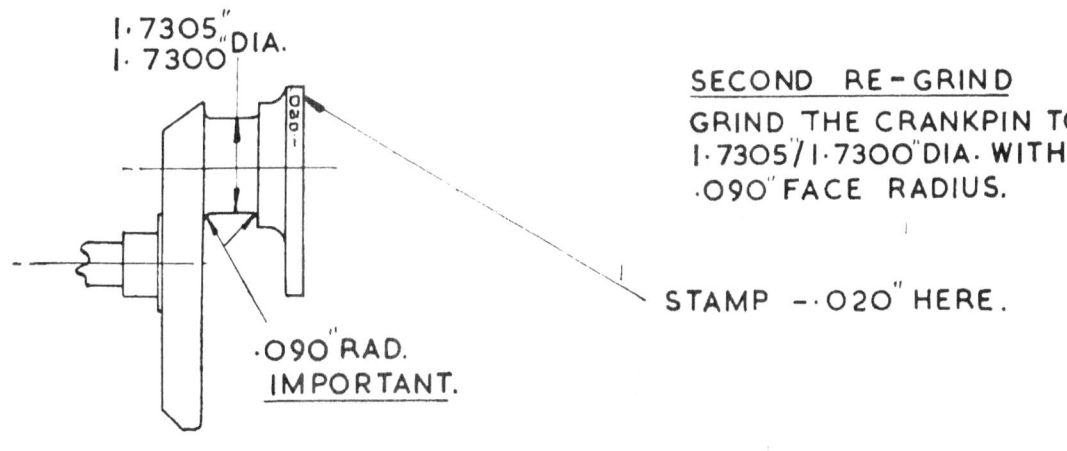

SECOND RE-GRIND

GRIND THE CRANKPIN TO 1·7305"/1·7300" DIA. WITH ·090" FACE RADIUS.

STAMP -·020" HERE.

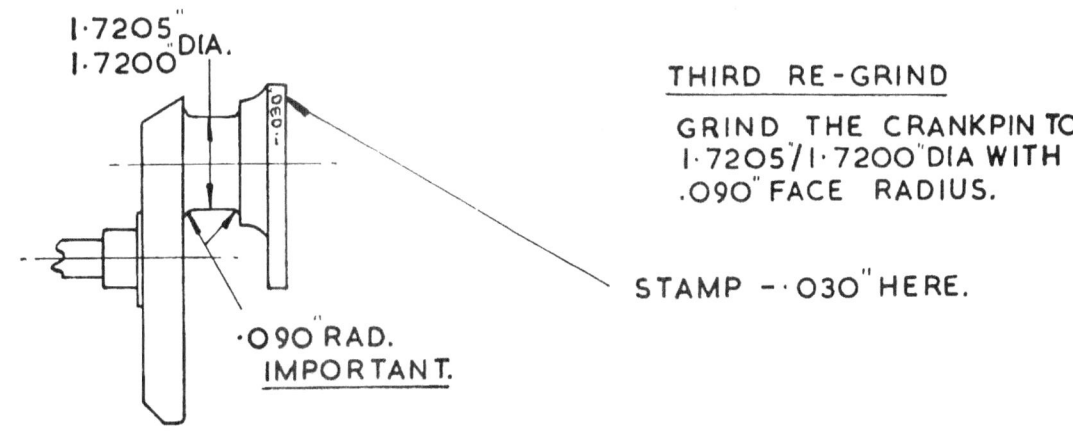

THIRD RE-GRIND

GRIND THE CRANKPIN TO 1·7205"/1·7200" DIA WITH ·090" FACE RADIUS.

STAMP -·030" HERE.

N106

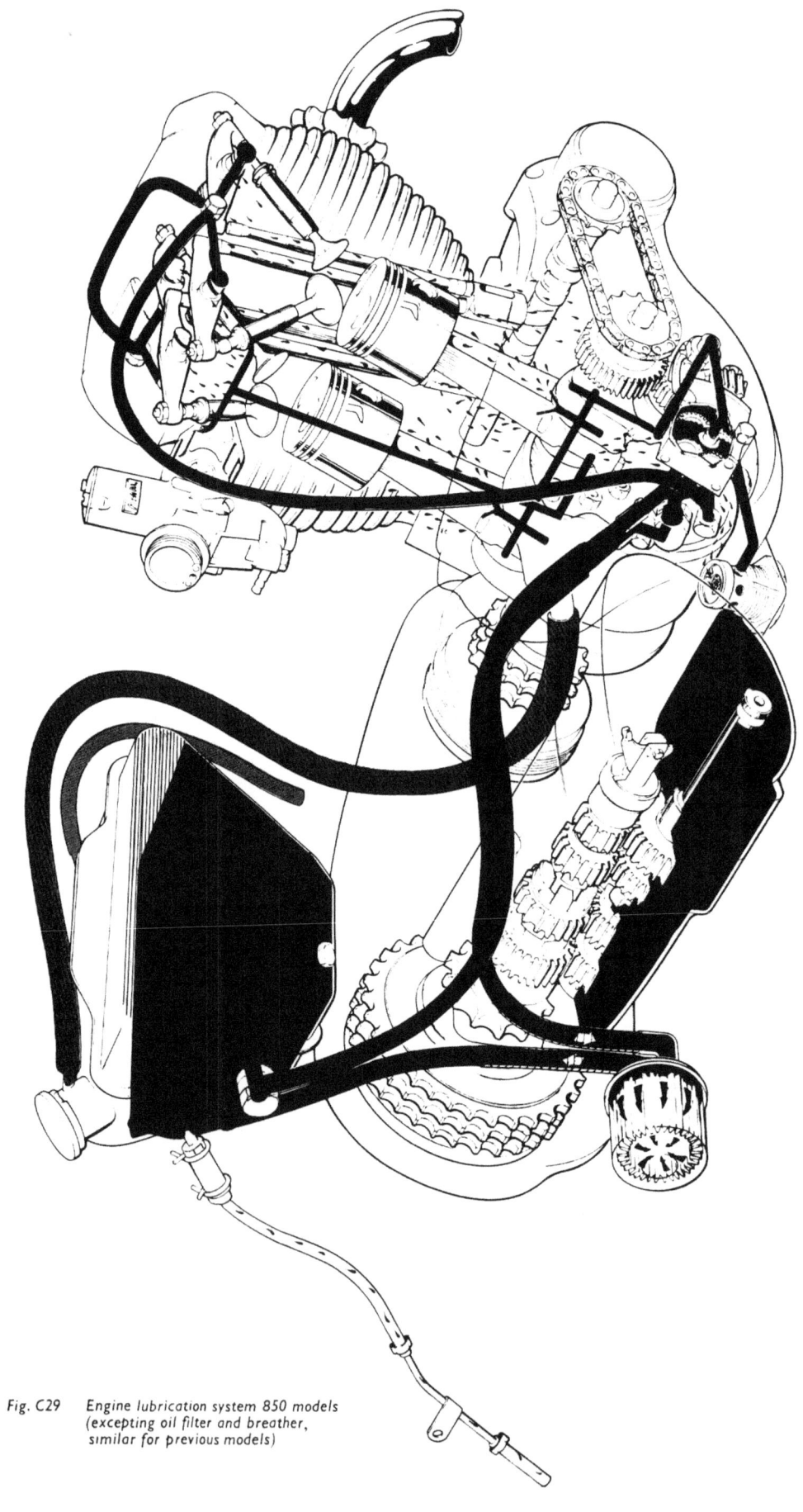

Fig. C29 Engine lubrication system 850 models (excepting oil filter and breather, similar for previous models)

Engine/Primary Transmission C

SECTION C22

OIL PRESSURE RELIEF VALVE

The relief valve is fitted to prevent oil pressure rising above 45/55 lbs. sq. inch. It is fitted to the rear of the timing cover below the rocker oil feed pipe banjo. The valve consists of a spring loaded steel sleeve pre-set at the factory using shims to regulate the blow off pressure and the valve requires no attention. Oil escaping from the valve returns to the feed side of the pump.

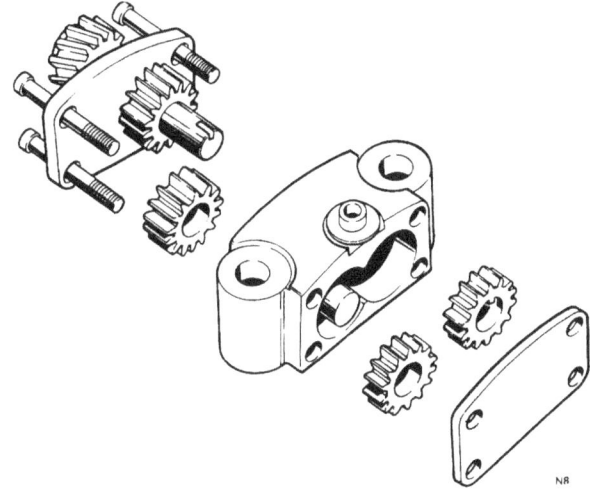

Fig. C30   Comprising parts of oil pump

SECTION C23

CRANKCASE BREATHER

A timed and ported mechanical crankcase breather is used prior to 1972. In this design, a rotary disc with cut-away segment driven by the camshaft and backed with a light spring mates with a similar stationary disc fitted behind the left camshaft bush in the crankcase. An elbow with flexible pipe from the left crankcase leads to the oil tank. The oil tank breather is connected to the air filter back plate. 1972 and 1973 750 models have a non-mechanical breather which is located on the back of the left crankcase. The 850 engine has a breather located at the top rear of the timing chest. As with earlier models, the breather is vented through the oil tank to the air filter back plate.

SECTION C24
OIL PUMP

The oil pump is of the gear type and is shown in detail in *Fig.* C29. The return side of the pump, which is of twice the capacity of the feed side to provide sufficient capacity to keep the crankcases clear of surplus oil, is identified by the wider gears. The oil pump is sealed to the timing cover bore with a conical rubber oil seal located on the pump body by a steel ferrule and compressed by the timing cover. Removal of the oil pump is included in Section C16 and the servicing routine covered in Section C25.

SECTION C25

SERVICING THE OIL PUMP

Removal of the oil pump is described in Section *C16*. The criterion of oil pump condition is the degree of end float on the oil pump pinions, most easily felt by movement of the oil pump driving gear relative to the pump body. After some period of use, the tendency is for the pinions to wear into the pump end covers and such wear can only be removed by taking off the covers and flattening down the actual pump body.

1   Detach the pump top covers and drive gear with drive spindle by tapping the spindles through the keyed pinion with a pin point drift. The remaining parts can be lifted from the pump body at this stage.

2   Wash all the components thoroughly in clean gasoline (petrol) and allow to dry.

It is most important to correct end float on the feed gears (the narrow ones) first.

Engine/Primary Transmission C

3 Remove the feed gears and rub down the back plate end of the pump body surface against a high grade quality emery cloth on a perfectly flat surface such as a small surface plate. Flattening of the surface should continue a little at a time until the stage is reached where, on re-assembly of the oil pump, there is barely discernible stiffness on the oil pump driving spindle. This barely discernible stiffness will indicate that there is just sufficient freedom of movement and that there is no excess clearance between the feed gears and housing.

4 Remove the feed gears and repeat the flattening down process on the return side of the pump body until with the return gears only in the pump body and the screws tight there is similar slight stiffness.

5 Strip the pump body again and wash with very great care. Reassemble the pump and tighten the screws completely. At this stage there should be some degree of stiffness in the complete pump.

6 Introduce oil into the feed hole then, holding the oil pump with one hand, place a ring spanner over the driving spindle nut, and revolve the oil pump a number of times to allow oil to circulate completely. The oil pump should now have freed off considerably. Slight stiffness remaining should decrease, if not disappear completely.

SECTION C26

TIMING COVER

There are two garter type seals in the timing cover, one at the contact breaker housing and one to seal the crankshaft to the cover.

Contact Breaker Seal – Failure of this seal is indicated by the presence of oil in the contact breaker housing. To remove the old seal it is necessary to prise out with a screwdriver or similar implement thus rendering the seal scrap. A new seal should be fitted, pressure side, that is spring side, towards the engine and the seal should be tapped fully home into the housing using Service Tool 064292.

Crankshaft Seal – This seal is retained in the housing with a circlip. After removing the circlip, the seal can be prised out of its housing but will be damaged beyond further use. Care must be taken to avoid damage to the housing. Fit the new seal pressure side towards the timing cover and drive fully home using Service Tool 064292. Refit the circlip "sharp" side towards the crankcase and make sure that it is fully seated all-round.

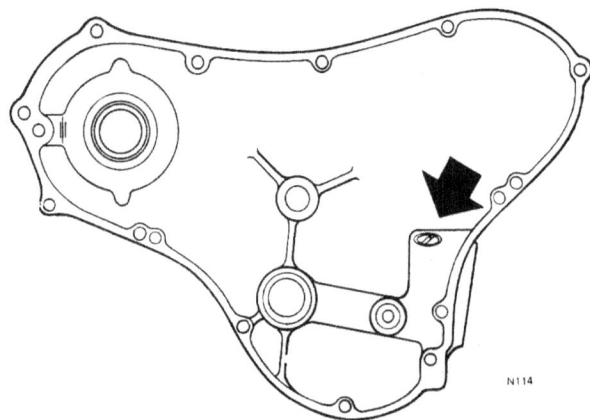

Fig. C31 Showing blanking plug in position in timing cover

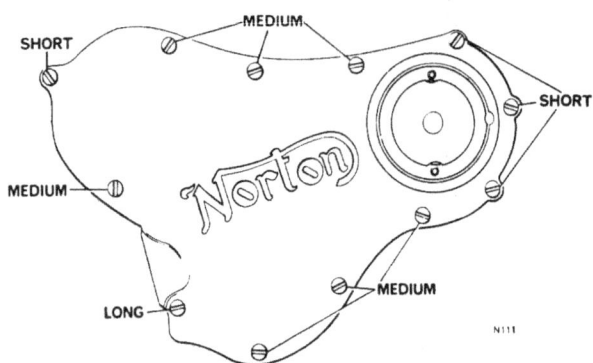

Fig. C32 Positions and lengths of odd timing cover screws

Where a new timing cover is being prepared for fitting, check that the blanking plug shown in *Fig.* C31 is in position. The timing cover odd screw lengths are shown in *Fig.* C32.

Engine/Primary Transmission C

SECTION C27

RE-ASSEMBLY OF THE CRANKSHAFT

Prior to assembly, it is vital to polish the crank journals using a fine grade emery tape then make absolutely sure that all parts are washed very thoroughly in gasoline (petrol) until clean. Ensure also that the oil ways are clean and blown through with an air line. Re-assembly proceeds as below:

1. Fit the drive side crank cheek to the flywheel, mating the markings previously made.

2. Fit the two inner studs through from drive side to timing side. Position the locking tab over both of the studs from the drive side and fit nuts.

3. Assemble the timing side crank cheek over the studs and the dowel in the flywheel.

4. Assemble the four remaining studs, driving side to timing side, noting that the studs are a good fit into the crank cheeks and will in all probability need to be tapped home with a drift.

5. Fit the second tab washer over the inner studs, followed by the timing side nuts.

6. Tighten the remaining nuts, commencing with the two washers and then proceeding diagonally, tighten the others.

7. Tap over the tab washers or use vice grips to bend the tabs over.

8. Ensure that the oil way blanking plug is fitted in the timing side crank cheek, particularly if a new timing side crank cheek is in use.

SECTION C28

RE-ASSEMBLING CONNECTING RODS TO CRANKSHAFT

As a matter of practice always use new bearing shells and at the time of fitting the shells, smear them with clean engine oil. Proceed as follows:

1. Press the drilled shell into the connecting rod big end eye and rotate into position, locating with the tab.

2. Fit the plain shell into the connecting rod cap and again locate the tab. The tab positions are shown in *Fig.* C33.

3. Fit the connecting rods but before doing so, note that it is unnecessary to renew the connecting rod bolts though new nuts should always be used. The connecting rods must be fitted with the oil holes from the big end eye outwards in each case. Fit the end caps with shells, ensuring that the mating marks align, and tighten the nuts evenly by hand.

4. Tighten the connecting rod nuts to a torque reading of 25 lbs./ft. (3·456 Kg/m).

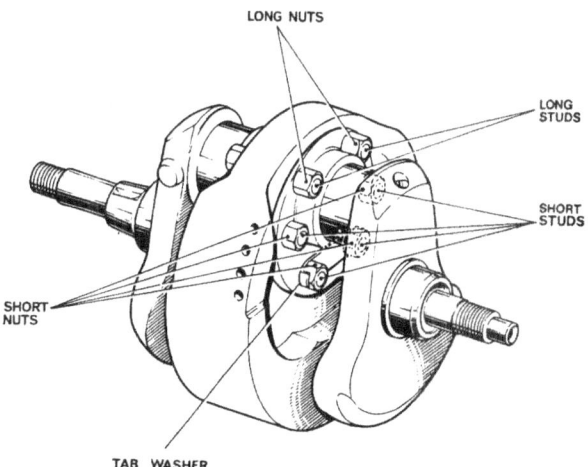

Fig. C33   Showing crankcheek to flywheel securing hardware

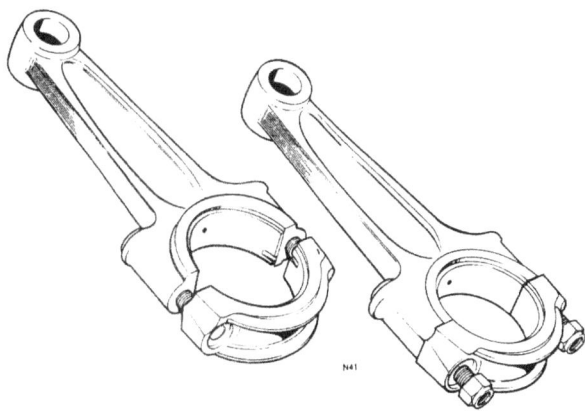

Fig. C34   Connecting rods showing both sides of big end eye and bearing shell tab locations

Engine/Primary Transmission C

SECTION C29

RE-ASSEMBLING CRANKSHAFT TO CRANKCASES

Since it is simpler to slide the drive side crankcase with the outer main bearing race over the complete assembly of the other crankcase with crankshaft than vice versa, we recommend the following routine:

1. Push the timing side crankcase over the crankshaft which must be supported upright on the bench. See *Fig.* C35. At this time check that the connecting rods clear the crankcase mouth of the crankshaft end of the bearing. If the bearing is too tight to push home over the crank, place a scrap main bearing inner race and a large washer over the crankshaft, outboard of the timing side crankcase then, using the oil pump driving worm on the crankshaft, pull it home through the bearing.

2. Position the camshaft thrust washer over the timing side camshaft bush and locate this, flat side towards the crankcase and bush, locating with a blob of grease. On engines between numbers 200000 and 300000, a flat thrust washer is fitted between this chamfered washer and the crankcase. Ensure that this flat washer is properly located with its tab in the hole provided below the bush.

3. Smear the timing side crankcase joint facing with a non-setting sealing compound. A little may be applied to the timing side case facing where there is no spigot.

4. Into the drive side camshaft bush fit the rotary disc followed by the spring on engines before 200000 and camshaft, oiling the bearing surface slightly.

5. Engage the camshaft with the driving dogs on the disc on engines before 200000.

6. Offer the drive side crankcase to the timing side after oiling the camshaft bearing area and the drive side roller main bearing. The operation of mating the crankcases is shown in *Fig.* C35. It will be noted that the camshaft is held in position against the breather disc and spring with one finger during this operation before 200000. Ensure that washer tabs are seated throughout this operation until cases are mated. It is most important that the drive side connecting rod does not come into contact with the crankcase mouth and at the final stage of mating the crankcases, it may well be necessary to turn the tachometer drive to locate into the camshaft worm drive.

7. Now tap the crankcases together with a hide hammer until the joint faces meet all-round.

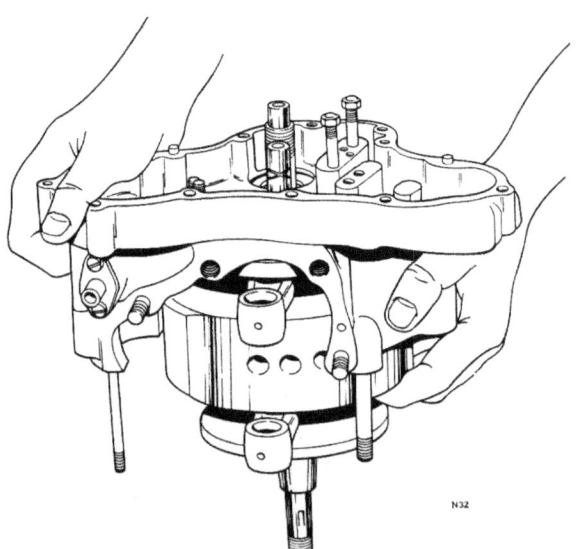

Fig. C35   Pushing timing side crankcase over crankshaft

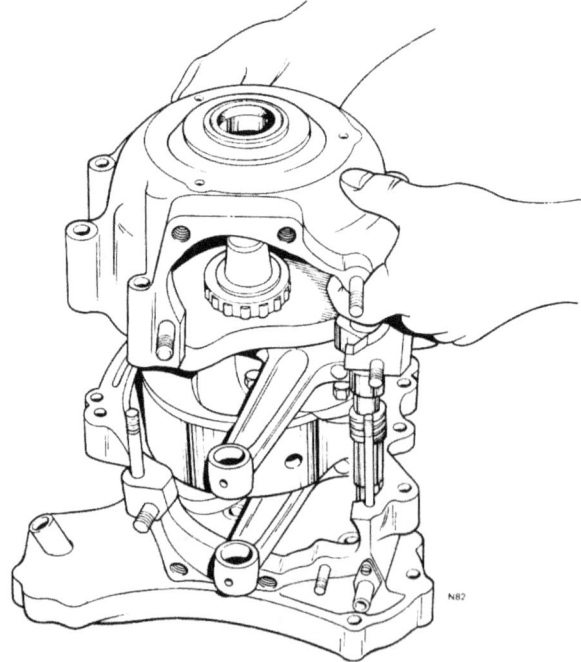

Fig. C36   Mating crankcases. Note the camshaft is held against the spring and disc with the finger

Engine/Primary Transmission C

8 Before tightening the crankcase securing nuts, ensure that there is end float on the camshaft, indicating its freedom.

9 Fit the crankcase front and rear screws, studs, nuts and washers.

10 Fit the short front crankcase mating bolt from drive side to timing side then fit the front bottom stud unless the crankcase is to be mounted in the vice in which case this front bottom stud should be omitted until a later stage.

11 Fit the two slot headed set screws from the timing side.

12 Tighten the mating nuts and screws evenly in rotation and wipe away surplus jointing compound remaining on the outside of the crankcase joint facing.

SECTION C30

ASSEMBLING RIGHT (TIMING SIDE) OF ENGINE

Having assembled the crankcases as detailed in Section C29, mount the crankcases in a plain jaw vice to facilitate handling. Re-assembly of the cam chain, sprockets and oil pump may now be undertaken as follows:

1 Fit the oil sealing disc over the timing side crankshaft, lip outwards.

2 Fit the cut-away backing washer.

3 Fit the woodruff key into the crankshaft then place on the crankshaft pinion, chamfered teeth and timing mark outwards. It may be necessary to tap the pinion fully home using a suitable tube as a drift.

4 Turn the crankshaft to top dead centre so that the timing pinion marking is uppermost.

5 Take the intermediate gear sprocket, the camshaft sprocket and cam chain, assembling as shown in *Fig.* C37. For correct timing the timing marks must be 10 rollers apart on the chain as shown in the illustration.

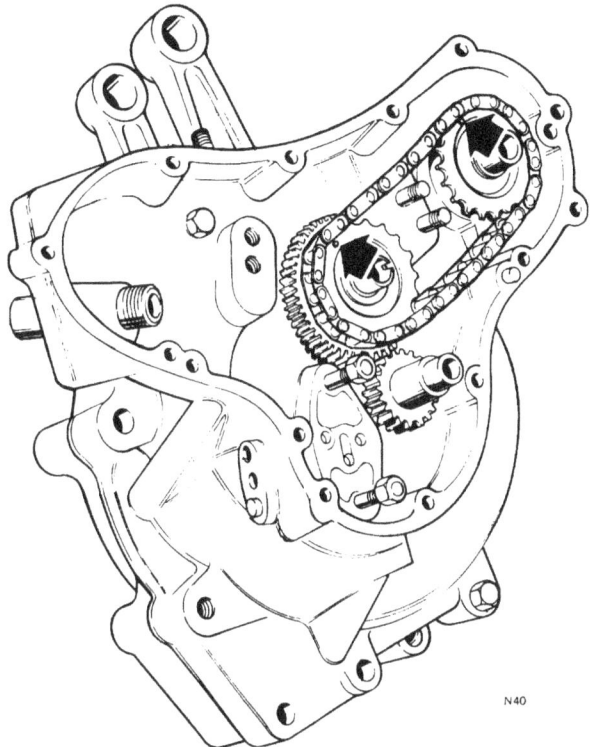

Fig. C37   Assembly of timing chain and sprockets. Note arrows

6 Locate the camshaft sprocket and intermediate gear and sprocket in position, mating up the marked space between the teeth on the intermediate gear with the marked tooth on the timing pinion. On all engines it will be found that there is a paint marking to illustrate more clearly the timing position on the intermediate timing gear.

7 Assemble the chain tensioner as shown in *Fig.* C38, noting that the clamping plates differ, the inner one being thinner than the outer and the inner being fitted long end down whilst the outer clamping plate is fitted long end up.

8 Fit the chain tensioner, fan disc washers and nuts moving the tensioner blade up to give a maximum $\frac{3}{16}$ in. (4·8 mm) up and down movement at the tightest point of the chain and nip up the tensioner securing nut. Before finally locking up these nuts, rotate the crankshaft a little at a time, checking at each stage the chain tension lest there should be a tight spot on some point of the chain. When chain tension is correct, finally lock up the tensioner securing nuts.

Engine/Primary Transmission C

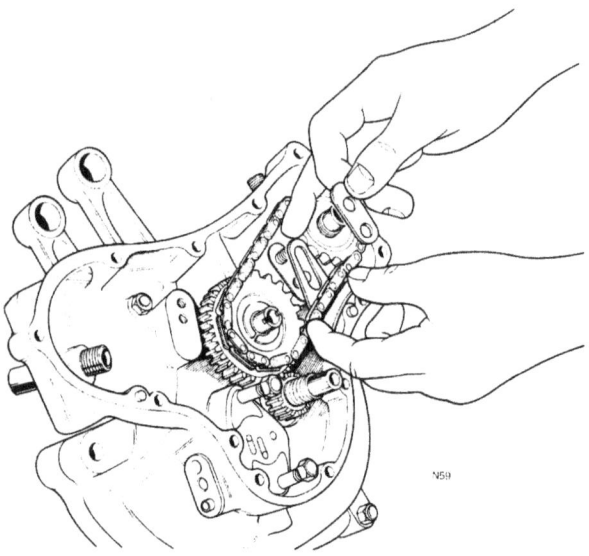

Fig. C38 Chain tensioner showing thin inner plate long end downwards

9 Fit the oil pump driving worm which is left hand threaded.

10 Fit the camshaft sprocket nut which is normal right hand threaded.

11 In order to tighten both the oil pump driving worm nut and camshaft sprocket nut securely it is necessary to sprag the crankshaft with a suitable bar placed in the deepest of the flywheel balance holes as shown earlier in *Fig. C22*.
Under no circumstances tighten the camshaft sprocket nut by shocking using a box spanner, tommy bar and hammer since an even pressure is required specifically for tightening this nut. Tighten securely the timing pinion nut.

Prior to fitting the oil pump it is desirable, if the pump has been stripped or parts renewed, to prime this. The pump should be turned by hand and oil fed into the gears by the use of an oil gun. Very late engines use a joint gasket between the oil pump and crankcase joint faces and where a joint washer is used at this point, under no circumstances should the conical rubber seal between the oil pump and timing cover be equipped with packing shims. Proceed as follows:

12 Fit the oil pump and secure with two nuts without washers. A torque figure of 10/12 ft. lbs. (1·383 to 1·659 Kg/m) is required.

13 Fit a new conical rubber oil seal part number NMT272 on the oil pump outlet stub and dispense with any shims which may have been fitted between the seal and pump body at the time of dismantling. Over compression of the seal will render it unfit for further use.

14 After the oil pump is secured, recheck the security of the driving gear nut.

SECTION C31

REFITTING THE TIMING COVER

The timing cover should be prepared by washing very thoroughly in clean gasoline (petrol) and if necessary by renewing the oil seals as described in Section *C26*. If a new timing cover is to be fitted, check that the blanking plug is fitted into the boss for the pressure relief valve. These features are shown in *Fig. C31*.

1 Fit the contact breaker oil seal protection tool 061359 into the camshaft and tighten. This will allow the contact breaker seal to pass over the camshaft without damage as the timing cover is placed in position. Lightly oil the tapered surface of this tool.

2 Pass the contact breaker lead through the hole in the timing case, then locate the cover in position.

3 Fit the timing cover screws. The odd screw lengths are shown in *Fig. C32* but the remaining screws are all of the same length. Secure the set of screws.

4 Remove the contact breaker seal tool 061359.

5 Prepare the auto advance mechanism by cleaning very thoroughly and lubricating sparingly with clean engine oil. Ensure that the taper for the auto advance cam is clean and dry then offer the auto advance unit loosely into position.

6 Fit the contact breaker plate, yellow lead rearwards and secure with the pillar studs central in the adjustment slots. For ease of handling at a later stage, centralise both contact breaker plate adjusters. These are indicated in *Fig. C50*.

Engine/Primary Transmission C

SECTION C32

RE-ASSEMBLY OF CRANKCASE ASSEMBLY TO FRAME

Re-assembly of the crankcase into the frame is virtually a reversal of the dismantling procedure though the operation of fitting the front mounting is given complete as below:

1. With the crankcase attached to the rear engine mounting plates, lift the crankcase assembly and gearbox, pivoting on the rear mounting to insert the bottom studs from right to left. The direction of fitting this stud is important only on 1970 models.

It is necessary to fit the front mounting at this stage before final tightening of all the engine plate to crankcase bolts and before fitting the inner chaincase. Attention to the front mounting and shimming has already been carried out on the bench as in Section F15.

2. Take the front mounting and slide the bottom mounting to crankcase stud into position.

3. Using the bottom stud as the pivot, lift the mounting into position on the crankcase bosses as in Fig. C39.

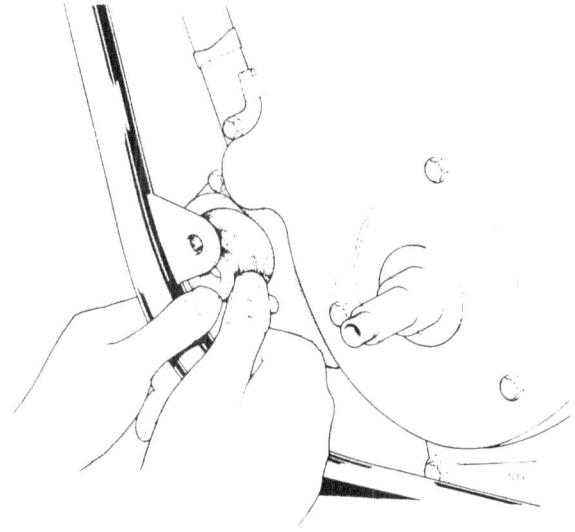

Fig. C40 Inserting front left gaiter mounting cap group

4. Grease the mounting cap and shims and assemble each group of plastic washers, spacers and gaiters ready for insertion in sets between the front mounting tube and frame.

5. Insert the right set first, then place the washer for the mounting front bolt against the frame, aligning the mounting centre bolt head with the timing case and inserting the centre bolt through to the left hand side just short of the Isolastic bush. Note that it may be necessary to lift the crankcases a little to ease fitting of this bolt.

6. As in Fig. C40 insert the left set of gaiter, mounting cap, shims, etc., and again, by lifting the crankcase for improved hole alignment, slide the centre bolt fully home.

7. Use a small screwdriver with care to feed the lip of the gaiter over the shim cap at both ends of the mounting, revolving the gaiter a little to facilitate this operation.

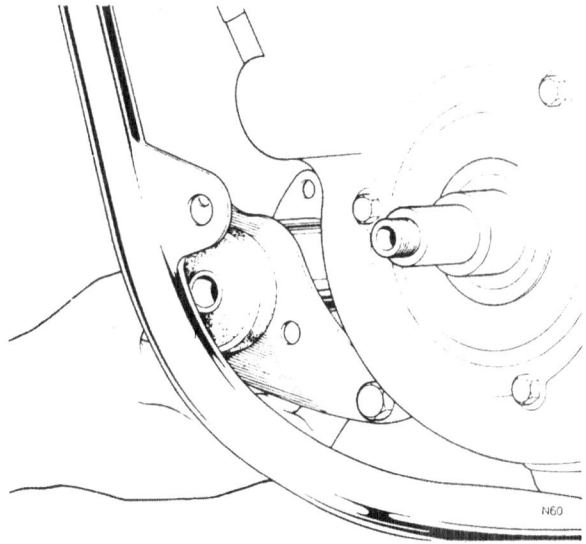

Fig. C39 Lifting front mounting into position using bottom bolt as pivot

Engine/Primary Transmission C

8   Fit and secure the centre bolt nut and washer and tighten to 25 lbs./ft. (3·456 Kg/m).

9   Fit the top bolt to the assembly.

The remaining items of the engine plates which have been assembled as a reversal of the dismantling procedure should now be tightened to the recommended torque settings. The $\frac{3}{8}$ in. diameter engine to frame stud nuts require a torque figure of 25 to 30 lbs./ft. (3·456 to 4·148 Kg/m) and the $\frac{5}{16}$ in. nuts to 15 lbs./ft. (2·074 Kg/m).

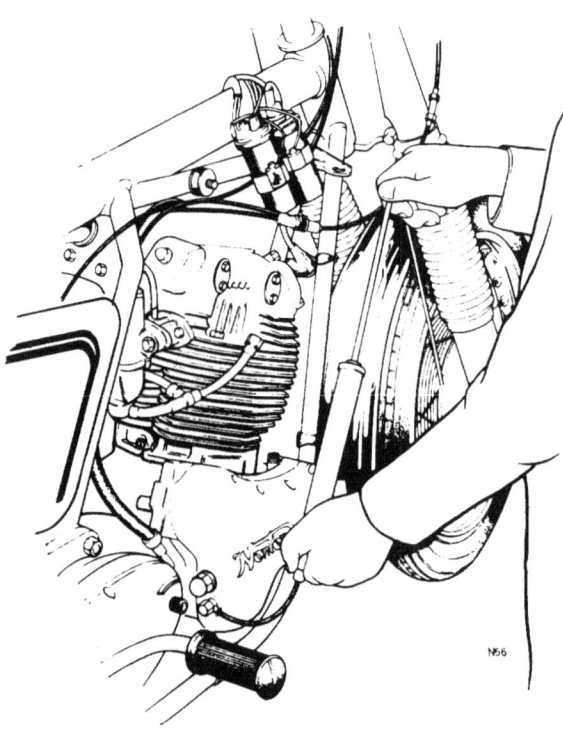

Fig. C41 Priming crankshaft with oil

Prior to fitting the bottom connection for the rocker feed pipe it is most desirable to prime the crankshaft with approximately a teacup full of oil. This is most easily achieved by the use of an oil syringe, short length of flexible pipe, and a spare rocker feed pipe banjo which can be connected at the rear of the timing case. The priming operation is shown in *Fig.* C41.

SECTION C33

REFITTING PISTONS AND CYLINDER

Throughout the fitting of the pistons and cylinder, take care to protect the connecting rods and pistons from damage caused by these parts coming into contact with the crankcase mouth or cylinder base studs. Proceed as follows:

1   Grease the crankcase studs lightly and apply a coat of Loctite "plastic gasket" material to cylinder base flange.

2   Fit one circlip to each piston, sharp edge outwards.

3   Heat the pistons in hot water to ease entry of the wrist pins (gudgeon pins).

4   Take special note that 750 pistons are handed and marked "LH" and "RH" respectively and "EX" at forward side.
If the marks are illegible the pistons may be recognised by the fact that the inlet valve cutaway is away from the edge of the crown in each case.

5   Oil the small end eye and wrist pin bosses and push each wrist pin home by hand.

6   As each piston is fitted, fit the second circlip sharp end outwards.

7   Turn the engine crankshaft backwards to lower the pistons, then support the pistons as in *Fig.* C41 on two suitable bars which must not overlap the timing case.

8   Position the piston rings with the top compression ring gap central at the front of the piston body and the second taper ring gap central at the rear of the piston body.

9   Position the scraper ring expander to the side of the piston body with the rail gap 1 in. to the left and right of the expander gap to prevent the rail ends spragging in the connecting rod clearance cutaways in the cylinders.

10   Smear both piston bodies with clean engine oil. Fit piston ring clamps (also shown in *Fig.* C41) to keep the piston rings closed. Do not overtighten the ring clamps which would tend to prevent the ring clamps sliding as the cylinder is offered.

Engine/Primary Transmission C

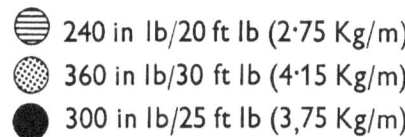

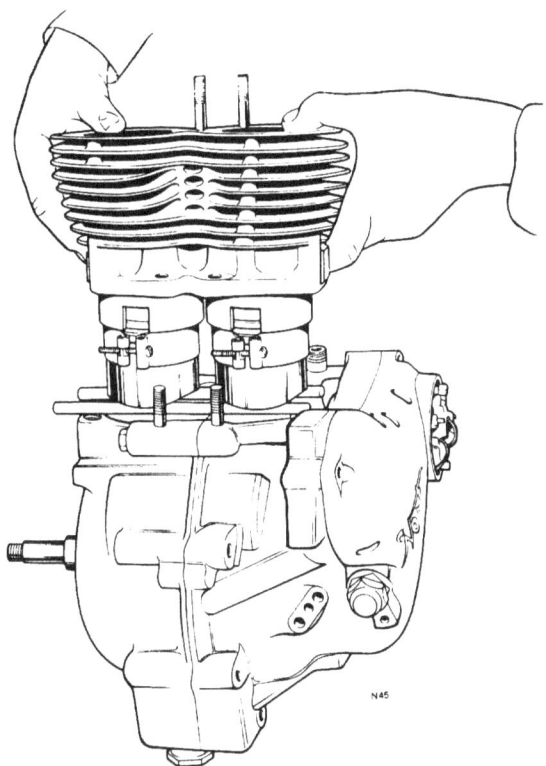

Fig. C42 *Fitting cylinder over pistons. Note piston supporting bars and ring clamps in use*

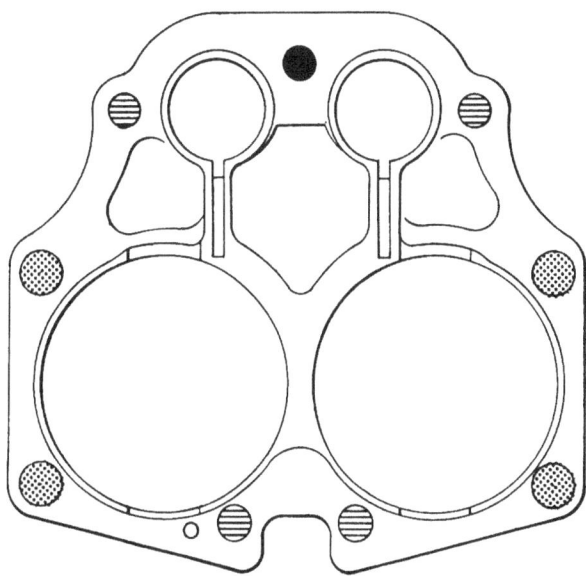

Fig. C43 *850 cylinder base securing torque.*

11 Offer the cylinder over the pistons as shown in *Fig. C42*, pushing the cylinder down to slide the ring clamps down quickly. The pistons are now entered in the cylinder bores.

12 Remove the support bars and both rings clamps.

13 Partially lower the cylinder but start cylinder base nuts before lowering the barrel completely. Only the large centre nut lacks a washer.

14 Tighten the cylinder base nuts in sequence. Tighten the ⅜ in. nuts to a torque setting of 25 lbs./ft. (3·456 Kg/m) and 5/16 in. nuts to 20 lbs./ft. (2·765 Kg/m). See *Fig. C43* for 850 torque settings.

SECTION C34

ASSEMBLING PRIMARY TRANSMISSION

The primary transmission is assembled in the order: inner primary chaincase, engine sprocket, clutch and primary chain, rotor and stator and finally the outer primary chaincase. The full routine is detailed below:

1 Check that the engine sprocket key will pass freely through the keyway in the sprocket and if necessary relieve any roughness.

2 Fit the engine sprocket key into the crankshaft.

3 Fit the inner chaincase to crankcase gasket, holding in position with grease or a non-setting jointing compound.

4 Check that the plain washer is on the chaincase support stud (on some units an additional thinner large diameter washer is used at this point).

5 Ensure that the inner and outer joint faces of the inner chaincase are clean.

6 Fit the inner chaincase, ensuring that the gearbox mainshaft seal passes over the mainshaft without damage and that the chaincase forward end is fully home.

Engine/Primary Transmission C

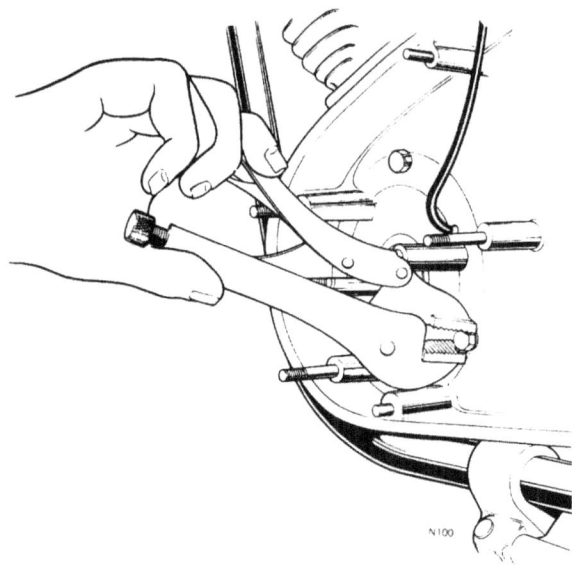

Fig. C44 Using grip wrench to squeeze over tab washers at inner chaincase

7. Fit the inner chaincase securing tab washers and set screws and squeeze over the locking tabs using a grip wrench as shown in *Fig. C44*.

8. Assemble the clutch location spacer, recessed portion towards the gearbox, followed by the spacing washer. The purpose of the spacing washers is to align accurately the clutch sprocket with the engine sprocket.

9. Assemble the engine sprocket and clutch sprocket to the triple row chain ready for fitting.

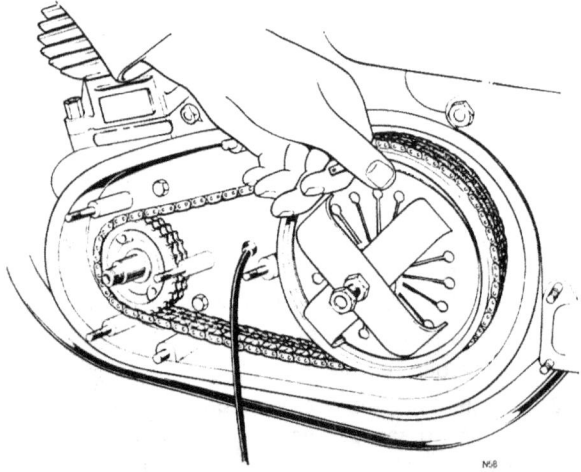

Fig. C45 Winding diaphragm spring circlip into position

10. Offer the engine sprocket, clutch sprocket and primary chain as a set, feeding the stator through between the chain runs. The stator is still attached to the inner chaincase by the lead passing through the chaincase grommet.

11. At this stage push the engine sprocket fully home over the woodruff key, if necessary using a tubular drift to push the sprocket fully home. At the same time the clutch will need to be pushed home firmly over the splines of the mainshaft.

12. Fit the clutch centre securing nut and single spring washer (early) or nut and tab washer (late models) in the case of the tab washer engaging the ends, in the 2 holes in the clutch centre.

13. Loosely position the rear brake pedal and footrest, apply the rear brake fully and tighten the clutch centre nut. The correct torque for the clutch centre nut is 70 lbs./ft. (9·678 Kg/m). Squeeze the centre portion of the tab washer to 2 flats on the nut (late models). Proceed to assemble the clutch.

14. If for any reason the clutch plates have been removed from the housing, re-assemble these, an inner splined friction plate first into the housing, followed by a plain steel alternately, finishing with the robust iron pressure plate.

15. The clutch diaphragm spring should be assembled to the spring tool and tensioned as shown earlier in *Fig. C13* until the diaphragm spring is flat.

16. Offer the diaphragm spring on the tool to the clutch housing and push home as far as possible.

17. Enter one end of the clutch spring circlip and continue to wind the remainder of the spring into the housing as shown in *Fig. C45*.

Engine/Primary Transmission C

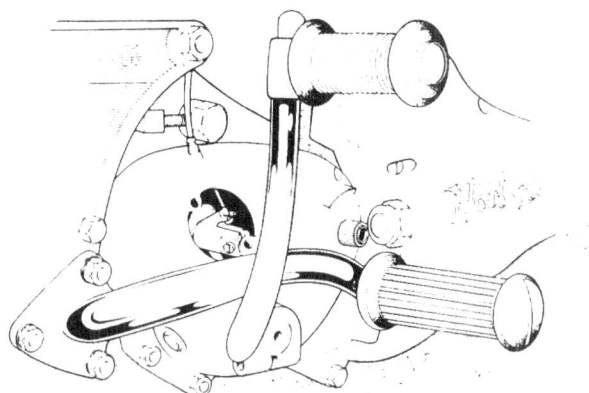

Fig. C46 Clutch operating lever in correct position

18 When the spring circlip is well bedded into the housing all-round, remove the spring tool by slackening the centre bolt.

19 Fit the clutch push rod adjuster screw and lock nut.

20 Adjust the clutch push rod with the handlebar adjustment slackened off completely. Screw in the adjuster until there is just perceptible lift on the diaphragm spring and slacken back one full turn, holding in this position whilst the lock nut is tightened completely.

It is possible for the clutch operating lever in the kickstart case to have dropped down between the thrust ball and roller against which the lever lifts and if this has occurred, it will be found that the clutch is inoperative, and it will be necessary to remove the inspection cover which is secured by two screws to the gearbox outer cover, slacken back fully the push rod adjuster and lift the lever back into position before adjusting. In *Figs.* C46 and C47 we show the lever in its correct position and the lever as it may be found if it has dropped

21 Assemble the shims on the crankshaft over the engine sprocket, followed by the spacing collar with the recess outwards.

22 Fit the rotor key, the inner end of which passes into the recess in the collar.

23 Ensure that the rotor is free of any magnetic particles it may have attracted whilst dismantled and fit the rotor to the shaft and key, name and timing marks outboards.

24 Assemble the rotor nut and fan disc washer and with top gear engaged and the rear brake applied fully, tighten the rotor nut fully to 70 to 80 lbs./ft. (9·678 to 11·060 Kg/m).

25 Fit the three stator spacers on to the stator mounting studs followed by the stator on which the lead must be outboard at the 5 o-clock position.

26 Assemble the plain washers and stator securing nuts and tighten to a torque setting of 15 lbs./ft. (2·074 Kg/m). Check the gap between the stator and rotor which must give a minimum air gap of 0·008 in. to 0·010 in. (0·2032 to 0·254 mm). Any misalignment of the stator mounting studs would account for reduced air gap at any one given point and can only be corrected by very careful slight re-alignment of the studs.

27 Check that the chaincase sealing band is snugly in position in the recess in the outer face of the inner chaincase with the join in the band at the top then place the outer chaincase in position.

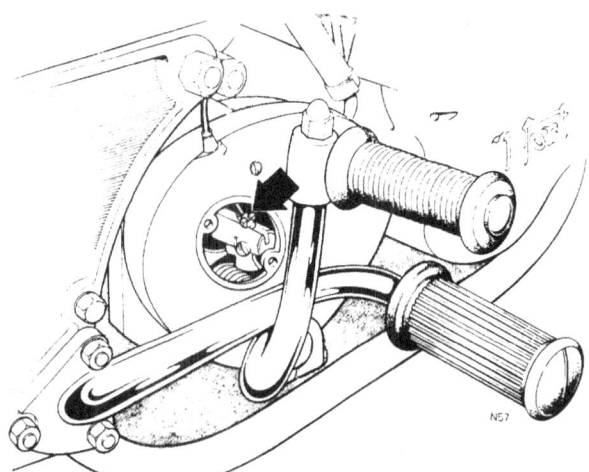

Fig. C47 Clutch operating lever in wrong position where lever has dropped down

28 Secure the outer chaincase using the single centre sleeve nut and washer.

29 In order that the point is not overlooked it is recommended that lubricant is added to the chaincase at this stage.

30 Refit the left hand foot-rest and brake pedal assembly, securing with three nuts, two washers and the stop lamp lead support bracket acting as the third washer on the bottom stud.

Engine/Primary Transmission C

SECTION C35

CLUTCH OPERATING MECHANISM

The clutch is connected from the left handlebar control to the clutch operating lever within the gearbox cover. As the lever is withdrawn, the clutch operating lever is lifted, exerting pressure on a ball bearing against the end of the clutch push rod. The push rod forces outwards the centre of the diaphragm spring, relieving the pressure and allowing the clutch plates to separate. For the clutch to operate correctly, the degree of free movement on the cable and clutch push rod must be controlled. Excessive slack may prevent the clutch freeing completely and excessively tight adjustment will result in the clutch plates being held apart. Adjustment is provided on the cable and push rod.

Clutch Adjustment

1. Slacken cable adjustment at the handlebar control as far as possible.

2. Remove the clutch adjuster inspection cap from the chaincase.

3. Remove the inspection cap from the gearbox end cover.

4. With the index finger, move the clutch operating lever to and fro inside the gearbox cover to establish whether or not there is slight movement. If there is, clutch push rod adjustment is correct. If there is not, rectify as follows.

5. Release nut (B) in *Fig.* C48 then turn the screw (C) gently anti-clockwise until movement is felt on the right side operating lever.

6. Turn screw (C) in a clockwise direction until it is felt that the screw just touches the push rod.

7. Unscrew adjustment screw (C) one full turn and, holding in this position retighten locknut (B). This ensures the correct free movement on the clutch push rod.

8. Adjust the clutch cable at the control to provide $\frac{3}{16}$ in. to $\frac{1}{4}$ in. (4·76 to 6·35 mm) free movement between the cable outer casing and adjuster.

CLUTCH PLATES

The clutch dismantling procedure is covered as part of Section C13 "Dismantling Primary Transmission and Clutch." However, it is sometimes considered necessary to remove the plates separately for inspection.

To gain access to the clutch plates, follow Section C13 & C14 items 1 to 9. Next remove the clutch pressure plate followed alternately by the internal splined friction plates and external splined plain steel plates.

After removal, wash all the clutch plates and the pressure plate in gasoline (petrol) until perfectly clean, then allow to dry.

Reassembly is a reversal of the foregoing but full nstructions are given in Section C33.

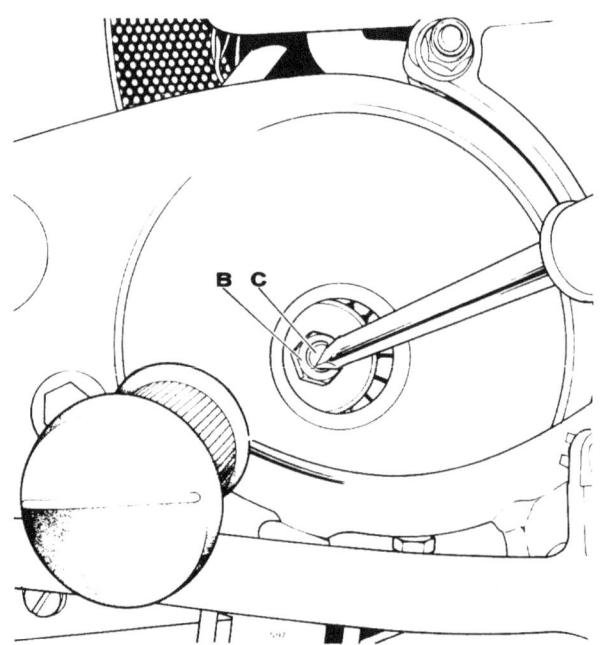

Fig. C48 Clutch adjustment

Plate Inspection

Examine the friction plates for obvious wear to the splines and for "charring" of the surface such as would occur during prolonged clutch slip. Examine the plain steel driven plates for deep scoring or grooving. Check the external splines for obvious wear, and check each plate in turn on a surface plate for flatness. Any badly worn or distorted plates must be renewed before reassembly.

Engine/Primary Transmission C

SECTION C36

TACHOMETER DRIVE

The tachometer drive is taken from the worm drive at the right end of the camshaft. The cable has an adaptor for the cable between the lower end of the cable and tachometer driven gear. The driven gear is removable after removing two screws and lifting clear the housing and 'O' sealing ring but damage to the drive gear can only be corrected by replacing the camshaft.

SECTION C37

REMOVING AND REFITTING ENGINE COMPLETE

For ease of handling the engine unit may be removed from the mounting plates as a unit so that it can be dealt with on the bench. Proceed as follows:

1. Remove the left footrest and brake pedal and allow these to hang on the cable.

2. Drain and remove the outer primary chaincase, alternator rotor nut and alternator stator. The stator can be left attached to the inner chaincase by the lead but disconnect the two connectors beneath the airbox and lever off the rotor.

3. Slacken off clutch adjustment, compress the clutch diaphragm spring (this requires tool 060999) and remove circlip.

4. Fit clutch hub tool 061015 and remove clutch centre nut and fit engine sprocket extractor tool 064297. Remove engine sprocket and lift entire engine sprocket – primary chain – clutch assembly away.

5. Flatten tab washers locking three bolts around crankshaft stub, remove the three bolts and lift off inner chaincase.

6. Remove rubber breather hose (near primary cover on early models; under rear of engine on 1972 and later; at rear of timing chest on 850).

7. Detach engine ground wire attached to lower left crankcase stud.

8. Remove fuel tank, ignition coils, carburettor top caps and withdraw slide assemblies. Remove exhaust pipes and upper Isolastic head steady.

9. Drain oil from oil tank and remove oil feed lines from boss beneath timing cover. Remove rocker oil feed pipe.

10. Disconnect the contact breaker lead wires and tachometer drive cable.

11. Slip a sturdy support (wood block or metal rod) between engine and lower frame tubes.

12. Remove bolts holding rear of engine to engine cradle so engine hinges on front Isolastic mount.

13. Loosen small bolts holding front engine mount. STEADY ENGINE and remove large Isolastic mount bolt, then the small bolts and lift out front Isolastic mount.

14. Engine is now free and can be lifted clear of frame to right side on to work bench.

Refitting is a direct reversal of the foregoing.

SECTION C38

IGNITION TIMING

Ignition timing can be checked and if necessary reset either with the engine stationary or, using a stroboscope, with the engine running. The stationary method is quite satisfactory where a stroboscope is not available. However, for greater accuracy, the stroboscope method is preferable, since it also checks auto advance function. A timing indicator plate is attached to the outer primary chaincase to align with the corresponding mark on the rotor, the marks being visible after removal of the chaincase inspection cap (see *Fig. C49*). The latest Lucas rotor has two timing markings opposite each other. Note that the presence of the surplus marking will not affect timing, either static or with a stroboscope.

To explain – the engine must be running for a stroboscope to be used. Setting the timing by the wrong marking would mean the spark was timed at bottom dead centre and the engine would not run. If the engine is timed on the correct stroke, the stroboscope will not pick up the wrong marking. Similarly with static timing, only the correct marking will align with the calibrated scale in the primary case with the piston near top dead centre on the firing stroke for the cylinder being timed.

Engine/Primary Transmission C

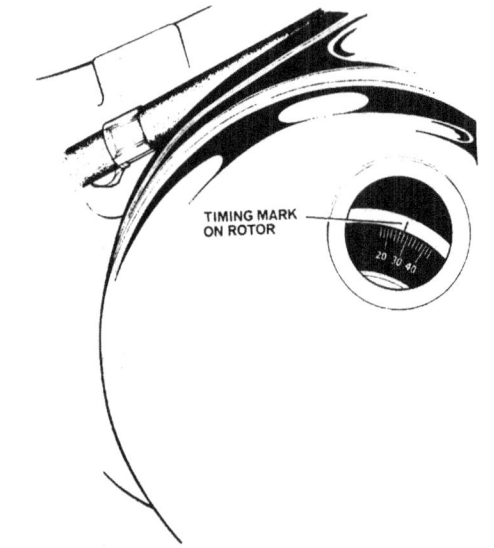

Fig. C49 Timing plate visible after removal of inspection cap from chaincase

Ignition Timing Basic Procedure Prior to Checking

Straightforward assembly of the auto-advance mechanism and contact breaker assembly is covered in Section C31 as part of the Timing Cover reassembly procedure. It is however, necessary to locate the auto-advance cam approximately prior to timing. It is assumed that the auto-advance mechanism is loose assembled to the taper in the camshaft and that the contact breaker backplate screws are central in the adjustment slots. Remove the inlet rocker cover and the right hand exhaust rocker cover and both sparking plugs then turn the engine forwards on the kickstart until T.D.C. is located on the right cylinder with both valves closed at the firing position. Identify by wire colouring the contact breaker points for the right cylinder then turn the auto-advance cam until it just starts to open this set of points. Secure the cam with washer and centre bolt. The engine is now ready for accurate timing.

Ignition Timing Procedure – Engine Static

1 Remove both spark plugs.

2 Remove the inspection cap on the chaincase.

3 Remove the contact breaker cover.

4 Clean and adjust the contact breaker points as described in Section C40.

Note that if, at any later time, contact breaker adjustment is disturbed or allowed to vary, ignition timing will be altered. This necessitates retiming of the engine.

5 Remove the auto advance cam centre bolt.

6 Replace the washer from this bolt with the special washer 06·0949 having a hole large enough to clear the central portion of the unit and thus abut to the cam.

7 Replace the auto advance cam bolt with special washer, rotate the auto advance to the full advance position (it will rotate only one way), hold and tighten the bolt. The washer bearing against the cam will hold this in the full advance position.

8 Establish that the cylinder on which the timing is being checked has both valves closed at Top Dead Centre (T.D.C.) and rotate the engine forwards by engaging top gear and turning the rear wheel until this is the case.

The contact breaker points leads are black and yellow or black and white and this feature allows the operator to check which set of points are feeding which coil and cylinder. The factory standard arrangement is for the left coil and cylinder to be fed by the yellow/black rear set of points.

9 Rotate the engine backwards gently until the machined mark on the rotor registers with 28° on the indicator plate. At this precise moment the contact breaker points should start to open in which case timing is correct.

Engine/Primary Transmission C

The exact point of separation can be determined by inserting a strip of very thin paper between the points. The points will grip the paper when closed. By moving the engine *slowly*, a light pull on the paper will dislodge this at the exact point of separation. Take care not to leave a shred of paper between the points when using this method. A preferable method is to use a low wattage bulb and holder with a short length of wire attached to the bulb body with a second length of wire attached to the bulb connection. Crocodile clips should be attached to the loose end of both wires. Connect one wire to the contact breaker spring of the set of points being checked and the second wire to a suitable earth point on the engine. Switch on the ignition and as the engine is turned, the bulb will light at the exact point of separation.

10 If the timing is incorrect, i.e. the points do not open at 28° before T.D.C., release the two screws in elongated holes which secure the main backplate and rotate it in the housing. To advance the timing, move the baseplate clockwise and to retard, move the baseplate anti-clockwise. When the timing is correct, secure the backplate screws.

11 Using the same technique, check that the contact breaker points open at 28° B.T.D.C. on the firing stroke for the second cylinder. If incorrect, make adjustment by movement of the secondary backplate. To do so, slacken screws (A) in *Fig.* C50 and use the eccentric headed adjusting screws (B) to move the mounting plate. When timing is correct, re-secure the screws (A).

Ignition Timing Procedure – Engine Running

(Stroboscope Method)

This method is greatly preferred for extreme accuracy in setting. Prior to checking timing, clean and set both sets of contact breaker points to the figure given in "General Data."
Note that late models have two marks on the rotor but that if the ignition timing is sufficiently correct for the engine to run at all, the stroboscope will only detect the correct marking. If the engine has been rebuilt and ignition timing is being set from scratch, firstly follow the basic procedure in the preceding text. Commence stroboscopic timing as follows:

1 Remove the inspection cap on the chaincase to reveal the degree indicator plate and timing mark on the rotor.

2 Connect the stroboscope to the H.T. lead on the right cylinder and use a battery separate to that on the motorcycle to power the lamp, thus eliminating possible incorrect readings. For the full method of connection follow the stroboscope lamp manufacturer's instructions.

3 Identify by lead colours the set of contact breaker points on which timing is being set by the colour of the wiring at the points and the ignition coil.

4 Start the engine and run at a steady 3000 r.p.m. indicated on the tachometer.

5 Shine the stroboscope lamp on the indicator plate. If timing is correct, the rotor marking will register with the 28° marking on the indicator plate. If the marks do not align, the timing must be adjusted.

6 To adjust the timing at the first set of points, release the two screws in elongated holes which secure the backplate and rotate it in the housing. To advance the timing, move the baseplate clockwise and to retard, move the baseplate anti-clockwise. Move the backplate on its slots until the rotor mark and 28° marks align when checked with the stroboscope then secure the backplate screws.

7 Reconnect the stroboscope for the left cylinder and again check for rotor mark alignment at 28°.

8 If timing is incorrect for the left cylinder, correct by slackening off the clamping screw for the secondary backplate for this set of points then use the eccentric headed adjusting screw to move the secondary backplate (see *Fig.* C50–secondary backplate screws are marked "A" and eccentric screws are marked "B"). Recheck timing with the stroboscope and when correct, secure the screws "A".

Engine/Primary Transmission C

SECTION C39

AUTO ADVANCE UNIT

The auto advance unit fitted behind the contact breaker plate in the timing cover automatically and progressively advances the ignition timing as the engine speed increases, and returns it to the fully retarded or static position when the engine stops.

To expose the mechanism, it is necessary to remove the contact breaker plate complete, but before doing so mark the exact position of the plate so that when it is refitted the timing is not disturbed.

Remove the contact breaker plate fixing screws and take off the plate complete with the contact sets. Ensure that the springs of the auto advance unit are intact with the taper loops attached to the pins. Check the automatic action by turning the cam by hand to the fully advanced position in which the bob weights will be fully extended. When the cam is released, the springs should return the bob weights to the static position.

Lubricate the mechanism sparingly. Do not over lubricate as an excess of oil may reach the contact breaker points. If the contact breaker plate has been removed from its original position without being marked, the ignition timing should be checked and reset as in Section C38 when the plate has been refitted.

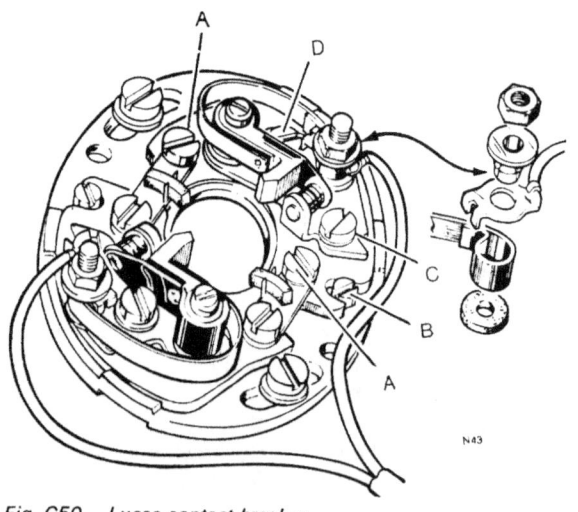

Fig. C50   Lucas contact breaker

SECTION C40

CONTACT BREAKER ASSEMBLY

Commandos have been fitted with two different Lucas contact breaker assembly systems. These systems are similar, but each requires a different contact point set and has its own peculiar adjustment procedure.

The Lucas 6 CA contact breaker was fitted to Commandos produced prior to 1973. All 1973 750's and all 850's have the Lucas 10 CA contact breaker assembly. Both systems have a separate and independently adjustable contact set for each cylinder, see *Fig.* C50. Each contact set is mounted on its own crescent-shaped assembly plate that is fixed to the circular base plate by two screws (A). When these screws are loosened, the assembly plate can be moved in relation to the ignition cam (and the base plate) by the eccentric screw (B). This permits a very accurate setting of ignition timing for each cylinder.

The difference in the two systems is in the fixing of the contact points set. The earlier 6 CA used only one fixing screw and an eccentric adjusting screw (C). The 10 CA uses two fixing screws to secure the contact set to the assembly plate. This system requires that the plate be moved by a screwdriver blade or similar tool to secure adjustment.

The circular base plate is secured by two screws (the tapped screws securing the outer cover). To advance the timing on both cylinders an equal amount, move the baseplate clockwise. To retard, move the baseplate anticlockwise.

Adjusting Contact Breaker Points Gap

Remove the spark plugs so that the engine can be rotated easily. A small mark located near the lubrication slot on the cam marks the highest lift position on the ignition cam. Rotate the engine until this mark aligns exactly with the nylon heel of the contact breaker; at this position the points will be fully open. Check the gap with a 0·015 in. (·38 mm) feeler gauge. If adjustment is necessary, slacken the contact breaker fixing screw(s), according to type of system fitted. Move the contact set by the method applicable to your assembly until the correct gap is obtained. Tighten the securing screws. Recheck the gap to ensure that the adjustment was not disturbed by the fixing screws. Adjust the other contact set in a similar manner.

Engine/Primary Transmission C

Maintenance of the Contact Breaker

Every 5,000 miles (8,000 kilometres) the contact breaker points should be examined to determine their condition. Remove the nut securing the contact breaker spring to the anchor post and lift off the spring heel, together with the terminals, insulating bush and the insulating washer. Remove the fixed contact plate locking screw and take off the fixed contact plate.

Points which are slightly burnt or pitted can be smoothed with a fine carborundum stone and afterwards cleaned with a brush moistened in petrol or white spirit; if they are badly affected they should be renewed.

Before reassembly, smear the contact breaker pivot post and the cam very sparingly with Retinax "A" grease and add three drops of engine oil to each lubricating felt. When reassembling ensure that the insulating washer, contact breaker spring, terminal and insulating bush are fitted in the order shown in *Fig*. C47 and that the terminal tags are inside the curve of the spring. Finally retime the ignition as described in Section C38.

SECTION C41

CHAINS

It is important to maintain the correct chain tension since if the chain is too tight the engine and gearbox bearings will be pre-loaded in the case of the primary chain and the gearbox and rear wheel bearings will be pre-loaded in the case of the rear chain. Pre-loading will inevitably cause premature bearing failure. Conversely, if the chains are too slack then premature wear is inevitable on the sprocket teeth.

The primary chain operates in an oil bath formed by the primary chaincase and requires no lubrication from an outside source providing the chaincase level is maintained. The rear chain is lubricated automatically from the oil tank via a restrictor located to the rear of the tank. However, the rear chain is not fully enclosed and from time to time requires cleaning and lubricating manually.

Chain Serviceability

Both in the case of single row (rear) chain and triple row (primary) chain, chain length extention of 2% is permissible before the chain is considered to have reached the end of its usefulness. This figure presumes that extension is checked only when the chain has been cleaned thoroughly and that any chain showing evidence of broken rollers has been discarded.

Primary Chain Adjustment

The separate gearbox design of the Commando permits adjustment by the medium of pivoting the gearbox on the bottom bolt and there is no necessity for a slipper type tensioner. Due to the high power output of the Commando and Combat engines the correct adjustment procedure must be followed to prevent subsequent gearbox movement in service. Proceed as follows:

1. Check the total up and down movement on the primary chain top run. This is felt by the finger when the upper centre inspection cap is removed from the chaincase. If incorrect, proceed to (2).

2. Slacken the gearbox top fixing bolt "B" (see *Fig.* C51). Note that nut on left is captive and must not be turned.

3. Slacken the nut on the gearbox bottom bolt.

4. Slacken the front nut on the adjuster eyebolt, two or three turns.

5. Tighten the rear nut on the adjuster eyebolt until, with the finger, the chain can be felt dead tight.

6. Now slacken off the rear nut and carefully tighten the forward nut until there is total up and down movement of $\frac{3}{8}$ in. (9·5 mm).

7. Tighten securely the rear nut to lock the assembly and recheck the adjustment in at least three places. Should there prove to be a tight spot, readjust to total up and down movement of $\frac{3}{8}$ in. (9·5 mm) at this point.

8. Tighten the gearbox bottom bolt nut. Lubricate the thread of the gearbox top mounting bolt, fit the nut and secure to 70 lb. ft. (87 in. lb., 9.678 kgms.) torque from the right side. *Note:* On 1972 and later models, do not attempt to turn the nut at the left side of the top bolt – this is spigotted to prevent movement.

Engine/Primary Transmission C

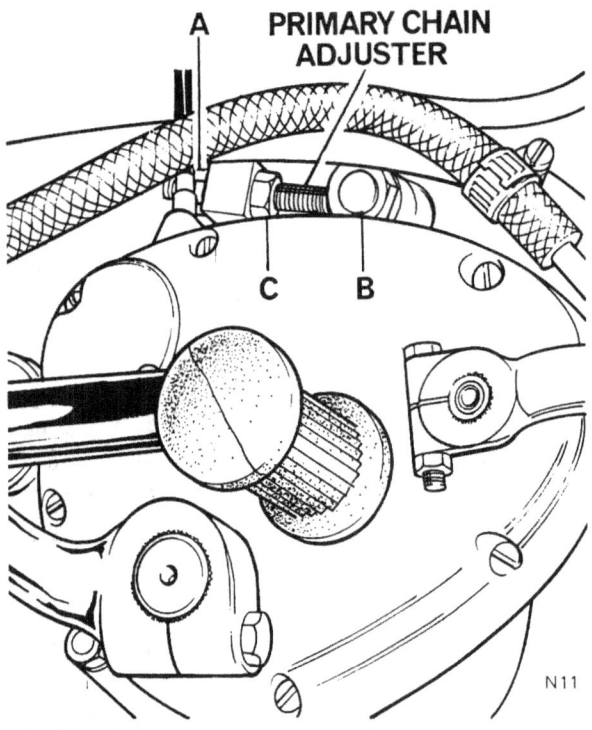

Fig. C51 Primary chain adjustment points

5 Tighten securely the adjuster locknuts (B).

6 Tighten the wheel spindle nuts and recheck the adjustment in at least three places. Should there prove to be a tight spot, readjust to give the correct up and down movement at this point.

7 Finally, recheck rear brake adjustment as in Section H13.

Rear Chain Adjustment

This adjustment is made by movement of the rear wheel. *Fig.* C49 shows the adjustment points. Proceed as follows:

1 Slacken the rear wheel spindle nuts (A).

2 Release the chain adjuster locknuts (B).

3 Pull downwards on the bottom run of the chain to bring the spindle hard up against the adjusters (C).

4 Turn each adjuster an equal amount until, with the rider seated, there is a total up and down movement, measured in the centre of the bottom chain run of ¾ in. to 1 in. (19·05 to 25·4 mm).

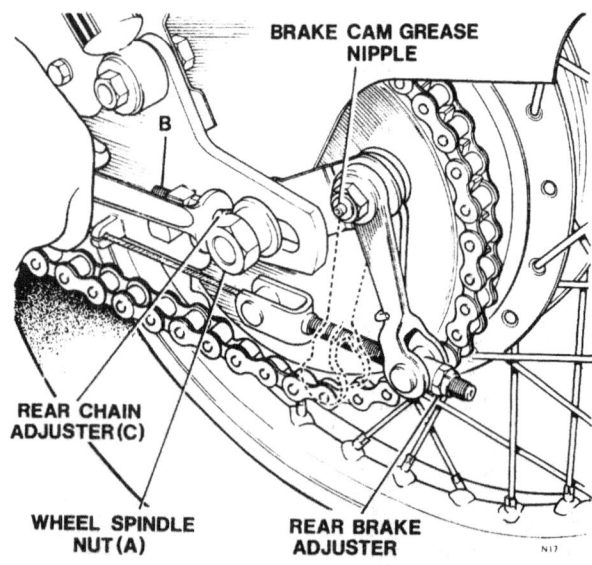

Fig. C52 Rear chain adjustment

Gearbox D

Gearbox

Gearbox

D

SECTION D1

GEARBOX DESCRIPTION

The transmission (gearbox) is a self contained 4 speed unit, completely separate from the engine crankcase and thus simple and inexpensive for servicing. A robust aluminium alloy casing with separate inner and outer covers contains a gear cluster of extra tough nickel chrome steel. Selection is foot controlled through a positive stop mechanism to a rotating cam plate. Hardened steel selector forks operated by the camplate position the gear pinions.

The kickstart drives through an internal ratchet on the layshaft first gear which in turn drives the mainshaft and clutch.

SECTION D2

GEARBOX DISMANTLING

It is not necessary to remove the exhaust system whilst giving attention to the gearbox, providing the gearbox is not to be removed from the engine plates.

SECTION D3

REMOVING GEARBOX OUTER COVER

Prior to gearbox dismantling it is recommended that the gearbox should be drained into a suitable sized drain tray using the drain plug at the bottom rear of the gearbox casing. Proceed then as follows:

1. Remove the kickstart by releasing the single securing bolt. The bolt locates into a groove in the kickstart spindle and thus it is necessary to remove this bolt completely.

2. If the battery is still connected, disconnect by removing the fuse before proceeding to the next operation.

3. Remove the two nuts and one bolt securing the right hand footrest and note that the bolt also secures the red earth lead tag from behind the footrest mounting plate.
   A nut without washer is used on the footrest securing bolt. It is vitally important during re-assembly not to overlook the refitting of this earth lead or otherwise a short circuit may result in the fuse being blown, or damage to the Zener diode.

4. Remove the gear indicator pointer from the gear shift spindle. This is secured by a set screw and plain washer.

5. Do not remove the gear shift lever at this time.

6. Remove the five cheese headed set screws from the gearbox outer cover.

7. Remove the two screws securing the outer cover inspection cap which may then be lifted away complete with gasket.

8. Disconnect the clutch cable from the fork within the gearbox outer cover.

9. Place the oil drain tray under the gearbox, and, using the shift lever as a handle, pull the outer cover off. It may be necessary to tap the cover gently to free it.

10. Withdraw the shift ratchet plate and spindle.

SECTION D4

REMOVING GEARBOX INNER COVER

Prior to removing the gearbox inner cover it is necessary to mark clearly the position of the clutch operating body by two punch marks which are shown in *Fig. D1*. This is due to the fact that the clutch operating body has no positive rotational location. Proceed as follows:

1. Remove the small lever, screw and nut securing the clutch operating arm and collect the arm, roller and bush.

2. Remove the clutch operating body locking ring as in *Fig. D1* and lift away the clutch operating body and the ball.

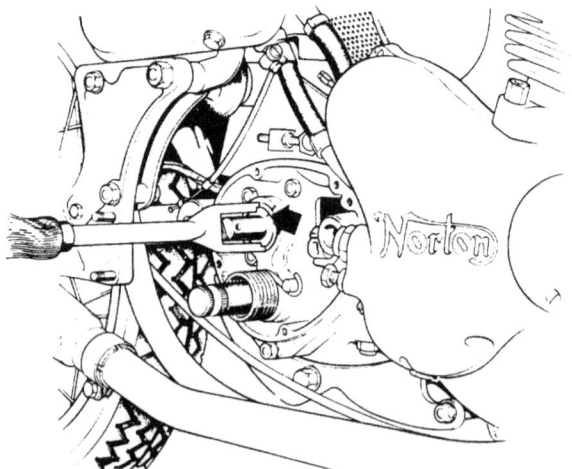

Fig. D1 Removal of clutch body lockring. Note alignment marks on lock ring and cover

Gearbox   D

3   Prevent the gearbox from turning by engaging top gear as follows and applying the back brake fully. Top gear can be engaged by levering the end of the quadrant carefully to the top of the window in the gearbox inner cover whilst rocking the rear wheel. At this stage the mainshaft nut can be removed.

4   In order to remove the gearbox inner cover it will be found simpler to revert to the neutral position, again by moving the end of the quadrant down the window.

5   Remove the seven securing nuts to the gearbox inner cover. These nuts are all of equal size, five within the case and two outside.

6   Remove the gearbox inner cover, if necessary tapping the end of the mainshaft to ease separation.
The inner cover should then be lifted away, complete with kickstart spindle, with the pawl assembled and also the return spring.

SECTION D5

DISMANTLING GEAR CLUSTER AND CAM PLATE

To dismantle the gearbox further it is necessary to remove the clutch from the gearbox mainshaft and if the sleeve gear is to be removed from the gearbox, the countershaft sprocket must also be removed. Clutch removal is covered in items 1 to 9 of Section C13 and C14 and countershaft sprocket removal in Section D8.

4   Remove the clutch locating shims, the clutch locating spacer, and circlip from the mainshaft end.

5   Remove the low gear pinions from the shafts.

6   Unscrew the selector fork spindle and remove.

7   Remove selector forks and withdraw mainshaft with gears.

8   Withdraw the layshaft with gears. If the shaft is a tight fit in the bearing heat the case and withdraw the shaft complete with bearing. The bearing can then be removed to complete disassembly.

9   Remove countershaft sprocket (Section D8).

10 Remove sleeve gear by tapping gently through the bearing into the gearbox.

11 Remove the acorn shaped detent plunger spring bolt. This will release the camplate detent plunger and spring.

12 Remove the two bolts and washers securing the camplate and quadrant to the gearbox shell.

13 Remove camplate and quadrant and collect "O"-rings.

14 Withdraw the sprocket spacer from inside the countershaft oil seal.

15 The bearings can be withdrawn for inspection or replacement by gently heating the case and tapping the open end on a soft wooden surface.

16 Prise out the countershaft oil seal.

SECTION D6

INSPECTION OF GEARBOX PARTS

After cleaning all components very thoroughly such as in gasoline (petrol) or kerosene (paraffin) check all items thoroughly as below:

1   Inspect the two mainshaft and one layshaft ball journal bearings for roughness indicating ball or ball track damage on either the inner or outer races. Feel for side play between the inner and outer races. If the bearings are in good condition, such play should be negligible.

2   Inspect both the layshaft and mainshaft for wear on the splines, damage to the threads, out of truth and severe wear and grooving on the bearing diameters.

3   Inspect all pinions for chipping or obvious wear to the teeth. Ensure that the dogs are not badly rounded and that the inner splines are a satisfactory fit to the shafts. Bushed pinions should be offered to the shafts and checked for excessive wear by attempting to rock them on the shafts.

Gearbox D

4 Inspect the gearbox shell and gearbox inner cover bushes for obvious wear. Note that wear on the bushes in the shell supporting the camplate and quadrant can result in bad gear indexing and a tendency to jump out of gear engagement.

5 Inspect the selector forks and mating grooves in the sliding pinions for seizure or wear.

6 Especially in cases of bad selection, inspect the camplate tracks for wear or distortion and ensure that the camplate spindle is a good fit in the bush in the gearbox shell.

SECTION D7

REMOVAL OF GEARBOX COMPLETE

Though not normally necessary during overhaul, we recognise that circumstances may arise which make it desirable to remove the complete gearbox without disturbing the engine although the primary transmission must be dismantled fully. In these circumstances remove the rear three crankcase to engine plate bolts (or studs, depending on year), the rear wheel and on 1971 and later models, support the motorcycle by the lower frame rails on a strong box and remove the centre stand. Remove completely the gearbox top and bottom mounting bolt and stud and remove the drawbolt assembly from the right hand side of the rear engine mounting and turn the gearbox anti-clockwise in the engine plates viewed from right side. Force the rear engine mounting rearwards until the cutaway part at the bottom right hand side is clear of the crankcase. The gearbox can then be turned further and withdrawn horizontally from the right hand side. Only in isolated cases will it be necessary to take out the front mounting main bolt to provide still further working space.

SECTION D8

COUNTERSHAFT (GEARBOX FINAL DRIVE) SPROCKET

The countershaft sprocket is mounted on the mainshaft sleeve (high) gear and secured by a tab washer and L.H. threaded nut. The Commando overall gearing should be varied by changing the sprocket size. For the road going editions of the Commando, the following sprockets are available:

040480	Sprocket	19 teeth
060931	Sprocket	20 teeth
060721	Sprocket	21 teeth
060759	Sprocket	22 teeth
063420	Sprocket	23 teeth
063421	Sprocket	24 teeth

Changing the countershaft sprocket

1 Remove the outer primary chaincase, clutch and primary transmission and inner primary chaincase as in Section C14 to gain access to the sprocket.

2 Remove set screw and lockplate from sprocket.

3 The sprocket must be prevented from turning whilst the left hand nut is released. If the gearbox is in the frame, leave the rear chain connected and apply the rear brake fully. If the gearbox is out of the frame, pass a length of chain round the sprocket, holding the ends securely in a vice.

4 Noting that the sprocket nut is *left hand* threaded, remove the nut and lift the sprocket clear.

5 Before refitting the sprocket, ensure that the sprocket spacer is in place on the sleeve gear bearing sleeve.

6 Place the sprocket in position and if necessary tap fully home with a tube drift.

7 If the original lockplate has been scrapped in removal, have a new one available.

8 Fit and tighten the left-hand nut fully, whilst preventing the sprocket from turning.

9 Secure the lockplate with the locating screw.

10 Refit the inner chaincase, primary transmission and outer chaincase as in Section C34 and fit and connect the rear chain.

Gearbox

D

SECTION D9

REFITTING GEAR CLUSTER AND SELECTORS

After inspection of components as in Section D6 commence reassembly as follows:

1. Heat the gearbox shell and press the sleeve gear and layshaft bearings fully into position.
2. Fit the sleeve gear bearing seal squarely into the housing, lipped side first.
3. Fit detent plunger, spring, and acorn nut loosely.
4. Fit the quadrant with "O"-ring and secure with bolt and washer.

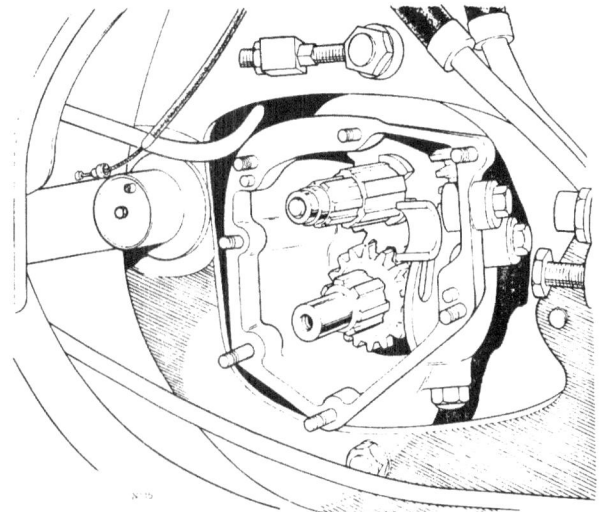

Fig. D3   Mainshaft and layshaft fitted to gearbox shell

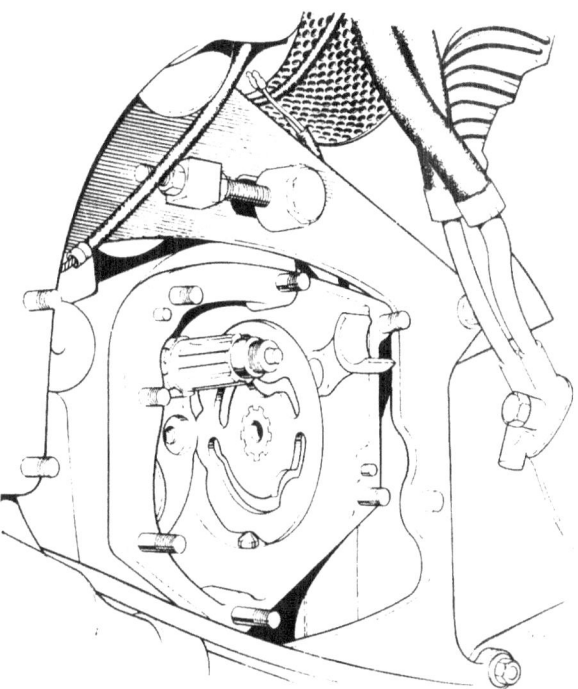

Fig. D2   Location of camplate to index plunger. Knuckle end of quadrant is aligned to top front cover stud

5. Lift the knuckle end of the quadrant until the top inside radius is directly in line with the top front cover stud (see Fig. D2), fit the camplate and sealing ring, engaging the teeth of the quadrant and camplate so that the notched edge of the camplate is towards the gearbox sprocket and the smooth edge towards the gearbox inner cover, the last notch at the bottom engaging with the camplate index plunger (see Fig. D2).
6. Secure the camplate with "O"-ring, washer and bolt.
7. Tighten detent plunger acorn nut.
8. Fit the countershaft (sleeve gear) through bearing and seal. Fit sprocket spacer in place inside seal.
9. Fit countershaft sprocket (Section D8).
10. Fit mainshaft through sleeve gear.
11. Fit the 3rd gear free pinion and bush to the layshaft (dog side first to face out of assembled gearbox).
12. Fit the fixed high gear pinion to the layshaft, flat side first (toward 3rd gear pinion). The shoulder is to fit against the bearing.
13. Push the layshaft into the bearing in the gearbox shell.
14. Assemble the mainshaft 3rd gear with selector fork to the mainshaft (selector fork groove side outwards) and engage the pin with the inboard cam track (see Fig. D4).
15. Assemble the main shaft 2nd gear with bush to the mainshaft, dogs inwards.
16. Assemble the layshaft 2nd gear with selector fork (selector fork groove side inwards) and engage the pin with the outboard cam track.
17. Fit the selector fork spindle through the selector forks and screw home into the gearbox shell.
18. Fit the layshaft 1st gear.
19. Fit the mainshaft 1st gear with shoulder outwards.
20. Since the quadrant roller cannot be fitted after the inner cover is fitted, it is imperative that the roller is fitted into the quadrant knuckle at this time.

Gearbox

D

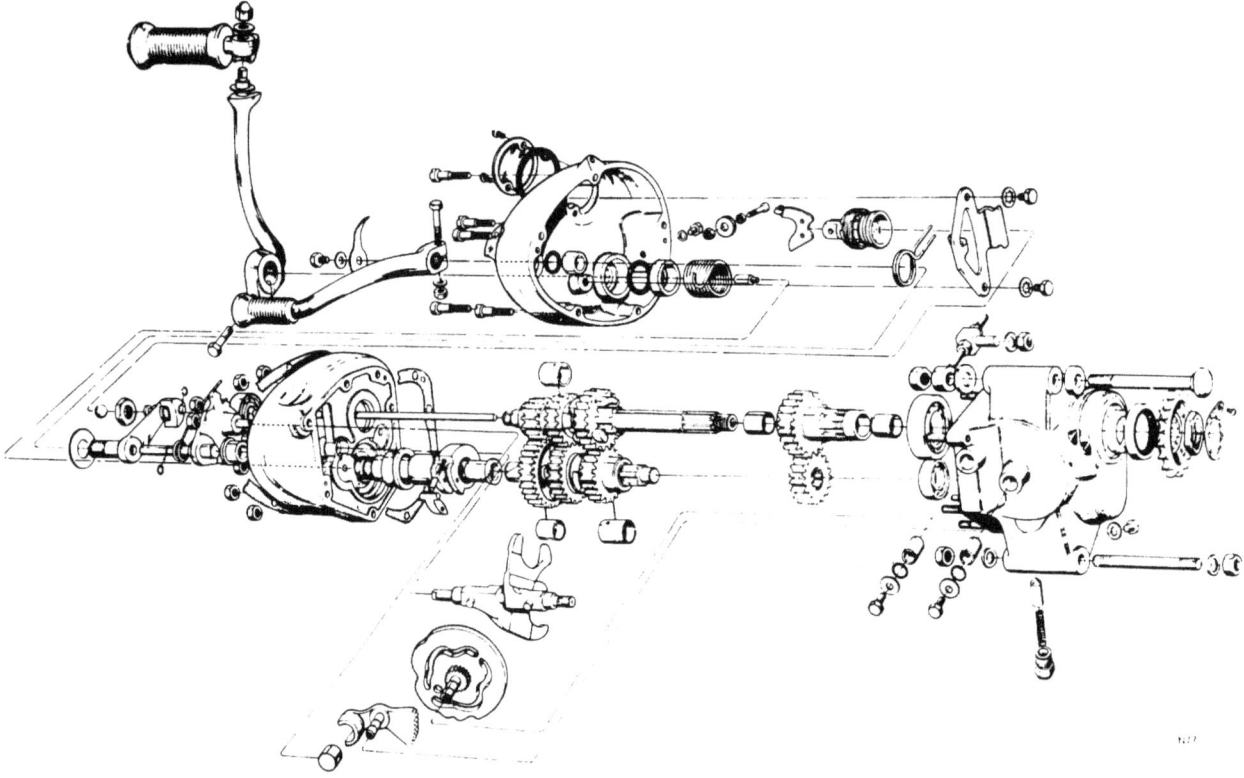

Fig. D4   Gear layout

SECTION D10

REFITTING GEARBOX INNER COVER

Ensure that the gearbox inner cover is clean on both inner and outer joint faces prior to assembly. Proceed as follows:

1   Fit the inner cover gasket.

2   If the kickstart spindle has been removed from the gearbox inner cover, it must be refitted at this stage. Assemble the kickstarter spindle to the inner cover, ensuring that the pawl is behind the stop on the inner cover as shown in *Fig. D5*.

3   Assemble the kickstart return spring, aligning the outboard end of the spring with the mating hole in the spindle and sliding the spring down until the spring engages in the hole. Wind the spring as illustrated in *Fig. D6* to tension and engage on the spring anchor pin.

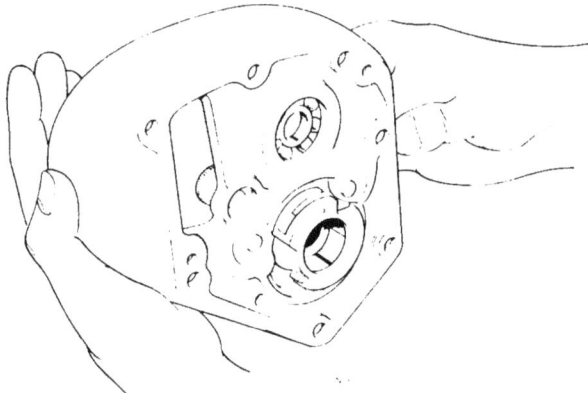

Fig. D5   Showing kickstart pawl stop on inner cover

4   Fit the inner cover gasket and hold in place with grease.

5   Ensure that the two shafts are fully home prior to attempting to assemble the inner cover to the gearbox shell.

Gearbox   D

6 Assemble the inner cover, ensuring that it enters over the location dowels, and fit snugly home during assembly, at the same time guiding the cover over the unsupported outboard end of the selector fork spindle.

7 Fit the seven nuts securing the inner cover, noting that two of these fit outside the casings. The seven nuts should be tightened to a torque setting of 10 to 15 lbs./ft. (1·383 to 2·074 Kg/m).

8 Engage top gear, apply the footbrake, and tighten the gearbox mainshaft nut to a torque reading of 70 lbs./ft. (9·678 Kg/m).

9 Assemble the clutch operating lever body complete with lock ring and ball to the gearbox inner cover.

10 Tighten the operating lever body ring until the body is fully engaged and finally tighten the lock ring to bring the body slot directly into line with the marks previously applied to the boss in the cover. *Fig.* D6 illustrates the alignment procedure during tightening of the lock ring. If a new cover is being fitted and no alignment marks are present, hold the body in the position where the clutch cable can exert a straight pull, as the lockring is tightened.

11 Assemble the withdrawal lever, roller, bush and pivot screw and secure the lock nut. Assembly should be in accordance with *Fig.* D7.

12 Assemble the ratchet plate and spindle, locating the peg into the knuckle pin roller. Ensure that the 'O' ring is fitted to the ratchet plate spindle.

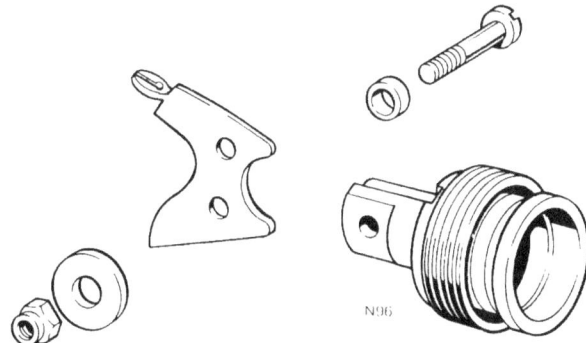

Fig. D7   Order of assembly of clutch withdrawal lever

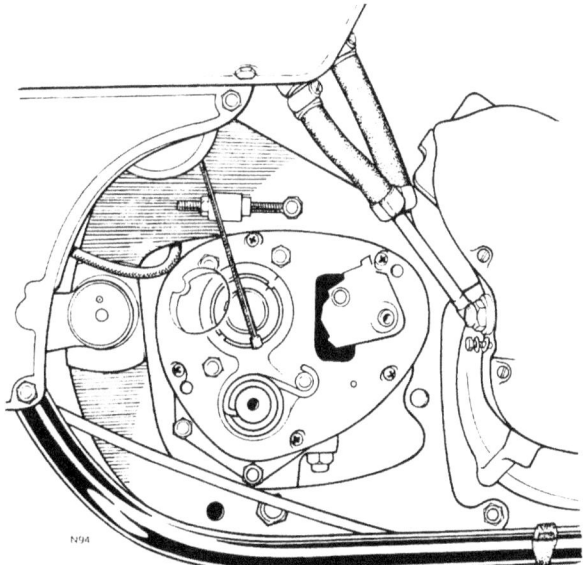

Fig. D6   Kickstart spring located. Note alignment of clutch body to permit straight pull on clutch cable and operating lever

SECTION D11

DISMANTLING AND RE-ASSEMBLING GEARBOX OUTER COVER

To dismantle the outer cover, remove the pawl carrier assembly and press the pedal spindle from the outside of the cover to disengage the spring peg from the legs of the pedal return spring. The pedal stop plate set screws can now be removed and the stop plate lifted away, complete with spring.

Gearbox **D**

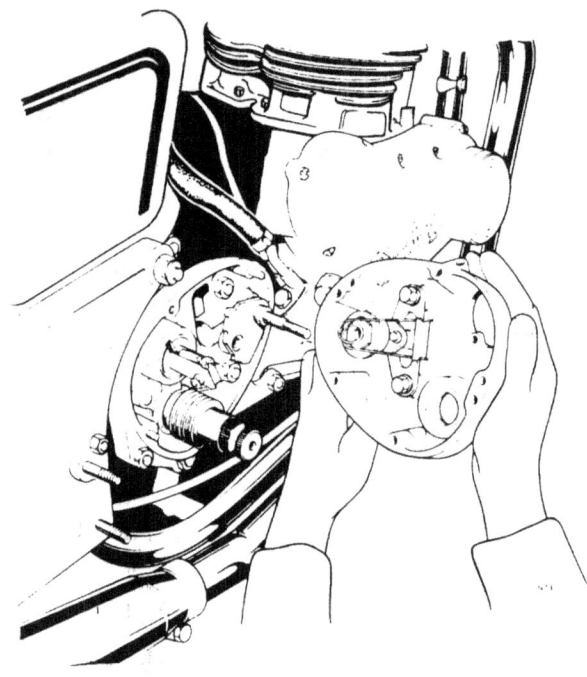

Fig. D8   Pawl carrier, spring and ratchet plate assembled

During re-assembly ensure that the spring retaining washer is fitted over the main spindle of the pawl carrier and that the spring has been assembled over the ratchet plate as illustrated in *Fig*. D8. Tighten the stop plate set screws and assemble the splined end of the pawl carrier past the 'O' ring in the cover. Locate the spring peg between the legs of the spring and push the pawl carrier fully home, engaging between the legs of the spring. Check the carrier action and that the spring is correctly located. The set screws should be tightened only when the action of the pawl carrier has been checked for full freedom of movement. Now fit the pawl spring with its double cranked leg downwards, ensuring a minimum but perceptible clearance, between the two legs of the spring and the pawl.

SECTION D12

REFITTING THE GEARBOX OUTER COVER

Having dealt with the outer cover as described in Section D11, ensure that the joint facing is perfectly clean and proceed with assembly as detailed below:

1. Fit the inner cover to outer cover gasket, retaining in place during assembly with a smear of grease. Ensure that the gasket engages satisfactorily over the cover dowels.

2. To ensure cover alignment during assembly, retain the ratchet spring in the central position with the index finger of the right hand and guide the case over the kickstart shaft with the thumb of the left hand engaged through the filler cap hole.

3. Drive the outer cover fully home and assemble the five screws of equal length to retain the outer cover in position. If the cover is very difficult to push into position, check whether the pawl has rotated due to the pawl scissor spring not having been held securely in position, during final assembly. The cover should be removed, the ratchet pawl reset and re-assembly undertaken.

4. Fit the gearshift pedal and kickstart crank, then check the action of the gearbox, rotating the rear wheel as the gear pedal is moved to the various gear positions.
   If all is well, assemble the gear position indicator pointer and replenish the gearbox with oil.

5. Connect the clutch cable through the inspection hole in the gearbox outer cover, engaging and locating the nipple in the operating lever.

6. Finally assemble the gasket, inspection cover and screws to the gearbox outer cover, and check the security of the drain and level plugs.

Carburetor   E

Carburetor

Carburetor E

SECTION E1

DESCRIPTION

The Amal concentric float carburetor proportions and atomises the correct amount of fuel, mixing it with the air drawn in through the air intake. The jet sizes, choke bore, throttle needle, and throttle slide cut away ensure that the correct fuel/air mixture is maintained at all throttle openings. Initial opening of the throttle brings into operation the mixture supply from the pilot jet system which controls the idling speed. As the throttle is progressively opened the mixture supply is augmented from the main jet which discharges through the needle jet into the primary air chamber and goes from there as a rich fuel/air mixture through the primary air choke into the main choke. The earlier stages of the throttle opening are controlled by the throttle cut away and the taper needle which passes through the needle jet, the taper allowing more fuel to pass through the needle jet as the throttle is opened.

Type 930 Amal concentric carburetors are fitted to early 750's. Type 932 Amal concentrics of 32 mm bore size are fitted to Combat engine 750's, other late 750's, and 850's. An exploded layout (illustrating both types) with part descriptions is shown in *Fig. E1*. A common airbox serves both carburetors, this being covered in detail in Section E9.

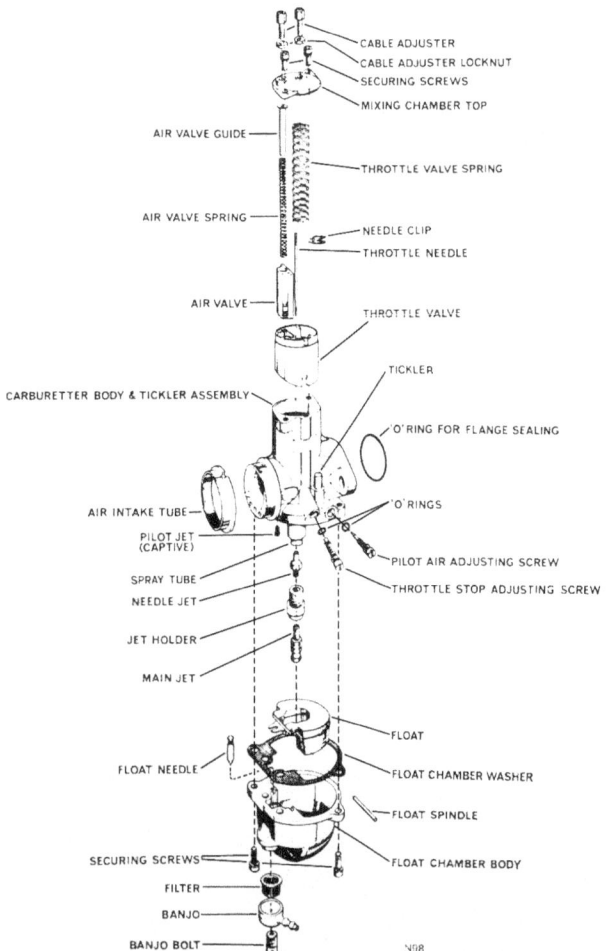

Fig. E1 Amal concentric float carburetor

SECTION E2

CARBURETOR REMOVAL

For ease of handling it is recommended that the carburetors are removed attached to the spacers as a pair as follows:

1. Disconnect the fuel lines from both fuel taps.

2. Remove four socket screws and washers securing the spacers to the head – a shortened socket key is needed for ease of access.

3. With the balance pipe and cables still connected, lift the carburetors and manifolds away from the cylinder head, disengaging the flexible air hoses at the same time. To service the carburetors individually:

4. Disconnect the balance pipe at one end.

5. Remove the two cross head screws and washers securing the carburetor top.

6. Lift off the carburetor top, throttle and air slides with cables attached.
   The top and slides can be left hanging from the cables but the exposed parts should be protected from damage by wrapping in clean cloth.

7. If required, remove the second carburetor in similar fashion, removing the fuel line by taking off the banjo bolts.

Carburetor　E

SECTION E3

CARBURETOR DISMANTLING

The carburetor as detached from the motorcycle is partially dismantled, in that the mixing chamber top and both throttle and air slides have been removed. If the top and slides are to be removed from the cables, proceed as follows:

1. Lift the throttle return spring, note the groove in the needle to which the clip is engaged then remove the clip. Collect the needle.

2. Disengage the throttle cable nipple and collect the throttle valve.

3. Lift the air valve cable and spring, disengage the cable nipple and collect the air valve.

4. The top is now free to be lifted clear. Dismantling of parts from the mixing chamber should proceed as follows:

5. Remove the two screws securing the float chamber to the carburetor body and collect the float chamber complete with float and float needle, also the joint washers.

6. The float and float needle are manufactured from white nylon. Lift the float, float needle and float spindle clear for later examination and drain the float chamber.

7. Remove the main jet, needle jet.

SECTION E4

EXAMINATION OF CARBURETOR PARTS

The following parts should be examined and replacements made where necessary:

Float: Check for leakage — fuel can be seen in the float if this condition exists. Check also that the float needle fits securely.

Float Needle: Check for wear on the seating taper.

Main, Needle and Pilot Jets: Examine for damage and blockage — never use wire to clear a blockage but instead use compressed air.

Throttle Valve: Remove any burrs and burnish carefully any scores. Deep scoring renders the valve unfit for re-use.

Throttle Needle: Ensure the needle is not bent or worn badly on the taper. Check that the clip grooves are clear and "sharp."

Carburetor Body: Blow out all internal galleries with compressed air. Check that all threads are sound. Examine for excess wear on the throttle valve bore.

Pilot Air Screw: Check for wear on the taper.

SECTION E5

CARBURETTOR REASSEMBLY

Assuming all parts are clean and in sound condition commence reassembly as follows:

7. Using new friction 'O' rings on both screws if the originals have deteriorated, refit the pilot air screw and throttle stop screw.

8. Fit the needle jet to the jet holder and jet holder to the carburetor body.

9. Fit the main jet.

10. Position the float, with float needle and spindle, in the float bowl.

11. If the original is damaged, fit a new float bowl joint washer ensuring it is the correct way round with the holes aligned to the jet passages in the bowl.

12. Fit the complete float bowl and secure with the two screws and washers.

Where the originals have deteriorated, replace the 'O' ring in the mounting flange of both carburettors and couple the carburetors to the manifolds, securing with two nuts and plain washers for each instrument. Connect the balance pipe to both manifolds. If the air and throttle valves and mixing chamber tops have been detached from the control cables, they should be re-connected as follows:

Carburetor E

13 Place the air valve guide tube and spring over the air cable (the brass guide assembles with the flanged end towards the cap).

14 Compress the spring to expose the maximum of inner cable then pass the nipple through the air valve to engage at the bottom.

15 Place the throttle valve spring over the throttle cable and compress it.

16 Feed the throttle cable nipple through the throttle valve centre hole then engage the nipple in the adjacent hole.

17 Fit the needle clip to the correct groove.

18 Compress the throttle spring to clear the throttle valve then place the needle and clip into the throttle valve from the top with the needle in the centre hole of the slide. Release the throttle spring and ensure that the spring fits over the needle clip.

19 Locate the air valve into the channel of the throttle valve. The carburetors with manifolds are ready to refit to the cylinder head. Proceed as follows:

20 Offer the throttle and air valves, assembled to the cables and tops to both instruments. Ensure that the throttle needle passes easily through centre hole of the body and that the key on the throttle valve mates with the keyway in the carburetor body. Ensure that the return spring fits over the abutment in the top.

21 Secure each carburetor top with two cross headed screws and washers.

22 Mount the carburetors on the cylinder head using the heat insulators between the manifolds and cylinder head. Secure with socket screws and washers.

23 Reconnect the fuel pipes to both petrol taps.

24 Fit both carburetors to the airbox flexible connectors and take great care that these locate both in the airbox front plate and over the carburetor intakes.

25 Reassembly is now complete and slack should be taken up in the control cables and the carburation adjusted as in Section E7.

SECTION E6

FUEL TAPS

Twin taps are fitted. The one on the right side provides the reserve supply and is recognised by the lack of a stand pipe inside the tank. Fibre washers seal the taps to the tank and must be checked that they are undamaged before being re-used.

SECTION E7

CARBURETOR ADJUSTMENT

Adjustment should be carried out in the sequence described below with the engine at operating temperature. The exhaust system to be used must be fitted and preferably the test should be carried out on a slight up grade so that the engine is pulling. The air lever must be fully to the tight wire position before adjustment takes place.

1. Main Jet – Throttle threequarters to full open.
If at full throttle, the engine runs "heavily" the main jet is set too large. If by slightly closing the throttle valve, the engine power seems to improve, the main jet is too small. With a main jet of the correct size the engine should run evenly, and be delivering maximum power at full throttle.

The appearance of the sparking plug is one of the best indications of mixture strength. To check, set the carburetors to shut off completely on closing or false readings will be obtained, then run the machine at full throttle over the test course, declutching and stopping the engine quickly. Then examine the spark plugs. If the plugs have a cool appearance with the central insulator free from loose black carbon and a light chocolate colour on the insulator, the mixture is correct. A rich mixture will be indicated by a black, wet oily appearance with deposits on the central insulator. Weak mixture will be indicated by a dry whitish deposit and the points may appear to have been overheated.

2. The Pilot Jet – Throttle up to one-eighth open.
Set the engine to run at a fast idling speed with the throttle shut by using the throttle adjusting screw. Turn this screw outwards until the engine runs slower and begins to falter, then screw the pilot air adjusting screw in or out to make the engine run more evenly and faster. If the idling speed is still too fast reduce it by means of

Carburetor E

the throttle adjusting screw and again adjust the pilot air adjusting screw until the idling is satisfactory.

Note: When new or re-assembled carburetors are used, start with pilot screw $1\frac{1}{2}$ turns out from the fully-in position.

3. Throttle Cutaway – Throttle one-eight to one-quarter open.

If, as the machine pulls away from the idling position, there is spitting back from the carburetors, slightly richen the mixture by screwing in the pilot air adjusting screw slightly. If this is not effective, return the screw to its former position and fit a throttle slide with a smaller cutaway. If, with the throttle in this position, the engine jerks under load and there is no spitting, either the jet needle is much too high or a throttle slide with a larger cutaway is required to cure richness.

4. Throttle Needle – Throttle one-quarter to three-quarters open.

The needle controls a wide range of throttle opening and therefore the acceleration. Placing the needle in the lower position, that is, with the clip in the top groove gives a weaker mixture. Placing the needle in the higher position, that is, with the clip in the bottom groove, richens the mixture. If the mixture is too rich with the needle in the lower position, the needle jet should be replaced and if the needle itself has had a great deal of use, replace it also.

5. Pilot Jet

Check again pilot adjustment as the last operation.

SECTION E8

ADJUSTMENT FOR ALTITUDE

It is necessary to adjust carburation on a motorcycle operated continuously in altitudes greater than 3,000 feet approximately. Motorcycles as supplied from the factory are already equipped for correct carburation up to 3,000 feet.

The main jet requires a reduction in size of 5 per cent at altitudes between 3,000 and 6,000 feet. Beyond 6,000 feet further reductions of 4 per cent should be made.

Altitude adjustments should only be made if the motorcycle is used permanently at high altitudes. It is not necessary to adjust merely for a journey through mountainous areas.

SECTION E9

TWIN CARBURETOR ADJUSTMENT

It is necessary periodically to synchronise the carburetors so that they open and close simultaneously. Start with the handlebars in the centre position so that there is no "pull" on the throttle cable which will interfere with adjustment. Proceed as follows:

1. Take up any slack in the throttle cables using the adjuster on the top of each mixing chamber, then tighten the adjuster locknuts.

2. Start the engine – this must be thoroughly warmed up before adjustment commences.

3. Follow the main adjustment sequence in Section E7 before setting slow running. It is all-important to have both throttle valves opening simultaneously. To ensure that this is the case, the twist-grip should be set to allow the engine to run fractionally over idling speed. Gently screw in the throttle stops in that position. Return the twist-grip to the closed position so that the engine runs on the throttle stops. Now proceed as follows:

4. Lift off one spark plug lead and commence setting the carburetor on the other cylinder as a single unit.

5. Adjust the pilot air screw and stop screw on the cylinder which is firing.

6. Reverse the process by replacing one plug lead and removing the other.

7. Adjust the pilot air screw and stop screw on the second cylinder.

8. Replace the plug lead – at this stage tickover may be too fast. If so, lower both throttle stop screws by an equal amount until idling is correct. Ensure there is about $\frac{1}{8}''$ (3 mm) slack in throttle cable. This slack must be equalized so that throttles open together.

Carburetor E

SECTION E10

AIR FILTER

The airbox comprises a detachable front plate, perforated metal band and replaceable automobile type air filter element, the backplate being mounted directly on to the front of the battery tray.

Removing and Refitting the Element:

1 Take out the two bolts securing the air filter front plate.

2 On Fastback only, remove the accessory cover to provide clearance

3 Lever the front filter plate outwards at the bottom and clear of the perforated band and element. Models with the power socket attached to the front plate need not have the socket disconnected.

4 As shown in *Fig. E2*, remove the gauze band together with the element.

5 The element should be cleaned as described below or replaced.

Reassembly is a reversal of the dismantling procedure.

Fig. E2   Removing air filter element and gauze band

Cleaning the Air Filter Element:

Whilst stressing that the pleated, resin impregnated paper element is replaceable and should therefore be changed for a new one and when it is badly clogged, the life of the element can be prolonged by superficial cleaning. After removal, taking care not to deform the element, tap it on a bench to dislodge as much foreign matter as possible, then blow clear with compressed air.

Frame and Ancillaries   F

Frame and Ancillaries

Frame and Ancillaries   F

SECTION F1

REMOVAL OF POWER UNIT

In some types of repair, for example, during an accident repair, where the frame must be changed, it is desirable to remove the engine/gearbox/primary drive and engine plates as a group. To remove this assembly, proceed as below:

1. Release the large side knobs and lift the seat off upwards and to the rear (Fastback seats lift straight upwards).

2. Turn the ring of the twist fastener to release the forward end of the accessory cover and lift the cover forward off the rear mounting pegs.

3. Disconnect the battery by removing the fuse from the fuseholder adjacent to the battery.

4. Remove the right side panel which is secured by two screws at the top and a peg and rubber at the bottom.

5. Remove the fuel tank (Section F9).

6. Remove both exhaust pipes with mufflers by releasing the tab washers at the finned lockrings and unscrewing the lockrings using service tool 063968. Remove the nuts and washers holding the muffler bracket to the two mounting rubber studs and lift each system away in turn.

7. Disconnect the rear chain at the split link and remove the chain completely.

8. Disconnect the rear brake cable from the expander lever by removing the adjuster nut completely and depressing the rear brake pedal so that the end of the cable clears the trunnion. Collect the trunnion.

The swinging arm must now be removed. The pivot is lubricated by SAE 140 oil and provision must be made to collect the oil released as the end cap is removed. Proceed as follows:

9. Unscrew the pivot end cap screw and lift the end cap, washers and long screw away together.

10. Whilst allowing oil to drain from the pivot, remove the rear wheel (see Section H1). Pre 1971 models may have the wheel removed complete with sprocket and brake. On 1971 and later models remove the wheel only, leaving the sprocket and brake assembled to the swinging arm.

11. Lift away the right footrest complete after removing two set screws or nuts of the same length, and one bolt, the nut for which secures also the ground (earth) tag for the Zener diode.

12. Disconnect the flexible rear chain oiler tube from the metal oiler pipe at the swinging arm.

13. Remove the suspension unit bottom bolts.

14. Take out the swinging arm pivot spindle. This is an easy sliding fit but is secured by a lock screw on top of the pivot tube which must be removed. It will be noted that the pivot spindle is threaded internally to aid removal. Screw a bolt with locking nut into the thread (the main front mounting bolt will be ideal) tighten the nut and twist and pull the spindle gently out.

15. Lift away the swinging arm complete with chainguard. Collect the left end plate and 'O' rings.

16. Disconnect the tachometer cable (at the top front of the crankcase).

Fig. F1   Removing oil junction block securing bolt

Frame and Ancillaries F

17 Dismantle the engine steady (see C1) by removing the nuts and washers from the rubber mountings first, to prevent them turning in the frame. Release the two studs and lift away with the side plates. Remove the main engine steady plate by taking out the three socket screws and washers. Note that the centre screw secures the ground (earth) lead tag.

18 Remove the rocker feed pipe after taking out the three banjo bolts. Collect the copper washers for re-use.

19 Release the coil cluster from the frame as an assembly (on pre 1971 models two bolts are used: on 1971 and later models, four bolts are used). Disconnect the H.T. leads at the sparking plugs then tie the cluster clear of the engine unit with all other leads still attached.

20 Detach the carburetors from the cylinder head complete with manifolds and balance pipe. Either removal or refitting of the securing screws is facilitated by the use of a shortened socket screw key. Lay the carburetors and manifold assembly still attached to the throttle and air cables over the headlamp clear of the engine unit.

21 Disconnect the contact breaker leads from the main harness in the area of the frame top rails.

22 Disconnect the oil tank end of the engine breather pipe.

23 Place a receptacle of sufficient size to contain the contents of the oil tank below the rear of the crankcases, remove the bolt securing the oil junction block to the crankcases, pull the block and pipes away from the crankcases and allow the oil to drain. Alternatively after parting the junction block from the crankcases, raise the junction block and tie with wire to the airbox to prevent oil draining from the tank, or protect the feed pipe with cardboard and compress the pipe with grips to prevent oil draining (see *Fig.* F1).

24 Slacken clutch cable adjustment and lift the cable nipple from the handlebar control.

25 Remove the front engine mounting by taking out the centre bolt, sliding back the left gaiter and removing the mounting collar, plastic washer and gaiter as a set. Remove the right gaiter etc. in similar manner. Remove the two mounting-to-crankcase studs (bolts on later models) and lift away the mounting.

26 On 1971 and later models, remove the centre stand. This is secured by bolts fitted from inboard. Lift the spring clear as the stand is removed.

27 On pre 1971 models, remove the earth lead from the side stand bracket to bottom crankcase stud.

28 Disconnect the two alternator leads at the snap connectors.

The power unit assembly is now secured to the frame only by the rear mounting. Before removing the rear mounting stud, coil the clutch cable by the gearbox. Unclip the C.B. leads from the frame and coil them by the timing case. Protect the lower frame rails against damage using cardboard or thick cloth.

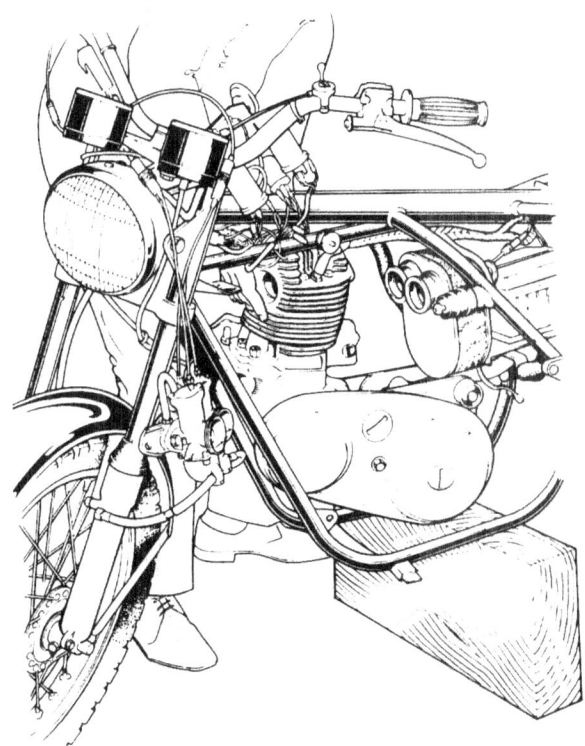

Fig. F2 Lifting out power unit to right side

Frame and Ancillaries F

29 Support the weight of the power unit and use a soft drift to drive out the rear mounting stud.

30 Collect the gaiters, collars, end caps and footrest plate spacers.

31 As shown in *Fig.* F2, lift the power unit bodily from the frame to the right hand side. Raise the front of the power unit and lower the rear to clear the airbox.

SECTION F2

ISOLASTIC ENGINE MOUNTINGS

The Norton Isolastic principle built into the Commando couples together the engine, transmission, swinging fork and rear wheel. This assembly, parted from the main frame is seen clearly in *Fig.* F3.

Isolation of the engine transmission swinging fork and rear wheel is achieved by the use of resilient mountings shown as A, B and C. Unlike earlier attempts at rubber mounting, the Commando is unique in that the swinging fork is mounted on the engine cradle and thus isolated from the main frame. This prevents twisting between the engine and rear wheel sprockets under load which would otherwise cause premature chain wear or displacement of the chain.

The power unit in its mounting plates oscillates on the rear mounting (B) which has three bonded and two buffer rubbers. This arrangement provides maximum support, particularly to the swinging arm and rear wheel, whilst isolating the power unit from the frame.

The front mounting (C) controls the degree of movement of the power unit on the rear mounting and the two bonded and two buffer rubbers allow more flexibility than does the rear mounting.

Both the front and rear mountings incorporate plastic thrust washers to permit side play to be kept within very restricted limits without transmitting engine and transmission vibrations to the rider. The degree of side play is controlled by shims to enable the figure to be kept within design limits even after considerable mileages.

The engine head steady (A) completes the triangular formation of the resilient mountings and controls lateral movement of the engine unit in the frame. The insulating rubbers are fitted between the side plates and frame tube.

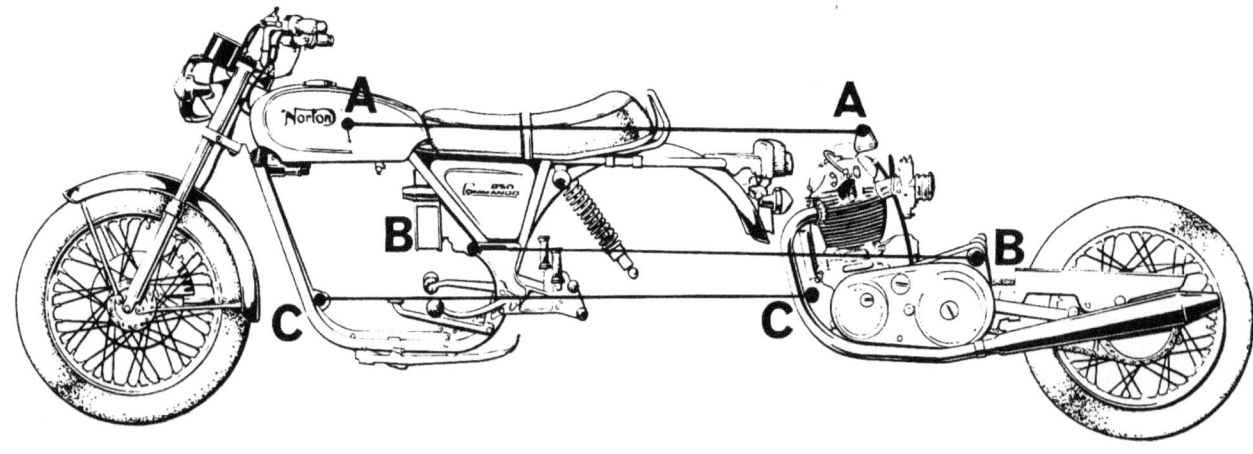

Fig. F3   Commando parted to show isolastic mounting points

Frame and Ancillaries F

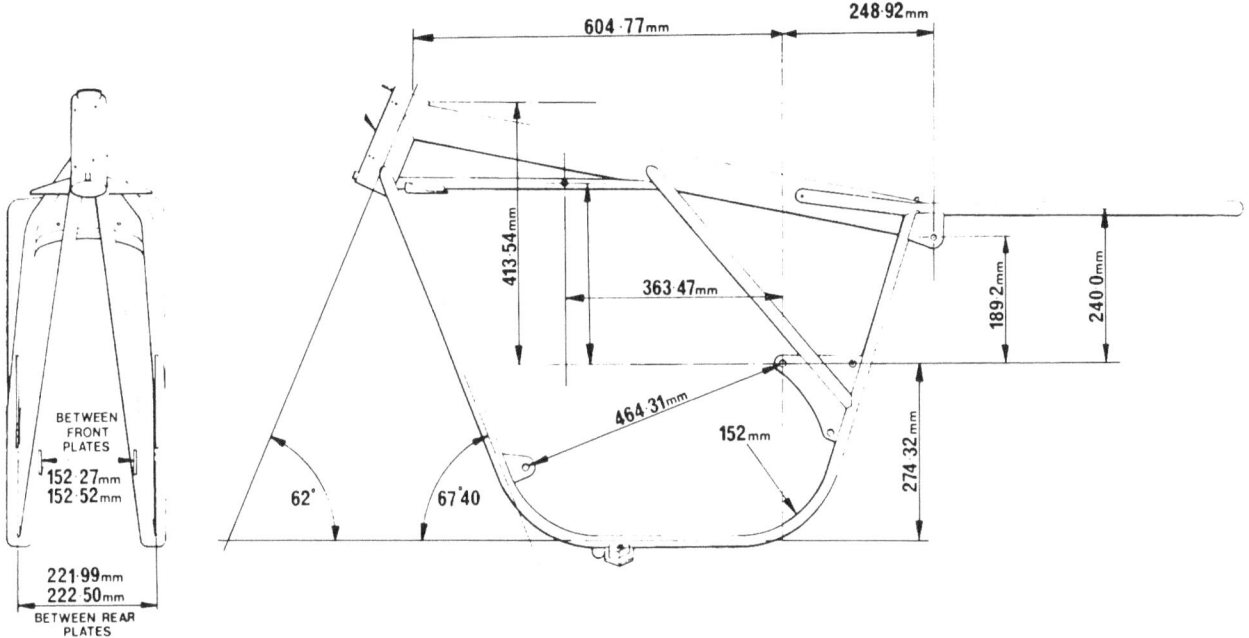

FRAME CHECKING DATA 850 MODELS

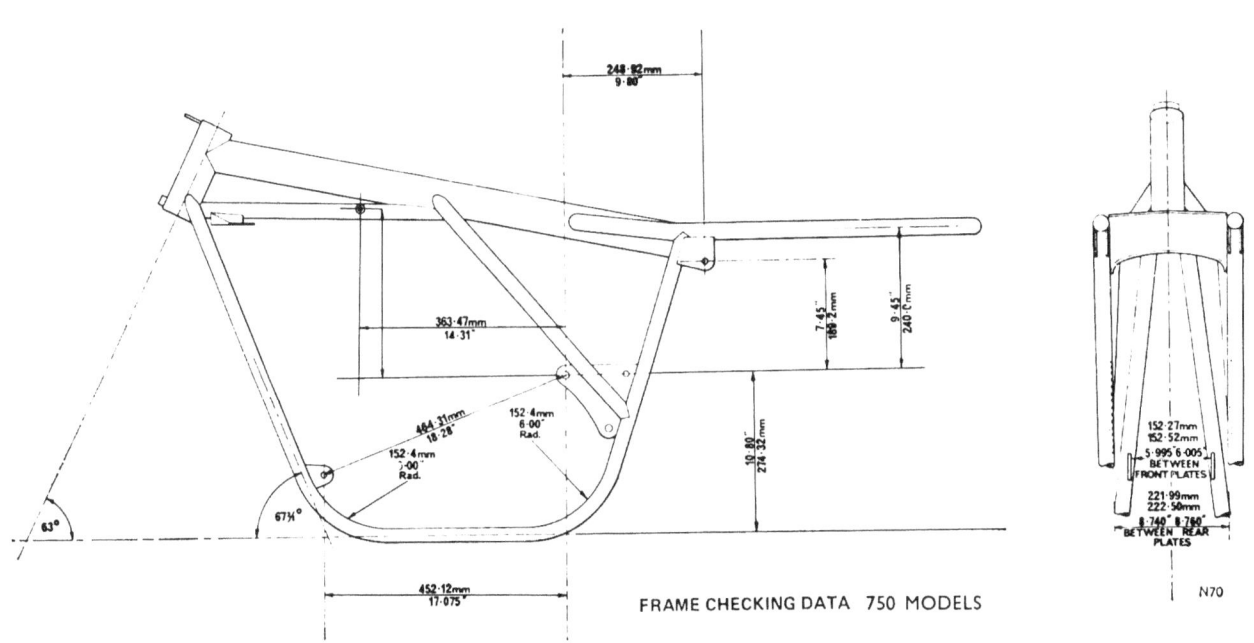

FRAME CHECKING DATA 750 MODELS

Fig. F4 Frame checking charts

Frame and Ancillaries F

SECTION F3

FRAME CHECKING DIMENSIONS

During the course of an accident repair, the frame must be examined most carefully for damage to tubes, welds and fixing lugs. It is then essential to check for distortion and misalignment. *Fig.* F4 shows the Commando frame measurements which should be used to establish whether or not damage has occurred. However, before stripping out the frame from the motorcycle, one quick visual check can be made on vertical alignment at the steering head tube after removal of the front fork assembly. This is accomplished by a long tube (approximately 4 ft. (121 cm)) inserted as a tight push fit through the steering head races. Viewed from the front, the tube should be seen to be perfectly aligned to the motorcycle centre line. Severe damage will immediately be shown up by this method and will obviate unnecessary dismantling at the estimating stage.

It is recommended that the frame is checked more accurately when removed from the motorcycle, to the dimensions given in the checking chart.

SECTION F4

REFITTING POWER UNIT

Prior to refitting the power unit, if any major mechanical attention has been given, wash the oil tank and oil pipes out very thoroughly to remove dirt and foreign matter. As with dismantling, protect the lower frame rails against damage. Proceed as follows:

1. Pass the power unit into the frame from the right side, raising the front slightly and lowering the rear to clear the airbox.

2. With the power unit loosely in position, move the rear end as far as possible to the right side of the frame to facilitate assembly of the rear mounting.

Engine mountings are covered in detail in Section F12-17.

However, if the mountings have merely been dismantled and are to be reassembled without varying the shimming, proceed as follows:

3. Grease using silicone grease (such as Releasil No. 7) and place in position the shims and left side end cap (the shims should be divided equally between left and right).

4. Grease using a silicone grease and insert as a group the left side gaiter, collar and plastic washer with the gaiter held back for maximum clearance. Note that the gaiter should be greased inside to slide easily over the cap and mounting. The order of assembly and method of holding the gaiter back on the edge of the plastic washer are seen respectively in *Figs.* F14 and F5.

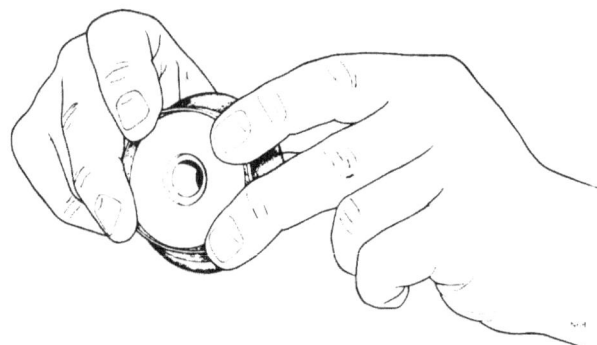

Fig. F5 Gaiter/collar group ready to fit. Note gaiter held back on edge of polyurethane washer

5. Position the spacer between the left hand alloy footrest mounting plate and battery tray bracket and slide in the mounting stud from the left side, moving the power unit as necessary to align the stud holes.

6. Grease using a silicone grease and fit the right side shims and cap.

7. Grease (including inside the gaiter) and fit the gaiter, spacer collar and plastic washer (see *Figs.* F14 and F5).

8. Tap the main stud right through aligning with the right frame bracket, insert the footrest plate spacer, then fit the washer and nut. Tighten to 25 lbs./ft. (3·456 Kg/m).

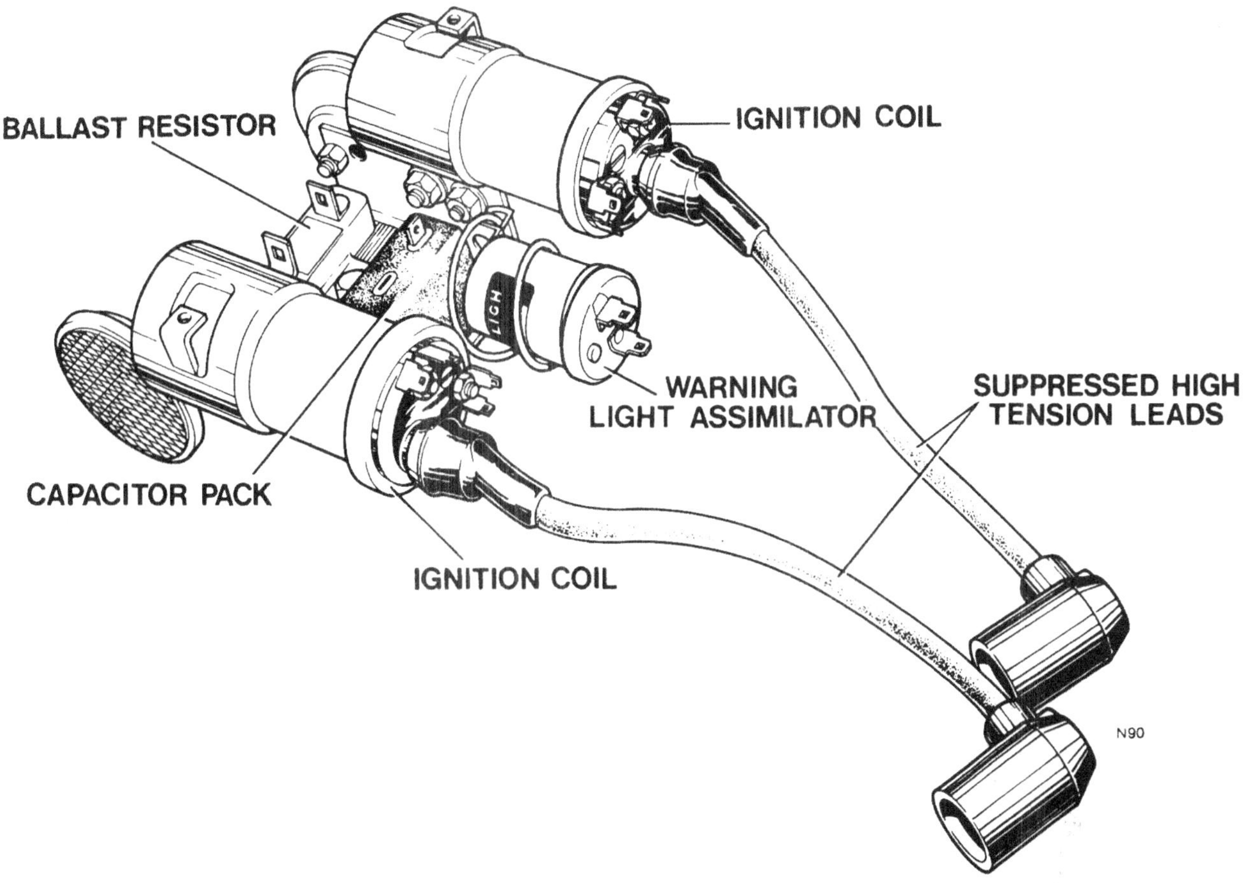

Frame and Ancillaries F

Fig. F6 Coil cluster from rear beneath

9 Fit the front engine mounting plates to the crankcases, sliding the long end of the mounting over the lower crankcase bosses. With the stud or bolt fitted, pivot the mounting up into position to insert the second stud or bolt. Almost certainly the power unit will need to be lifted to insert the crankcase studs (or bolts).

10 Grease the components with a silicone grease and reassemble the front mounting as in Section C32. Tighten the centre bolt to a torque of 25 lbs./ft. (3·456 Kg/m).

11 Refit the oil pipe junction block, using a new gasket if necessary and securing with the single bolt which must not be overtightened.

12 Prior to refitting the carburetors and spacers, grease the manifold screws lightly and run them into the cylinder holes to ensure that they can be tightened by finger pressure only when the carburettors and manifolds are assembled. During this operation and before attempting to fit the engine to the frame block the inlet ports with clean non-fluffy cloth to prevent a screw dropping down one of the ports. Remember to remove the cloth before fitting the carburetors.

13 Holding the Tuffnol insulating block in place (some models use blocks with one flat edge which must fit inboard) fit the air hose to the airbox using a screwdriver blade to enter the lip, then assemble the right carburetor and manifold to the head tightening the socket screws completely.

14 Fit the air hose to the airbox, then offer the insulating block, carburetor and manifold to the cylinder head, tightening the socket screws as far as possible with the fingers. When locking up the screws an abbreviated socket key is essential.

Frame and Ancillaries   F

15 Fit the main head steady plate to the cylinder head, securing with three socket headed screws. Note that the centre screw secures the ground (earth) tab on the red leads.

16 Position the two spacer tubes in the head steady plate and offer the side plates over the rubber mounting studs. Pass the two studs through the side plates and spacer tubes and secure with the washers and nuts. Lastly, fit and tighten the nuts at the rubber mountings.

17 Pass the rocker feed pipe behind the fuel line 'T' piece and between the manifolds. The double end of the pipe fits to the right side of the rocker box. Ensure copper washers are fitted to both sides of each banjo and secure with the banjo bolts.

18 Refit the coil cluster, (the cluster is illustrated in *Fig.* F6) and reconnect the contact breaker leads colour to colour.

19 Reconnect the crankcase breather pipe at the oil tank.

20 Reconnect the tachometer cable to the abutment at the top front of the crankcase, ensuring that the cable adaptor is fitted square upwards and that it has engaged with the drive before the cable union nut is tightened.

21 Reconnect the clutch cable at the handlebar control and adjust the cable to give $\frac{3}{16}$ in. to $\frac{1}{4}$ in. (4 to 6 mm) free play.

1971 and later models

22 Refit the centre stand with the pivot bolts passing through the engine plates, spacers and stand, inboard to outboard. Fit the nuts and tighten fully on to the spacers.

23 Hook the long end of the centre stand spring into the L.H. rear engine plate then use a length of twine over the stand end of the spring to expand it whilst locating the hook in the stand cross tube.

Prior to refitting the swinging arm, ensure that the pivot area is perfectly clean, that the sintered bushes are oiled lightly and that the four 'O' sealing rings are in position.

24 The left side pivot end cap must be held or "stuck" in position with a dab of grease as the swinging arm is positioned (see *Fig.* F7). Push the swinging arm forward so that the left end cap is held in position by the inner chaincase.

25 Using a suitable bolt with locknut screwed into the right end of the swinging arm pivot spindle, position the lock screw hole upwards to align with the pivot tube hole (see *Fig.* F8). Align the pivot spindle with the swinging arm bore and push fully home.

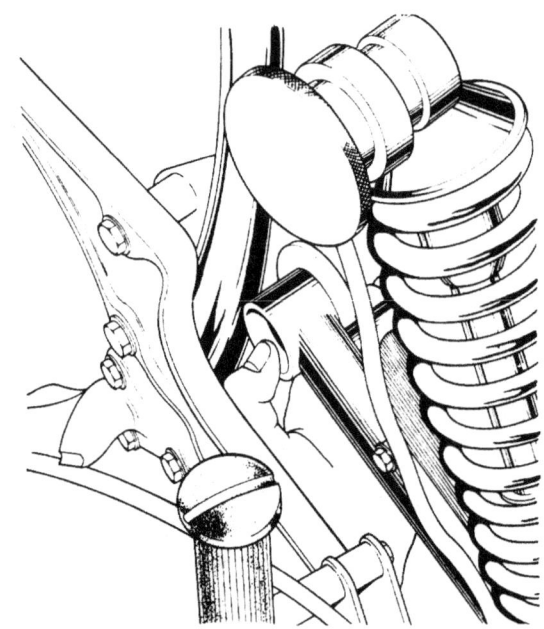

Fig. F7 Swinging arm offered into position with end cap held in place with grease

26 Align the lock screw hole in the pivot spindle and mounting cross tube by movement on the bolt used during refitting the spindle, locate and secure the lock screw and washer. (see *Fig.* 9).

27 Remove the bolt and nut used during fitting of the pivot spindle.

Frame and Ancillaries   F

28 Ensure the right side 'O' rings are still in position then screw home the right end cap and extra long thin screw with copper washer. During tightening, position the lubrication nipple between the 11 and 1 o'clock position and check that the fibre washer is in position beneath the nipple.

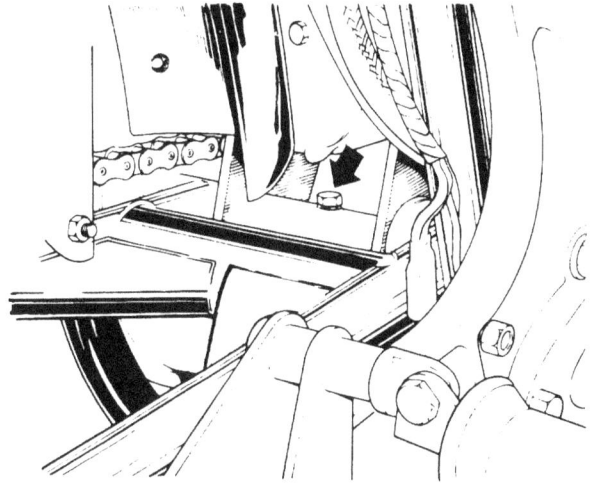

Fig. F9   Spindle lock bolt fitted

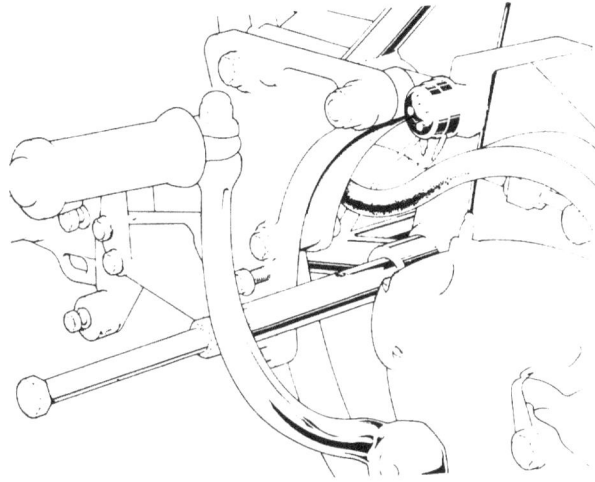

Fig. F8   Aligning swinging arm spindle with swinging arm bore

32 Refit the rear wheel (see Section H2).

33 Refit the exhaust system but check that the copper sealing rings (corrugated steel rings on later models) are in position in the ports and that lockring tab washers are fitted. Tighten the lockrings using service tool 063968 then tap the lockring tabs as appropriate between the cylinder head and lockring fins.

29 Refit the rear chain. This must pass over the bolts within the chainguard and over the countershaft (gearbox) sprocket. This is facilitated by engaging top gear, tying the clutch lever back to the handlebar then cranking the kickstart to revolve the sprocket and pull the chain over. Engage neutral and pull the chain through sufficiently to connect the bottom run. Release the clutch lever.

34 Adjust the rear brake as desired then adjust the stop switch position (see Section J18).

35 Refit the fuel tank (see Section F9) and reconnect the fuel pipes.

36 Refit the fuse.

37 Refit the accessory cover and right side cover.

30 Push the rear chain oiler flexible pipe onto the metal pipe at the swinging arm.

38 Check all oil levels and top up or refill as necessary. This includes the swinging arm pivot which requires SAE 140 oil.

31 Refit the right footrest and secure — do not overlook the ground (earth) tag secured to the longest bolt from behind by a nut.

39 Replace the seat and secure with the knurled side knobs.

Frame and Ancillaries F

SECTION F5

REMOVING AND REFITTING SUSPENSION UNITS

In order to replace or dismantle the suspension units it is necessary to remove them from the motorcycle as follows:

1. Remove the nut securing the bottom of the suspension unit and pull the unit clear of the swinging arm.

2. Release both large knobs and lift the seat up and to the rear (Fastback model straight up) clear of the motorcycle.

3. Slacken off the knurled knob as far as possible to gain spanner access to the integral hexagon of the suspension unit top bolt.

4. Holding the bolt by the hexagon to prevent turning, remove the nut and plain washer from behind.

5. Support the weight of the suspension unit and remove the bolt.

The suspension unit is now free to lift clear of the top frame lugs.

Refitting is a reversal of the foregoing but on reassembly ensure adequate clearance between the suspension unit top collar and any carrier equipment which may be fitted.

SECTION F6

REAR SUSPENSION UNITS (GIRLING)

The rear suspension units are of the spring controlled, oil damped, telescopic type. Adjustment of static spring loading is accomplished by rotating the three position castellated cam ring at the bottom of the spring. To adjust, support the motorcycle on the centre stand and use a 'C' spanner to turn the cam ring. Turning the cam ring to the left increases the loading to cope with additional loads and vice versa. Both units must be on the same loading – if in doubt, start both units from the light load position. The damper units are factory sealed thus cannot be serviced. The springs can however be removed. Bonded rubber bushes are used top and bottom for mounting the suspension units. These can be pressed out for replacement and new ones pressed in, smeared with a lubricant such as soap to ease entry.

SECTION F7

CHANGING THE SPRING

In order to change a spring it is recommended that the suspension unit is gripped in a vice by the bottom mounting. Turn the castellated cam ring to the light load position. The help of a second operator is needed so that as the spring is grasped firmly in both hands and compressed down, the second operator lifts clear both split collars. Pressure on the spring is now released and the spring can be lifted clear. Reassembly is a reversal of these instructions.

SECTION F8

REBUSHING THE SWINGING FORK

After long usage, where lubrication has been neglected or where grease has been used instead of the recommended SAE 140 oil, the two flanged bushes working on the spindle may wear. After removal of the swinging fork (Section F1 (9-15) wash all parts very thoroughly in gasoline (petrol). Insert the pivot spindle and check the fit. Excessive working clearance will permit unacceptable side movement at the rear wheel and this must be rectified by renewing the spindle, bushes and oil sealing 'O' rings. Renewal of these items should be dealt with as follows:

Frame and Ancillaries   F

1. If not displaced during removal of the fork, lift out the outboard 'O' rings (see *Fig.* F10).

2. Using a light press and a suitable shouldered press tool, press out the first bush, releasing the large 'O' ring and dust cover.

3. Repeat for the second bush.

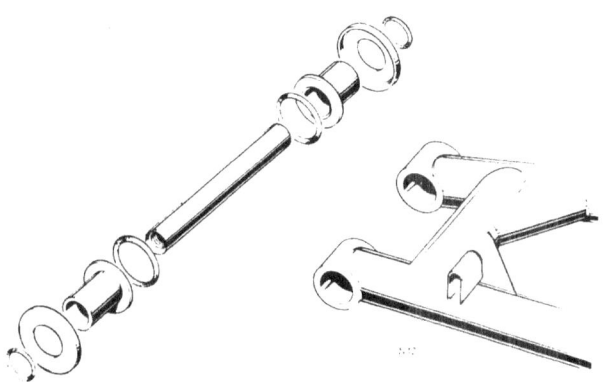

Fig. F10   Swinging arm bushes showing order of assembly

New bushes are pre sized and do not require reaming after fitting. Assemble as follows:

4. Place the dust cover over the bush as in *Fig.* F10 and press the bush in fully.

5. Place the large 'O' ring in the dust plate.

6. Repeat for the second dust cover, bush and 'O' ring.

7. Place the smaller 'O' rings in the bush recess of the swinging arm.

The swinging arm is now ready to refit to the motorcycle, using a new spindle if the original shows signs of wear.

SECTION F9

REMOVING AND REPLACING FUEL TANK

Prior to removal of any fuel tank, remove the seat after releasing the two large knurled securing knobs. This will permit easier access to the rear tank fixings. Disconnect the fuel pipes from both fuel taps at the pipe union nuts.

The various fixing methods used for glass fibre and steel tanks are shown in *Fig.* F11. Note specially the thicknesses and positions of the foam rubber support pads.

The front of the tank in all cases is of the stud and self-locking nut variety. Roadster, Fastback and Interstate types utilise rubbers of the washer type whereas all other models use bonded rubber front mountings.

The rear of the tank prior to 1972 and excepting SS and Hi-Rider models is secured by a single rubber band. SS and Hi-Rider models use a resiliently padded steel cross strap beneath the main frame tube to the rear of the tank, secured by bolts and washers.

Existing glass fibre tanks continue with the same fixings from 1972 but Roadster steel tanks and Interstate steel and glass fibre tanks utilise the rear cross strap. To provide additional space and thus aid removal on such models, removal of the side panels is desirable.

See illustrations *Fig.* F11

Frame and Ancillaries F

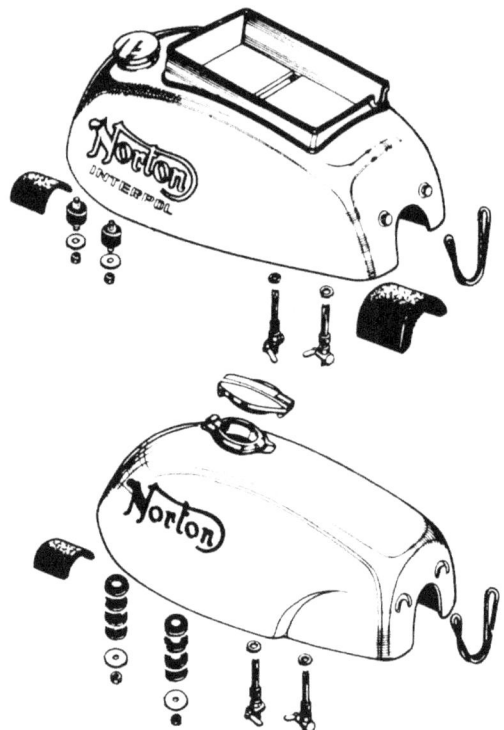

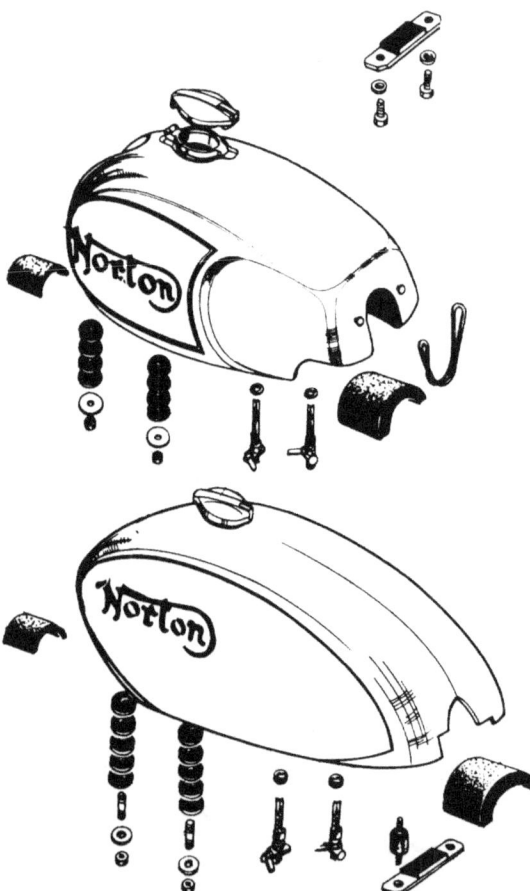

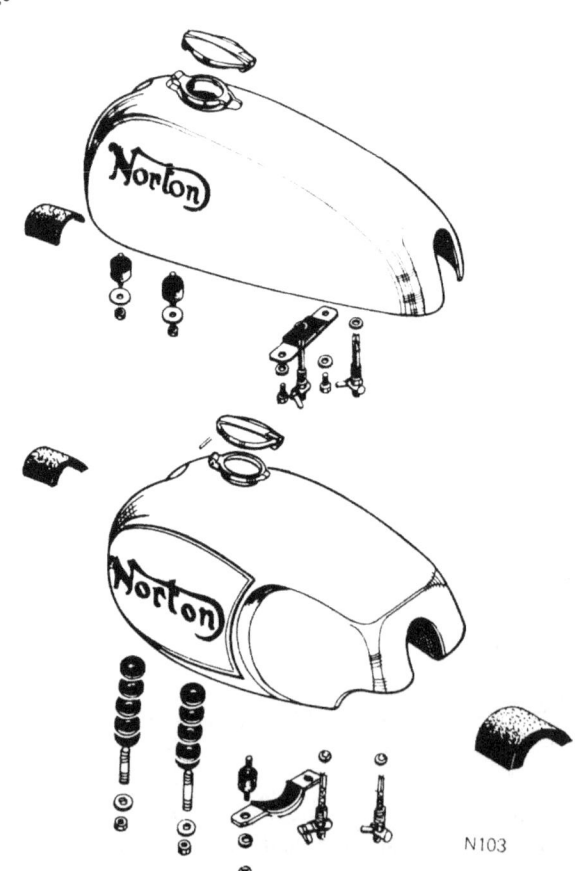

Fig. F11
Fuel tank fixings

Frame and Ancillaries

SECTION F10

REMOVING AND REFITTING OIL TANK

Prior to draining the oil tank, take the motorcycle for a short run to warm the oil which should then flow more freely. Have available a receptacle of sufficient size to receive the contents of the oil tank. Remove the seat after releasing the large knurled side knobs.

Pre 1971 Roadster oil tank

Due to the lack of a drain plug the large hexagon oil tank filter must be removed and the oil pipe union lifted away to drain the oil. The position of the filter boss makes it desirable to place a cardboard "chute" below the boss, thus directing oil straight into the drain tray and minimising mess. Proceed as follows:

1 Remove the oil feed pipe nut and filter and drain the tank.
2 Remove the fuel tank, carburetors and manifolds as in Section F9 and E2.
3 Dismantle the air filter and remove the element (Section E10).
4 Disconnect the rear chain oiler pipe from the oil tank.
5 Disconnect the crankcase breather from the oil tank.
6 Detach the oil return pipe union from the tank.
7 Remove the two bolts and locking plate securing the air filter backplate portion of the oil tank to the battery carrier and collect the spacer.
8 Remove the nut, bolt and washer securing the oil tank top bracket to the frame gusset.
9 Remove the oil tank forwards, bottom end first.
10 Reassembly is a reversal of the removal procedure, but if necessary use new oil sealing washers at both sides of the oil pipe unions. If the motorcycle is ready for service when the oil tank is refitted, fill to the level indicated on the dipstick.

Pre 1971 Fastback oil tank

1 Remove the oil tank drain plug and drain the oil into the receptacle previously obtained.
2 Remove the left side accessory cover by releasing the Rotolok catch and lifting the cover off the rear mounting pegs.
3 Part the rear chain oiler pipe by compressing the spring clip and pulling the pipe clear of the felt cartridge (in front of the battery).
4 Remove the oil tank breather pipe and air filter breather pipe.
5 Remove the oil feed and return pipes from the oil tank.
6 Remove the top front and top rear nuts securing the tank to the flexible mountings.
7 Lift the oil tank upwards, clear of the bottom rubber mounting and pull the bottom of the tank out so that the filler cap clears the frame.
8 Reassembly is a reversal of the foregoing.

1971 and later models

A common oil tank is used on all later models and the following instructions apply to all editions.

1 Remove the two hexagon headed screws and washers securing the right hand side panel.
2 Remove the drain plug and allow oil to drain into the receptacle previously obtained.
3 Part the rear chain oiler pipe by compressing the spring clip and pulling the pipe clear of the felt cartridge.
4 Pull the crankcase breather pipe and oil tank breather pipe away from the oil tank.
5 Remove the large hexagon headed oil tank filter at the rear of the oil tank.
6 Pull off the oil return pipe from the stub at the rear of the oil tank.
7 Remove the nut and washer securing the oil tank to the top rear mounting.
8 Slacken only the nut on the top front flexible mounting (the bracket is slotted and will then slide clear).
9 Using an extension socket wrench, remove completely the bolt fitting through the bottom mounting into the base of the oil tank.
10 Pull the bottom of the oil tank outwards so that the filler neck clears the frame, slide the tank forwards and outwards, lifting the bottom clear first.
11 Reassemble as a reversal of the foregoing. Take care not to omit the spacer from the bottom mounting rubber.

Frame and Ancillaries F

SECTION F11

L.H. ACCESSORY AND R.H. SIDE COVERS

The left hand accessory cover is retained by a Dzus fastener at the top front of the cover. To remove, pull and turn the ring of the fastener. The cover is then pulled away from the frame at the front and lifted off the two rear pegs. On all but certain Interpol models, the cover can be lifted clear. On Interpol models with alternating horns, the horn relays and control boxes are located within the accessory cover and the cover cannot be removed completely without disconnecting the horn wiring.

Pre 1971 Fastback and Interpol models had no right hand side cover, the oil tank itself being styled to match the left cover. Roadster models and all 1971 and later models have a right hand side cover secured at the top by hexagon headed screws and washers, and supported by an extension with rubber grommet at the bottom, fitting inboard of the footrest support plate. Note that the securing screws are both the same length on Fastback, Fastback L.R., Interpol and Interstate, but that the rear screw is longer on other models.

SECTION F12

SHIMMING ENGINE MOUNTINGS

Prior to checking shimming note that whilst pre 1971 models can be supported on the centre stand during this operation, 1971 and later models must be supported by a stand or strong box placed below the main frame tubes with the centre stand folded. This is necessary due to the stand being mounted direct onto the engine plates on later models. On such models the mountings would be under tension with the centre stand in use. Proceed as follows:

SECTION F13

CHECKING FRONT SHIMMING

1. Slide the left side gaiter back to give access to the shims and plastic washer.
2. Push or lever the engine to the right until all slack in the Isolastic mounting has been taken up. Holding the engine unit in this position, use feeler gauges to measure the clearance between the plastic washer and bright plated collar. (See *Fig. F12*).
3. The ideal clearance is 0·010 in. (·25 mm). Make a note of the actual clearance.

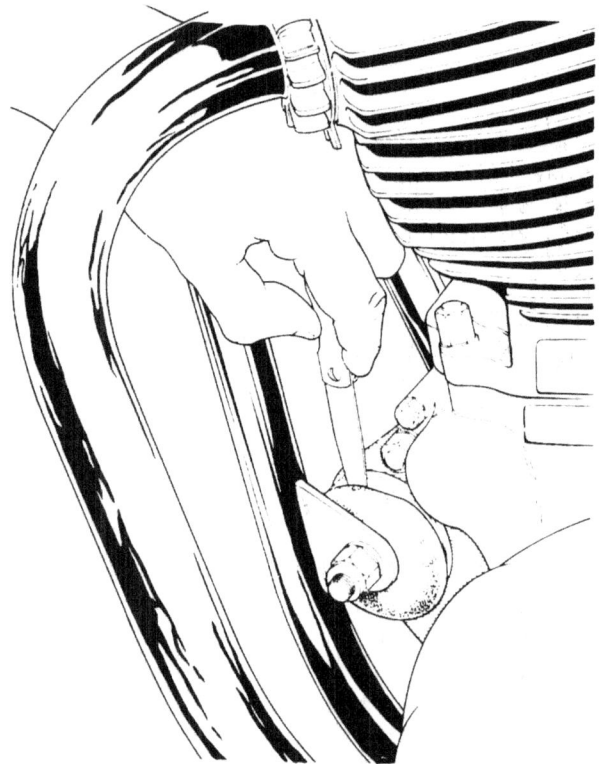

Fig. F12 Checking front mounting clearance

SECTION F14

CHECKING REAR SHIMMING

1. Slide the right side gaiter back to give access to the shims and plastic washer.
2. Push the rear wheel to the left firmly and measure the clearance between the plastic washer and bright plated collar.
3. The ideal clearance is 0·010 in. (·25 mm).

SECTION 15

ADJUSTING FRONT SHIMMING

There are two methods of adjusting front shimming, the quicker method (Method 1) deals with the mounting in situ and is intended for checking as an item of routine maintenance. Method 2 deals with removal of the complete front mounting without removing the power unit. This method is preferred where the mounting has seen a great deal of service and requires a thorough cleaning and the replacement of worn components.

Frame and Ancillaries F

METHOD 1

1. Remove the self locking nut and plain washer from the mounting bolt.

2. Align the flats on the hexagon of the mounting bolt with the timing case casting of the engine.

3. Using a soft metal drift to avoid damaging the threads drive the bolt through sufficiently that the gaiter, spacer and plastic washer can be removed together.

4. Remove the end cap and note the shim thicknesses.

Shims are available in 0·005 in., 0·010 in., 0·020 in. and 0·030 in. thickness. If at the time of stripping, the clearance was found to be, for example, 0·030 in., then a shim of 0·020 in. thickness should be added. It is obviously more desirable to use one 0·020 in. shim than a collection of shims to this thickness which tend to deteriorate faster. Prior to reassembly, clean all the parts including inside the gaiters, and grease lightly. Examine the plastic washer for excessive wear producing uneven thickness and replace if necessary. Proceed as follows:

5. Reassemble the gaiter, spacing collar and shims after attention, in the order shown in *Fig. F14*. Note that the reassembly procedure is a reversal of that used in dismantling but take care to fit the cap with shims well over the actual mounting to allow room for the gaiter, spacing washer and plastic washer to be fitted together.

6. Secure the mounting bolt to a torque reading of 25 lb./ft. (3·456 Kg/m).

METHOD 2

This operation involves removal of the complete front mounting. In order to remove the mounting bolt completely, it may be necessary to remove the right exhaust system as described in Section F19. Proceed as follows:

1. Remove the main mounting bolt nut and washer.

2. Using a soft metal drift drive the mounting bolt out to the right side whilst supporting the weight of the engine to prevent damage to the bolt threads.

3. Slide back the gaiter at the left side and remove the collar, plastic washer and gaiter as a set.

4. Slide back the right hand gaiter and again remove the parts.

5. Collect the end cap and shims from both sides.

6. Remove the two ⅜ in. studs securing the mounting to the front of the crankcase and lift the mounting away.

7. If the rubbers and buffers are to be changed in the mounting, refer to Section F17.

At this stage clean the engine mounting, end caps and spacing collars thoroughly to remove any corrosion, and replace the plastic washers if this is obviously necessary due to wear, uneven thickness or damage. Proceed as follows:

8. Assemble the front mounting less shims in a plain jawed vice. The order of assembly is shown in *Fig. F14* and the method of holding the mounting in *Fig. F13*.

9. Fit and tighten down the mounting bolt washer and nut. Note: Due to variations in thread length on the bolt the nut may "bottom" on the threads. If this occurs, add spacing washers to compensate for the thickness of the main frame lugs. Secure the self-locking nut to a torque setting of 25 ft./lbs. (3·45 Kg/m) so that the spacing collars abut to the centre spacer tube of the mounting.

10. Using feeler gauges, measure the clearance between the end cap and plastic washer at one side only.

If the measurement is found to be, for example, 0·050 in. then it will be necessary to add shims to a total thickness of 0·040 in. This would best be achieved by the insertion of a 0·020 in. shim at each side of the mounting beneath the end cap. Having settled the number and thickness of shims to add, remove the mounting bolt, recheck that all parts are perfectly clean, grease lightly using a silicone grease such as Releasil No. 7, including inside each gaiter, and proceed as follows:

11. Lift the gaiters, collars, etc. away from the mounting to increase clearance during fitting.

12. Offer the mounting to the lower crankcase lug and hold loosely in position with the bottom stud.

Frame and Ancillaries F

13 Pivot the mounting up to engage with the crankcase lug and fit the top stud.

14 Secure both top and bottom stud nuts to 25 ft./lbs. (2·07 Kg/m) torque.

15 Fit the right side cap shims, gaiter etc. first (the order of assembly is shown in *Fig.* F14) and ensure that the lip of the gaiter fits well over the mounting.

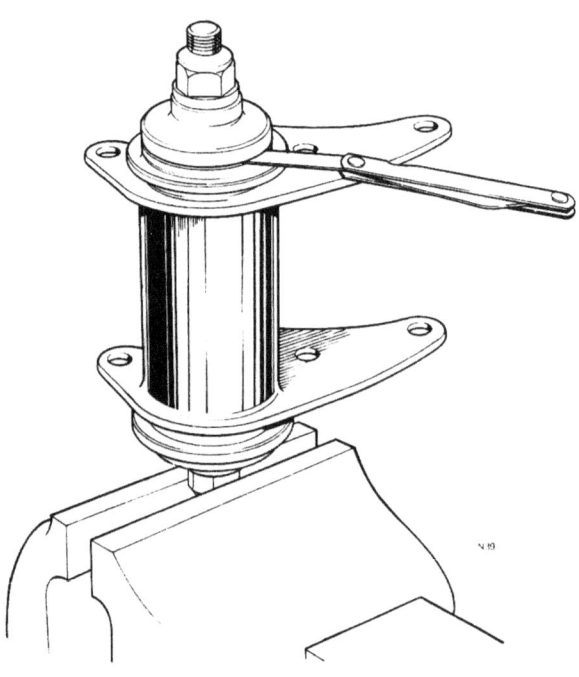

Fig. F13   Method 2. Holding front mounting in a vice for checking.

16 Fit the main mounting bolt from the right side. It will be necessary to align a flat on the hexagon to pass the timing case and the bolt should pass through until it is just flush with the left end of the spacer tube.

17 Assemble the left end of the mounting – this is facilitated by "peeling" the gaiter back and if necessary by levering the power unit over in the frame to the right.

18 Ensure that the gaiter lip is located properly over the mounting, using a small screwdriver to assist this operation.

19 Push the mounting bolt fully home, fit the washer and nut and secure to 25 ft./lbs. (3·456 Kg/m) torque.

20 Although the assembly has previously been shimmed and greased, ensure that both gaiter/end cap assemblies can be revolved with finger pressure. If this is not the case, recheck to ensure that the gaiters have not been trapped.

SECTION F16

ADJUSTING REAR SHIMMING

Unlike the front mounting, the rear can only be dismantled completely after stripping the primary transmission as described in Section C13 and C14. The shims can, however, be changed at the right side only without the need for this further work. The normal method of shimming, after the clearance has been checked following Section F14, is:

1 Remove the self-locking nut and washer from the right end of the main mounting stud.

2 Using a soft metal drift drive the mounting stud partially through, right to left until it protrudes some 4 in. from the left hand side.

3 Slide the right gaiter lip off the mounting tube then push down and rearwards clear of the frame the gaiter, spacing collar and plastic washer as a group.

4 Collect the right side shims and end cap. Examine the plastic washer for excessive wear and replace if necessary.

As with the front mounting, the thickness of shims required should be determined from the measurement at the time of stripping as against the ideal clearance 0·010 in. (0·025 mm). For example, to correct a clearance of 0·030 in., a single 0·020 in. shim would need to be added. Reassemble as follows:

5 Clean and grease lightly the parts of the right end cap/gaiter group, using a silicone grease such as Releasil No. 7.

Frame and Ancillaries   F

6   Fit the shims and end cap to the mounting with the thinest shim to the cap.

7   In order to refit the gaiter, plastic washer and collar, the gaiter must be held back as far as possible on the lip of the collar, as shown in *Fig*. F5 to gain sufficient room for fitting.
If it proves extremely difficult to insert the parts, have a second operator push the rear wheel as far as possible from right to left, thus providing maximum clearance at the end of the rear mounting.

8   After entering the end cap, gaiter etc. ensure that the gaiter fits completely over the mounting and cap without being trapped at either end. Check then that the collar, plastic washer etc. are free to revolve with the gaiter.

9   Using a soft metal drift, tap the main mounting stud right through from the left side and have the assistance of a second operator to align the frame lug with the mounting bolt, levering if necessary between the engine plate and frame tube to aid alignment, and inserting the spacer between the alloy footrest mounting plate and frame bracket.

10   Fit the plain washer and self-locking nut and tighten to a torque of 25 lbs./ft.

After considerable usage it may be expected that the mounting end groups have suffered wear and deterioration due to corrosion and after dismantling of the primary transmission and removal of the mounting stud the left end group can be removed for cleaning, greasing and replacement of the worn parts. If the rubbers and buffers are to receive attention as in Section F17 the power unit must be removed from the frame as described in Section F1. However, the need for attention to these particular is comparatively rare.

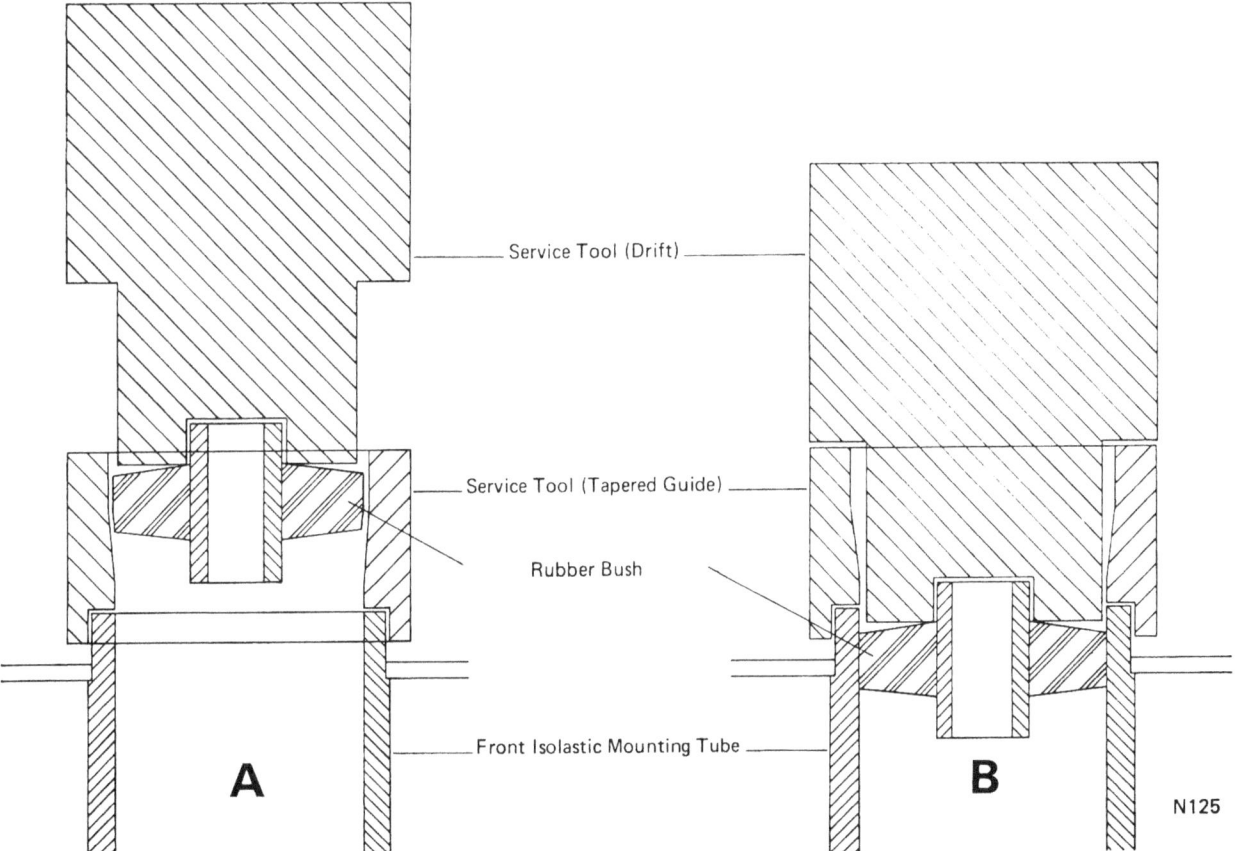

Fig. F14   *Using service tool 063971 to insert front isolastic rubber bushes*

Frame and Ancillaries   F

Note: Later model Commandos have been fitted with bronze-loaded PTFE plastic washers (brown in colour) in place of the cream coloured polyurethane washers fitted to earlier models. These washers resist wear and deterioration; therefore, we recommend they be fitted as replacements.

SECTION F17
RENEWAL OF RUBBERS AND BUFFERS

This section assumes that the end cap groups have already been removed and that, in the case of the rear mounting, the power unit complete has been removed to gain access.

Renewing Isolastic Mounting Rubbers

Pre 1970 models not covered by this manual used mounting bushes with outer steel sleeves which often proved extremely difficult to remove. 1970 and later models use bonded mounting bushes which are lubricated at the time of assembly and which present no such problems. Removal does not necessitate the use of special tools though reassembly requires the use of special tool 063971. Proceed to remove as below but refer to *Fig.* F14 for the positions of bushes and buffers.

Front mounting

1. Place a suitable sized bar into the steel centre of either bonded bush only sufficiently to occupy the bush sleeve. Apply strong side pressure on the bar and the bush will turn in the mounting tube and can be prised out.

2. Lift out the spacer tube complete with two rubber buffers.

3. Repeat the operation of removal by side pressure applied by a bar through the remaining bush. Examine all parts for deterioration and renew parts as necessary before reassembly.

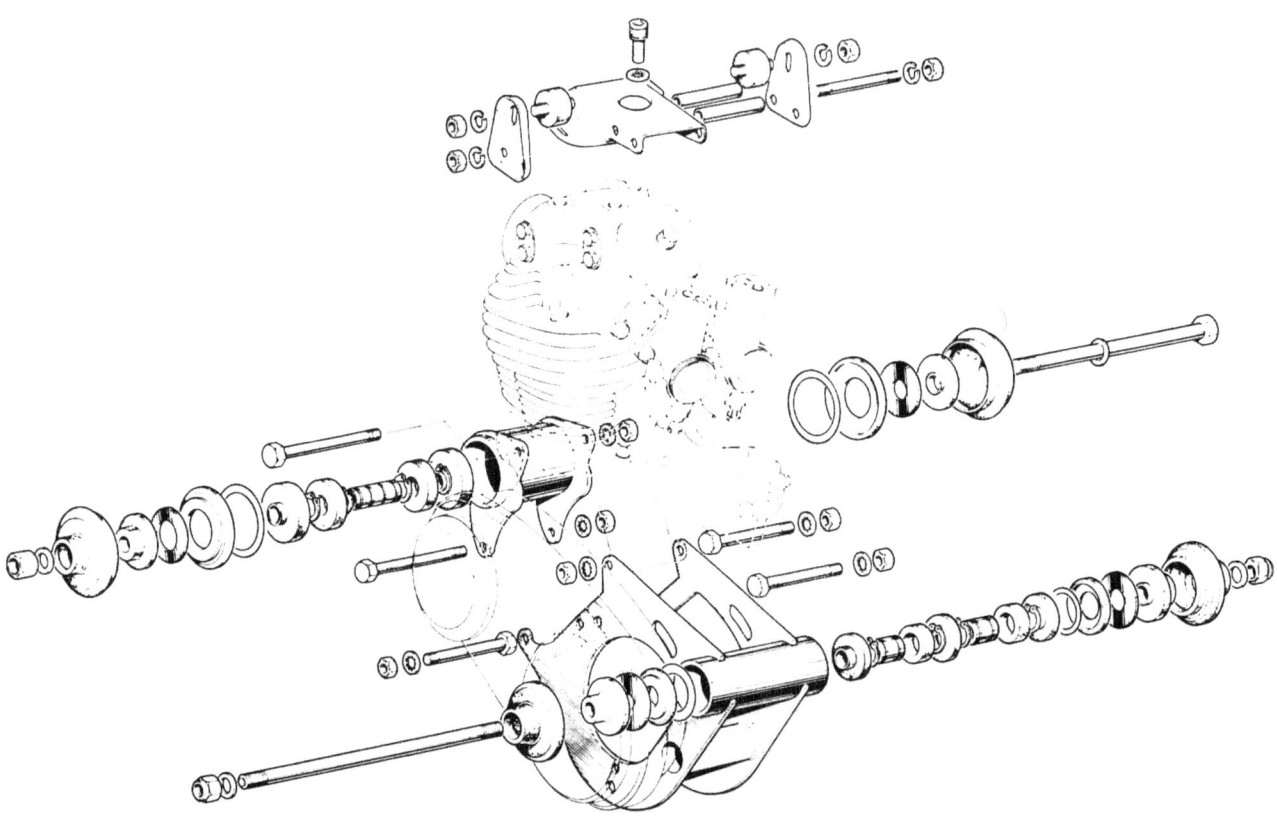

Fig F15   Isolastic mountings exploded view

Frame and Ancillaries   F

4 Fit the tapered guide body 063971 over the end of the mounting tube as shown in *Fig.* F15.

5 Take the first bush and paint the edge with a rubber lubricant.

6 Press the bush either way round into the tapered guide to compress the rubber to the diameter of the mounting tube.

7 Using service tool 063971 as in *Fig.* F15, either press or drive with a hammer so that the bush slides home into the mounting tube and the shoulder of this tool abuts to the top of the tapered guide. The first bush is now in the correct position.

8 Now invert the mounting and slide the two buffer rubbers over the spacer tube until they are central, with a gap of ½ inch (12·70 mm) between the buffers.

9 Place the spacer tube complete with buffers in the mounting tube, resting on the first bush fitted.

10 Repeat operations 4, 5, 6, 7, for the second bush. The front mounting is now complete with rubbers and ready for reassembly.

Rear mounting

1 Place a suitable sized bar into the steel centre of either bonded bush only sufficiently to occupy the bush sleeve. Apply strong side pressure on the bar and the bush will turn and can be prised out.

2 Lift out the first short spacer tube complete with buffer.

3 Remove the centre bush. Since this is recessed far into the mounting tube, access by a bar as for the end bushes will be more difficult. An alternative is to use the bar as a drift, then strike one side of the bush on the rubber portion and the bush will turn sideways in the tube. The bush may then be pulled easily from the mounting tube.

4 Collect the second spacer complete with buffer.

5 Repeat the operation of removal by side pressure applied by a bar through the remaining bush. Examine all parts for deterioration and renew as necessary before reassembly.

6 Paint the edge of the centre bush with rubber lubricant (all the rear mountain bushes are identical but of smaller outside diameter than the front mounting bushes).

7 By hand pressure only and without the need for a tapered guide, push the centre bush into the end of the mounting tube. Then using a suitable length of large diameter tubing push the bush into the centre of the tube $3\frac{1}{4}$ inches (75·15 mm) from each end of the tube.

8 Place one spacer tube, with buffer rubber centrally positioned, against the centre bush.

9 On the same side of the mounting, lubricate and press in the second bush until it abuts to the spacer tube.

10 Invert the mounting tube and repeat operations 8 and 9 for the second side of the mounting. The rear mounting is now complete with rubbers and ready for reassembly.

Fig. F15. Front mounting assembly tools. "A" shows bush in tapered guide. "B" shows bush entered in mounting tube.

SECTION F18

REAR FENDER

Removal and refitting of the rear fender is similar for all models excepting Fastback on which there is the additional problem of the tail section fairing. The separate routines are given below:

Fastback:

1 Release the two large knurled knobs securing the seat and lift the seat straight up and clear of the frame.

2 Remove the suspension unit top bolts to release the forward ends of the tail section.

3 Remove the clip from beneath which secures the tail section to the rear frame loop.

4 Disconnect the tail lamp leads and direction indicator leads where used at the snap connector terminals inside the tail section.

5 Remove the nuts and washers at the bottom front and lift the fender away.

Frame and Ancillaries

6 Reassembly is a reversal of the foregoing but do not omit to reconnect the tail lamp leads. Where direction indicators are fitted, ensure that they work correctly when reconnected.

Roadster:

1 Release the two large knurled knobs securing the seat and lift the seat straight up and clear of the frame.

2 Release the tail lamp with fairing and number plate support as a group, by removal of six bolts and plain washers.

3 Disconnect the tail lamp leads (and the direction indicator leads where fitted) and lift away the tail lamp and tail lamp fairing group.

4 Remove the bottom front two self-locking nuts and plain washers securing the rear fender to the bracket from the frame gusset.

5 Reassembly is a reversal of the foregoing but do not omit to reconnect the tail lamp leads. Where direction indicators are fitted, ensure that they work correctly when reconnected.

3 Remove the nuts securing the muffler (silencer) mounting plates to the rubber mountings, so that at the next stage the mufflers are removed with plate attached.

4 Lift each exhaust system clear.

5 When assembling the exhaust system, fit the copper/asbestos sealing ring into the exhaust port, offer the exhaust pipe to the port and, holding in the correct position, tighten the lockring sufficiently to hold the exhaust pipe in the correct position whilst permitting it to be rotated slightly. Now assemble the muffler to the exhaust pipe and to the muffler mountings.

6 Tighten completely the muffler mountings, forward clip and lockring.

When refitting the exhaust system, if the exhaust system is not assembled correctly to the frame, it can lie in the wrong plane. The tendency is to push the system to its lowest position during fitting so that the centre stand and other equipment can come into contact with the exhaust pipe and mufflers. Assembly as above will prevent both misalignment and strain on any of the fittings.

SECTION F19

EXHAUST SYSTEM

The dismantling and reassembly routine for 750 Commando models with the various low level exhaust systems is similar but the high level system of the "S" model, upswept to the left side requires a different technique. The downswept exhaust systems are shown in *Fig.* F16 and the "S" type system in *Fig.* F17.

Removing and Refitting – all 750 models except "S" type:

1 On late models with exhaust lockring tab washers, flatten back the tabs.

2 Using service tool 063968 unscrew the finned exhaust lockrings and allow these to hang on the exhaust pipes.

Removing and Refitting "S" type Exhaust:

1 Using service tool 063968 unscrew the finned exhaust lockrings and allow to remain loosely in place.

2 Remove nut from rubber mount block on bracket adjacent to suspension unit.

3 Lift off pipe and muffler complete.

4 Repeat for other pipe and muffler.

5 On reassembly, the use of new type tabbed washers to secure the lockrings is recommended.

Frame and Ancillaries F

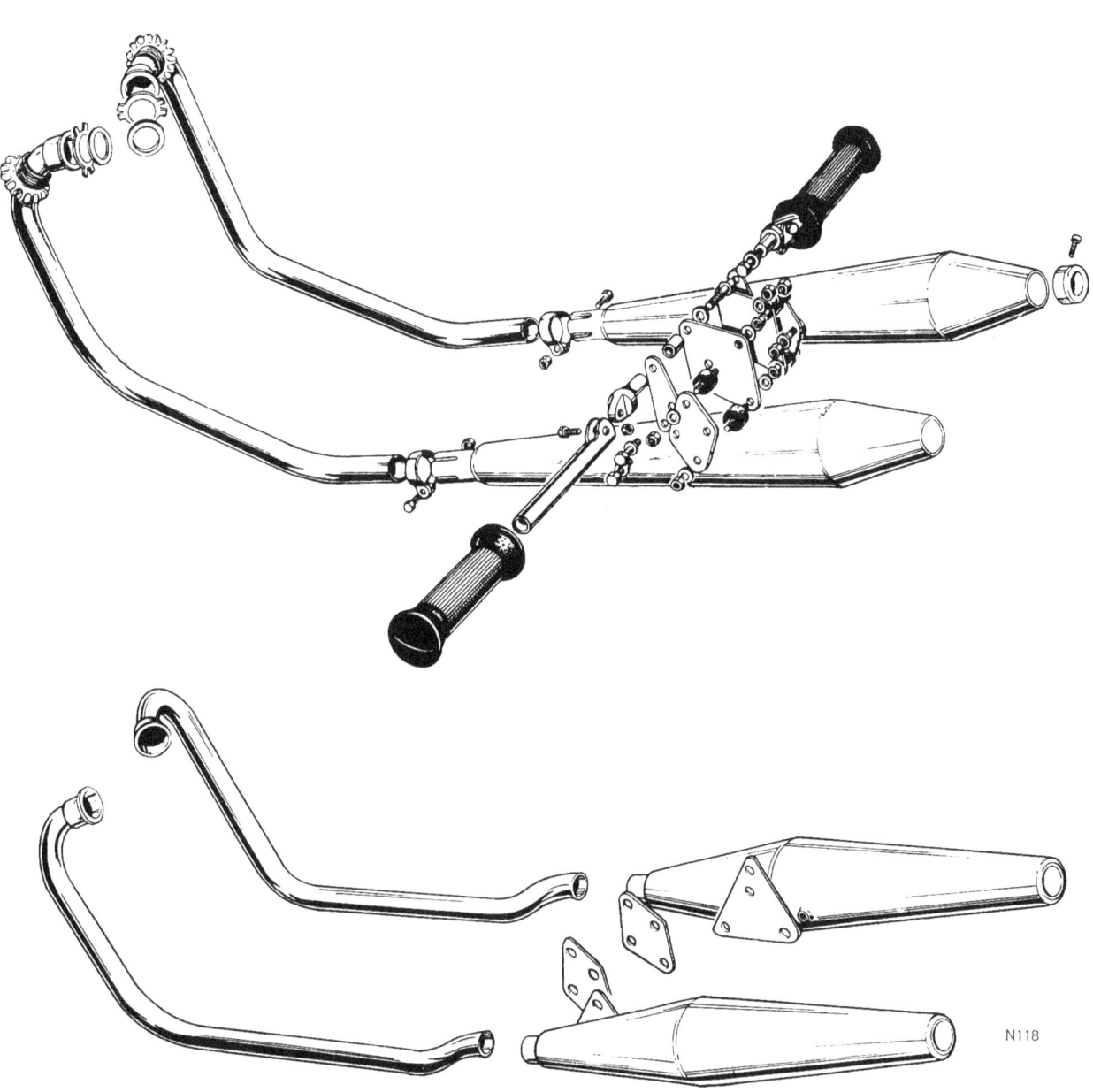

Fig. F16   750 Low level exhaust systems

Frame and Ancillaries   F

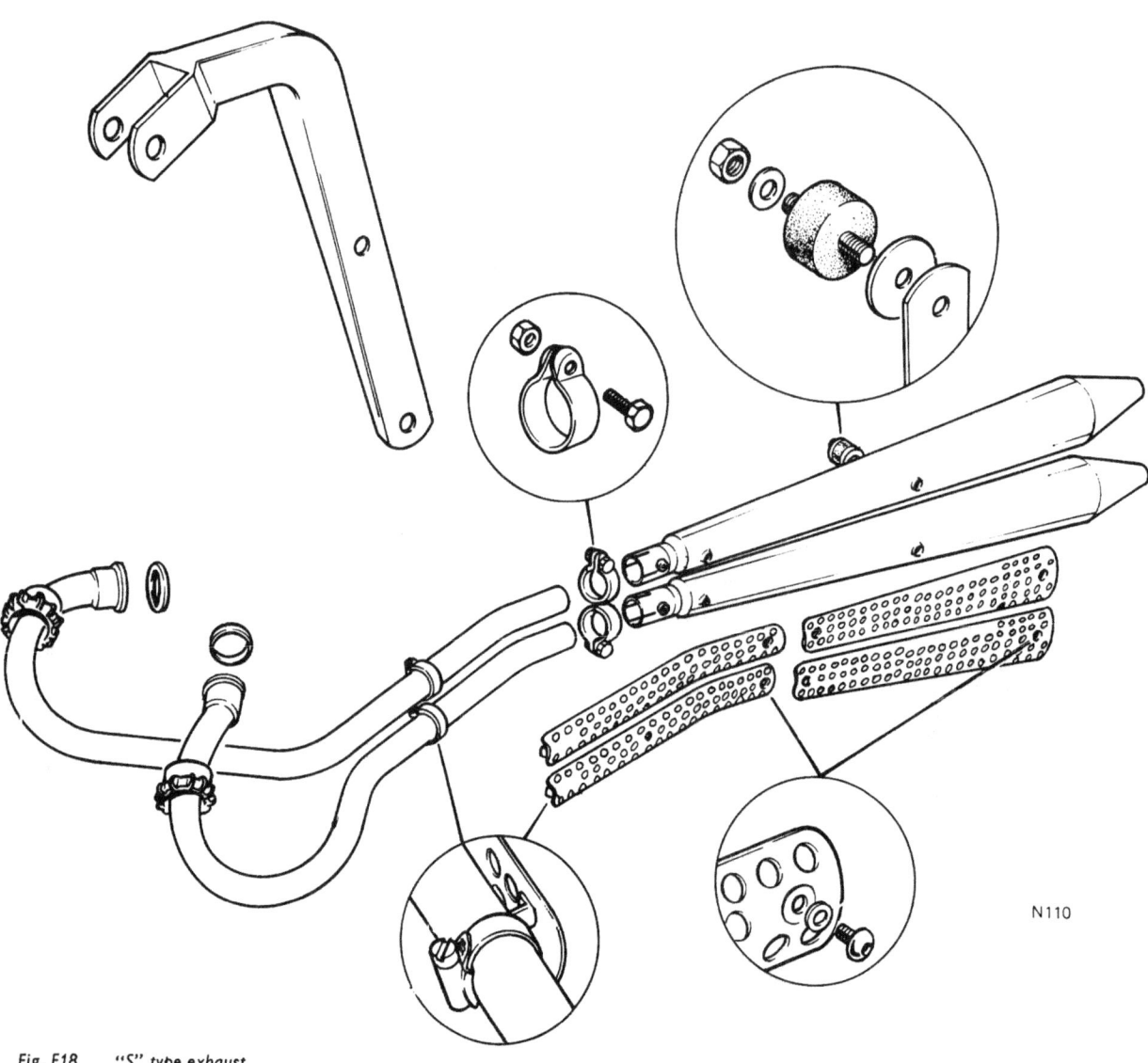

Fig. F18   "S" type exhaust

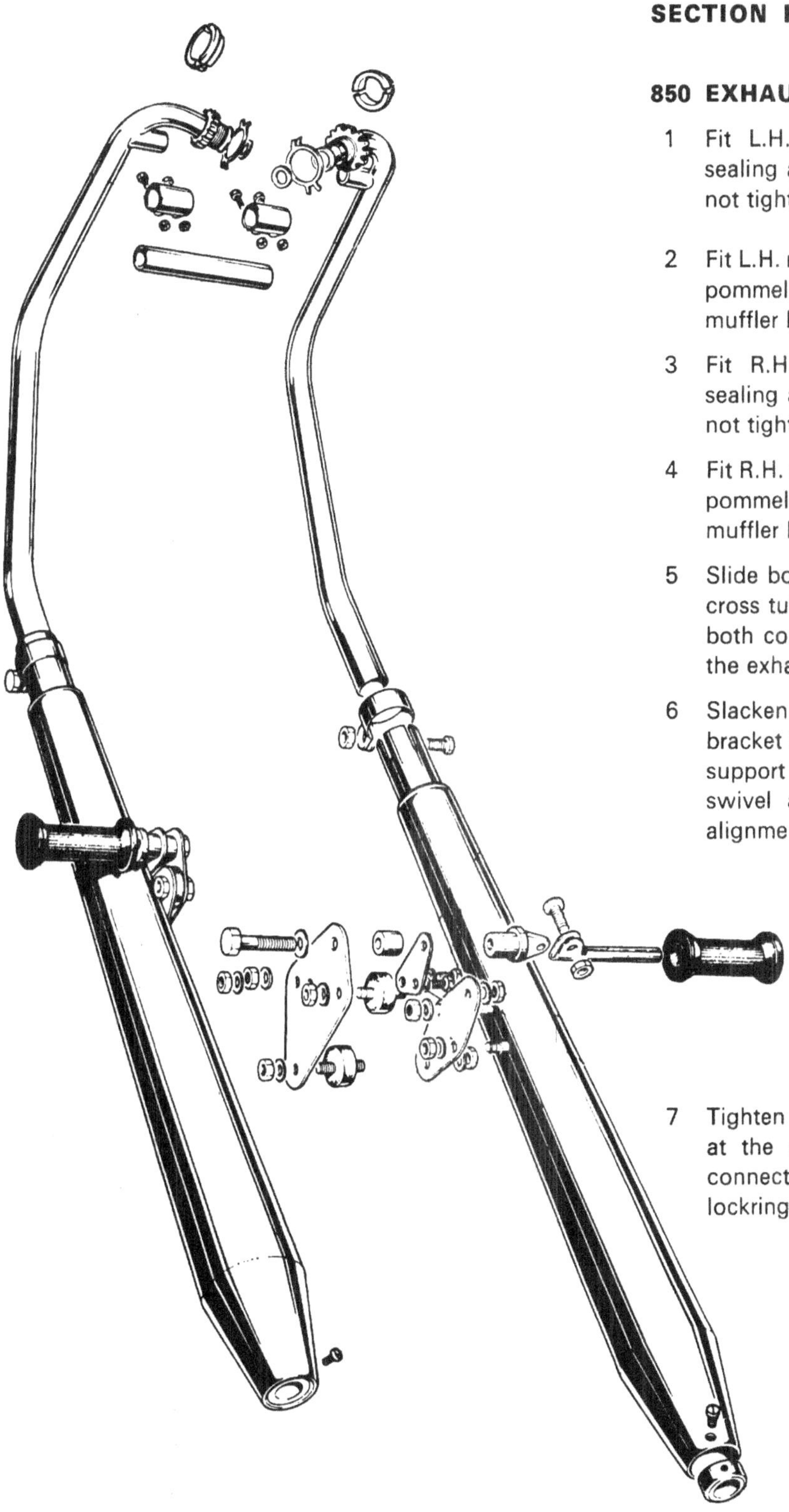

Frame and Ancillaries F

SECTION F20

850 EXHAUST SYSTEMS

1. Fit L.H. exhaust pipe complete with lockring, sealing and tab washers. Run up lockring but do not tighten at this stage.

2. Fit L.H. muffler to exhaust pipe, align the mounting pommels and assemble loosely to the L.H. muffler bracket mounting rubbers.

3. Fit R.H. exhaust pipe complete with lockring sealing and tab washers. Run up lockring but do not tighten.

4. Fit R.H. muffler to exhaust pipe, align the mounting pommels and assemble loosely to the R.H. muffler bracket mounting rubbers.

5. Slide both connector sleeves to the centre of the cross tube. Place cross tube in position and slide both connector sleeves outwards to engage with the exhaust pipe stubs.

6. Slacken off all footpeg support and muffler bracket bolts in the left and right hand aluminium support plate castings – to allow the brackets to swivel and adjust to the exhaust pipe/muffler alignment.

7. Tighten up the total exhaust system, commencing at the cylinder head lockrings and cross tube connector sleeves. Do not forget to bend up the lockring tab washers.

8. Finally retighten the muffler bracket/support plate bolts.

Fig. F18   850 exhaust system

NOTES

Front Forks/Steering   G

Front Forks and Steering

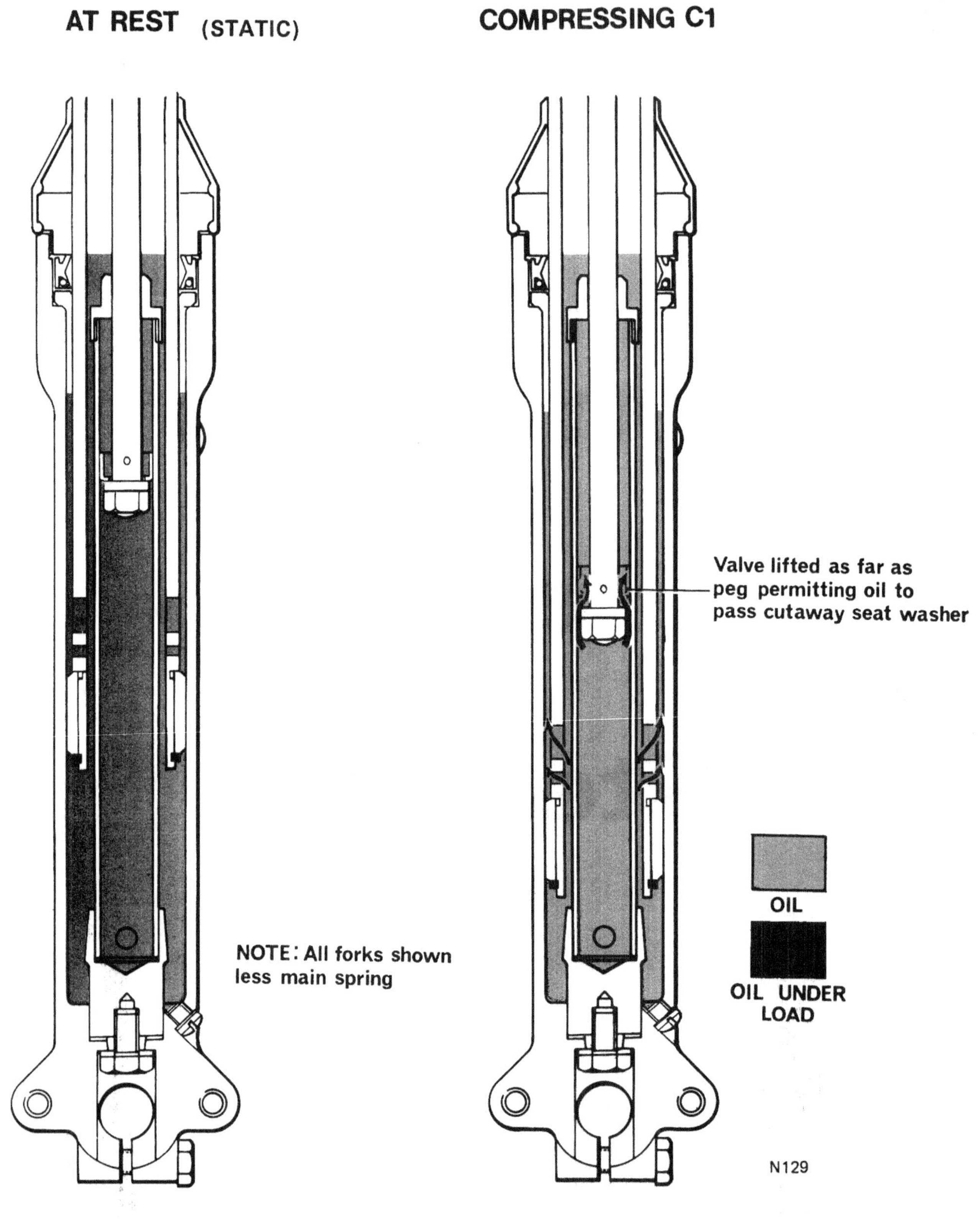

Front Forks/Steering

AT REST (STATIC)

COMPRESSING C1

Valve lifted as far as peg permitting oil to pass cutaway seat washer

NOTE: All forks shown less main spring

OIL

OIL UNDER LOAD

Fig. G2   Fork at rest, compressing, extending, and almost fully extended

Front Forks/Steering G

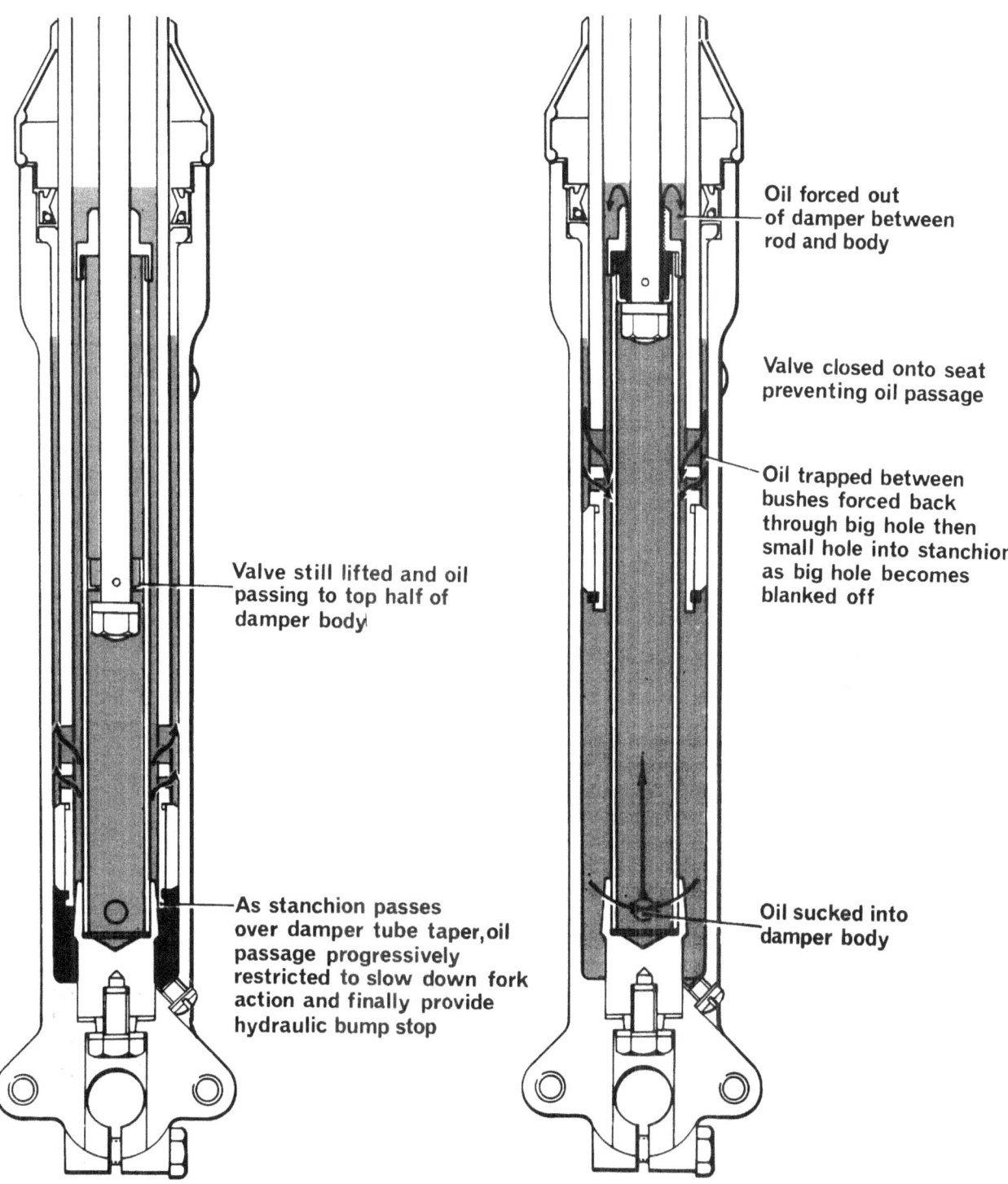

FINAL COMPRESSION C2

Valve still lifted and oil passing to top half of damper body

As stanchion passes over damper tube taper, oil passage progressively restricted to slow down fork action and finally provide hydraulic bump stop

EXTENDING

Oil forced out of damper between rod and body

Valve closed onto seat preventing oil passage

Oil trapped between bushes forced back through big hole then small hole into stanchion as big hole becomes blanked off

Oil sucked into damper body

Front Forks/Steering G

SECTION G1

FRONT FORK DESCRIPTION

The Commando Fork is a development of the "Roadholder" Fork which is world famous as an extremely strong and precise steering unit under all conditions. The forks comprise high quality seamless chrome steel main tubes with light aluminium sliding members for reduced unsprung weight. Fork movement is controlled by long single rate springs and two-way oil damping. The sliding members are supported on oil impregnated sintered bronze bushes at the top and steel at the bottom to give maximum support and to minimise wear. The fork yokes are substantial cast components which provide great rigidity. The steering head pivot comprises two pre-packed and sealed ball journal bearings. The steering head arrangement illustrated is that used on 1971 and later models with the stem captive in the upper yoke and incorporating non-adjustable bearings.

SECTION G2

HOW FORK WORKS

Consider that as the front wheel meets a bump in the road surface the front forks are compressed against the main springs. As the wheel passes the bump the forks are permitted to return to the static position. Should the motor-cycle become "front end light" such as negotiating a hump-backed bridge, the fork extends fully but once again on level road, returns to the static position. The natural tendency for a spring controlled suspension system is to over react and oscillate before returning to static position. Such a system would result in a pitching motion on rough roads and a subsequent loss of stability. To counter this condition, oil damping is provided which in the case of the Commando fork slows down the spring return both on compression and extension. Each fork slider contains 150 cc of oil which is metered by a rod and valve damper assembly. The damping sequence is detailed in the following text and the complete fork assembly is shown in *Fig.* G5. In the latter diagram "A" illustrates the fork at rest with parts descriptions, "B" the form compressing and "C1" and "C2" the fork extending.

FORK AT REST (A)

The oil lies in the bottom of the slider and occupies the spaces between top and bottom bushes, damper tube and main tube and occupies the lower end of the damper tube.

FORK COMPRESSES (B)

Consider that the main tube and damper rod remains stationary thus as the fork compresses, the slider and damper tube rise. As the slider rises, oil passes into the lower end of the damper tube. There is no passage of oil between the damper rod and damper tube cap but oil passes from the slider through the main tube bleed holes between the bushes. The vacuum caused between the fork bushes during compression causes oil to be sucked from the space between the fork bushes. As the fork compresses further, the damper tube passes further into the main tube until the cone shaped bottom area enters and the oil passage into the main tube is progressively cut off until only the bleed hole into the damper tube remains. Oil is then able to pass through the bleed hole slowly, thus slowing or "damping" the fork action, finally providing a hydraulic bump stop on full compression.

FORK EXTENDING (C1 and C2)

The main tube remains stationary whilst the slider and damper tube descend. Oil remains trapped between the top and bottom bushes. The damper valve within the damper tube remains closed thus as the damper tube descends, oil passes between the damper rod and damper tube cap into the space between the damper tube and main fork tube. As the fork continues to extend, oil trapped between the fork bushes is forced back into the slider through the large hole then the small hole to slow down the fork action and prevent the fork "topping" heavily.

Front Forks/Steering G

SECTION G3

REMOVAL OF FRONT FORKS

Removal of the front forks is most easily achieved by dismantling in parts rather than attempting to remove the fork assembly complete. Pre 1971 models had the steering stem captive in the lower yoke whereas 1971 and later models have the stem captive in the upper yoke. This alters the dismantling procedure for the yokes. In the case of disc braked models, it will be found easiest to remove the hydraulic system as an assembly, thus relieving the necessity for refilling and bleeding the system. Release the hydraulic pipe bracket from the right fork slider at the fender bridge. Remove the two bolts and spring washers securing the caliper to the slider and lift the caliper away, complete with pads and still attached to the brake hose. At this stage if the brake lever is operated accidentally, the pads and pistons will be forced from the caliper and the fluid lost. To protect against this, place a spacer between the brake pads – a suitable piece of clean wood or preferably a piece of plastic tubing would be ideal. Remove the four cross-headed screws securing the master cylinder to the right switch cluster, hold the master cylinder but allow the switch cluster to hang on its leads. Pull back the plastic switch cover from the master cylinder and disconnect both Lucar terminals. Release the large spring clips securing the hydraulic hose to the right fork leg and lift the complete hydraulic system away. The system is sealed and can therefore be laid down until it is to be refitted see *Fig. G3*. Support the motorcycle by using a box or block of wood beneath the lower frame rails and proceed as follows:

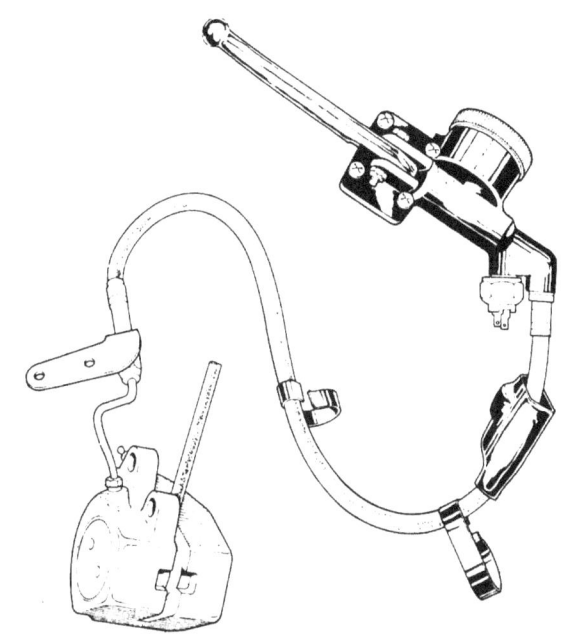

Fig. G3 Hydraulic system removed complete—note spacer between brake pads

1. Remove the front wheel (see Section H5 for disc brake wheel or Section H8 for drum braked wheel).

2. Unscrew and lift the fork tube large chrome top bolts and using two spanners as shown in *Fig. G7* release the damper rod from each top bolt.

3. Lift clear the speedometer and tachometer in their cases and allow them to hang on the cables.

4. Slacken the lower lug socket headed pinch screws (see *Fig. G8*).

The fork main tubes are a tapered fit into the upper yoke and require a shock to free them. The shock may be delivered by grasping the fork slider with both hands and snatching downwards several times. If this fails to break the taper, replace the chrome top bolt at least six threads without the instrument case and using a block of wood to protect the chrome finish (see *Fig. G4*) deliver several blows with a hammer. This will release the main tube from the upper yoke.

Front Forks/Steering

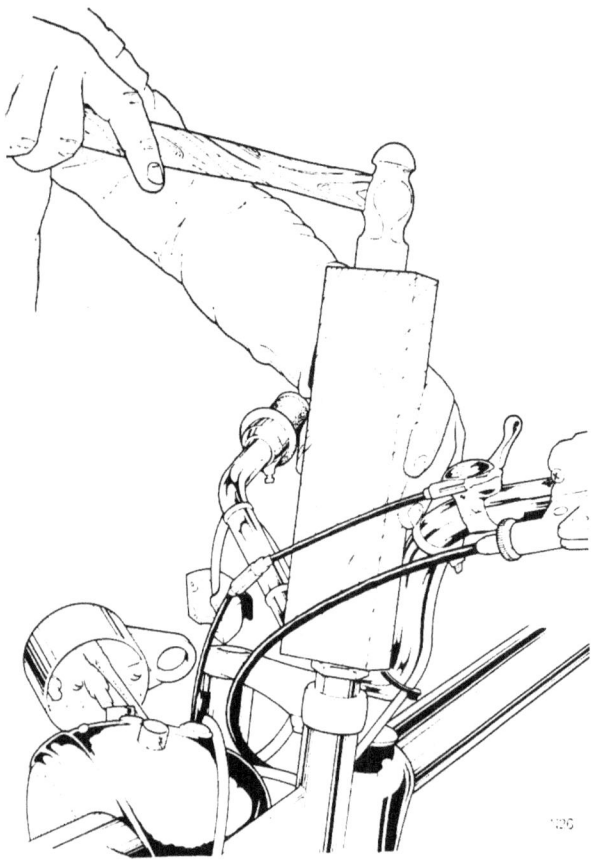

Fig. G4   Shocking main tubes free of upper yoke

8   Collect the two bottom and one top 'O' ring released by each headlamp bracket and top cover and allow the headlamp to hang down on its harness, with fork covers attached.

9   The upper yoke is now captive only by the tightness of the stem in the steering head bearings. Use a hide mallet or soft drift to drive the stem up through the bearings, allowing the upper yoke to be removed. Collect the dust cover and washer.

7A   **Pre 1971 models.** Remove the large chrome blind nut and washer and drive the upper yoke up off the stem.

8A   Remove the nut and dust cover from the stem.

5   Remove the first fork leg, replacing the top bolt to prevent oil loss.

9A   Using a hide hammer or soft drift, drive the stem down through the bearings, to release the lower yoke and stem.

6   Repeat the operation for the second leg.

Note that the steering head bearings are of the sealed ball journal type which will not be disturbed by removal of the yokes and stem.

Note: 850 models use a special pair of fork yokes identified by "ANG" stamped on lower surfaces of both yokes. These yokes must be used for 850's and must not, under any circumstances, be interchanged with earlier types.

7   **1971 and later models.** Remove the lower yoke. This is accomplished by releasing the tab washer and removing the large nut from the bottom of the fork stem. Support the headlamp and tap the lower yoke downwards clear of the stem.

Assembly is identical with later 750 design as outlined above.

Front Forks/Steering   G

SECTION G4

DISMANTLING FORK LEG

Removal of the fork leg assemblies is described in Section G3. Pour oil, from the fork leg to be dismantled, into a suitable receptacle and proceed as follows:

1. Secure the bottom of the slider in a plain jawed vice, with the leg vertical.

2. Lift the plastic gaiter up the main fork tube.

3. Remove the threaded collar by hand pressure only, or, if necessary, by the use of strap wrench 064622 which will not damage the finish.

4. Grasp the main fork tube in both hands and with a number of upward jerking movements, free the oil seal, paper washer and top collar.

5. Lift the main tube away from the slider.

6. Remove the damper tube anchor bolt (the various components are shown in *Fig.* G5) and collect the thick washer.

7. Lift the main spring and damper tube attached, clear of the slider.

8. Collect the bottom fibre washer from the damper tube for re-use.

9. Remove the slider from the vice, secure the damper tube *carefully* in the vice, taking care not to crush it.

10. Unscrew and lift away the alloy damper tube cap.

11. Withdraw the damper rod.

12. Grip the rod in a vice and remove the damper rod locknut, collecting the squared washer and damper valve.

13. The damper valve stop pin is free to be removed.

41. Removal of the square section circlip at the bottom of each fork tube permits removal of the steel bush.

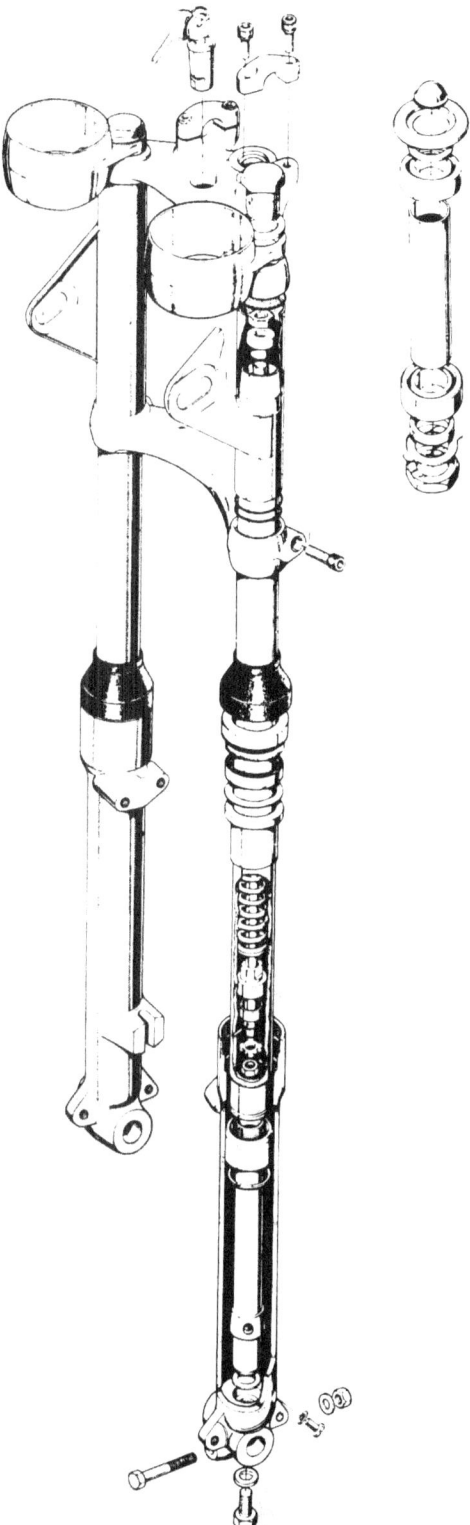

Fig. G5   Front fork exploded view

Front Forks/Steering   G

SECTION G 5

REASSEMBLING FORK LEG

Prior to reassembly, wash all parts very thoroughly in gasoline (petrol) and allow to dry. Examine for wear on the fork bushes and main tube. Check that the damper valve and stop pin are undamaged and that the damper rod is not bent. When all parts are sound, proceed to reassemble as follows:

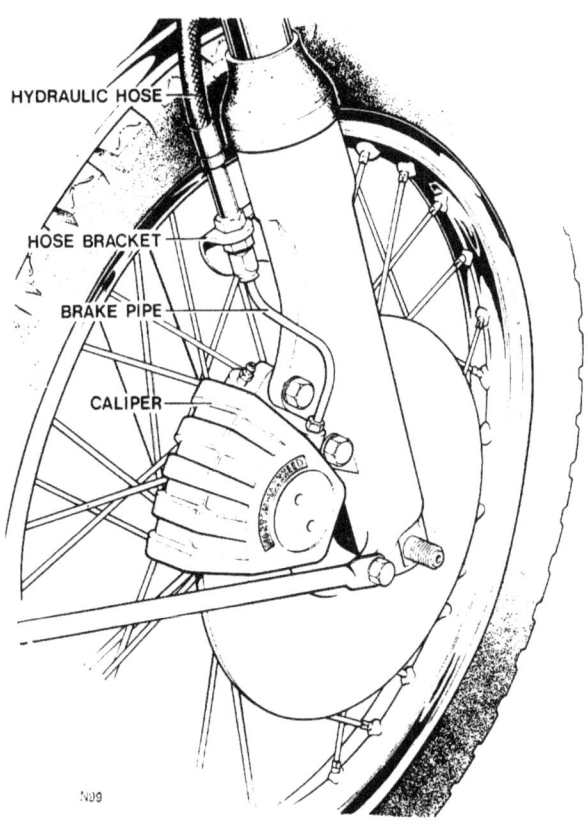

Fig. G6   Hydraulic system fittings to fork leg

1. If the lower bush on the main tube has been removed, fit a new bush and refit the circlip ensuring that it is bedded well all round.

2. Grip the damper rod in a vice and fit the damper valve stop pin. The order of assembly is shown in Fig. G5.

3. At the peg end of the damper rod assemble the damper valve, lip end down (when in the vice) followed by the squared washer and nut which must be tightened securely.

4. Assemble the damper rod to the damper tube then fit and secure the damper tube alloy cap.

5. Place the spring over the damper rod and secure with the thick washer and nut.

6. Place the fibre washer over the end of the damper tube and offer the damper tube assembled, to the slider, securing with the thick washer and bolt.

7. Smear the main tube with clean oil then enter it into the slider.

8. Fit the top bush, paper washer and oil seal: the oil seal will need to be tapped home using a suitable tubular drift.

9. Fit the threaded collar and tighten down.

10. Refit the plastic gaiter.

The fork leg is now ready to refit as described in Section G8.

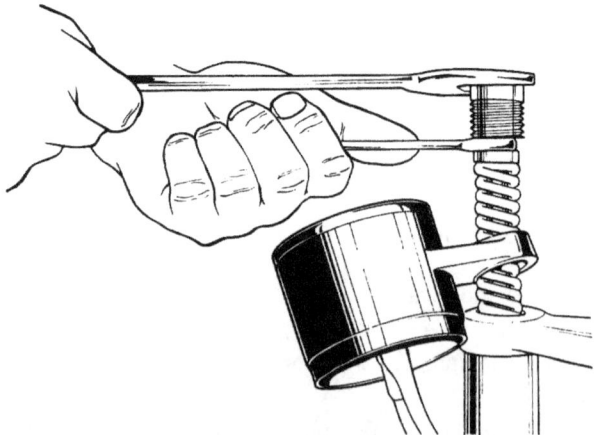

Fig. G7   Releasing damper rod from fork top bolts.

Front Forks/Steering G

SECTION G6

RENEWING STEERING HEAD BEARINGS

1971 and later models utilise sealed non adjustable ball journal bearings with a spacer tube to prevent the bearings being forced into the frame head tube. On such models, after removal of the forks as in Section G3, the bearing spacer tube must be pushed to one side so that a drift can be applied to the inner race of the bottom bearing and the bearing driven out with care. The bearing spacer will be released at the same time. By using the drift from the other end of the steering tube the second bearing can then be driven out.

To replace the bearings, fit the bottom bearing fully home into the housing absolutely square. Use a shouldered drift through the bearing to hold it in line with the housing whilst abutting against the outer race. Place the spacer tube loosely in position and drive the top bearing in to abut to the spacer tube.

As the fork yokes are assembled the bearings will be pulled up to the spacer tube.

1970 models used adjustable sealed ball journal bearings and these had no spacer tube. Removal and reassembly is similar to the sequence used on later models except that both bearings must be fitted up to the abutments within the steering head tube prior to assembly of the steering yokes.

SECTION G7

STEERING HEAD ADJUSTMENT

1971 and later models — The steering head bearing arrangement, where the bearings abut to a centre spacer tube, is non-adjustable. The stem nut fitted from beneath the lower yoke has a tab washer to prevent slackening.

Pre 1971 models — The steering head bearings take the form of ball journal bearings but are adjustable when necessary. If there is play in the steering head bearings the movement which takes place when traversing rough roads or when the front brake is applied will damage the bearings. To check the adjustment, support the motorcycle under the crankcase with the front wheel clear of the ground. Stand astride the front wheel, grasp the fork legs and attempt to move them backwards and forwards against the steering head races. Movement will most easily be detected by holding the fingers at the joint between the fork and steering head tube whilst checking.

Adjusting Pre 1971 Steering Head Bearings

1 Slacken top nut (A) in *Fig.* G8 (this is facilitated by removing the handlebar).

2 Release fixing nuts (B) to allow the fork tubes to slide in the yoke.

3 Using a Service Tool 060942, tighten adjusting nut (C) a little at a time to take up play. Continue to adjust until the forks turn freely from lock to lock without binding.

4 When adjustment is correct, tighten nut (A), clamping nuts (B) and refit the handlebars.

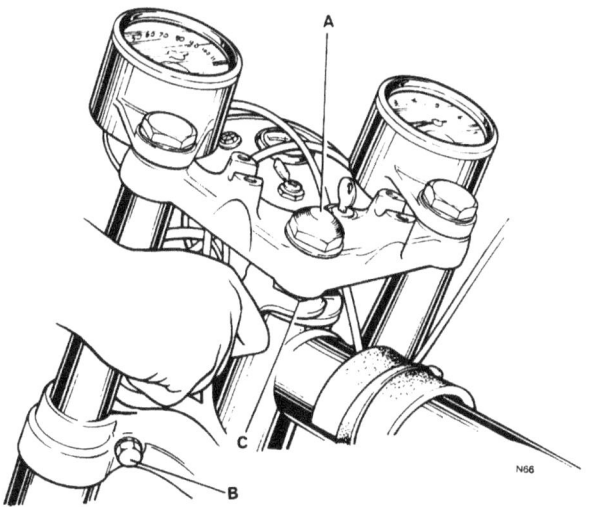

Fig. G8   Steering head adjustment—pre 1971

Front Forks/Steering G

SECTION G8

REFITTING FRONT FORKS

Reassembly of the front forks is virtually a reversal of the dismantling procedure though for clarity, the full procedure is detailed below:

1971 and later models

1 Place the top dust cover and washer over the top steering head bearing. Note that the washer fits below the cover.

2 Pass the stem of the upper yoke through the bearings. This will almost certainly require the use of a block of wood and a hammer to tap the stem fully home.

3 Lift the headlamp and top covers roughly into position, place the single 'O' ring in each side of the upper yoke to locate the tops of the fork covers Use heavy grease to hold the 'O' rings in place.

4 Place the lower yoke, with two 'O' rings to locate each fork cover, over the steering stem. Fit the tab washer and nut to the stem and commence to tighten. As the lower yoke is raised, locate the top covers, both top and bottom.

5 Tighten the nut sufficiently to pull the lower yoke into position, but do not secure fully yet.

1970 Models

1A Pass the stem of the bottom yoke up through the bearings.

2A Place the top bearing dust cover over the stem.

3A Fit the fork stem nut and tighten down to pull the stem fully home through the bearings. Since the bearings are adjustable, tighten the nut to eliminate any shake between the stem and steering head but not sufficient for the bearings to bind as the yokes are turned lock to lock.

4A On Fastback models only, place both top shrouds with headlamp brackets loosely in position, complete with top rubbers.

5A Place the top yoke over the stem and loose assemble with the large stem washer and large blind chrome stem nut.

6A Before proceeding to operation 6 "All Commando," ensure that the assembled spring cover tubes are in position.

All Commando models

6 Offer both fork legs through the lower and upper yoke and pull the main tube tapers into the upper yoke using the instrument cases and large chrome top bolts.

7 With the fork legs secured by the top bolts, snug the socket headed pinch screws.

8 Now tighten the fork securing points shown in *Fig* G8/9 in this sequence: Chrome top bolts, main fork stem nut, lower yoke pinch screws. Note that the stem nut must not be over-tightened. On 1970 models this would damage the steering head bearings, which must adjust until the forks are free to turn with no perceptible play.

Front Forks/Steering G

9   On 1971 and later models, tighten the stem nut to 15 lb/ft (207 kg/m) and tap over the stem nut tab washer.

10 Again lift the large chrome top bolts, firstly to add oil and secondly to connect the damper rods. Measure the required quantity of oil for each fork leg (150 cc of SAE 20). Pouring the oil into the leg will prove a long operation. To speed up the filling operation, pour in as much of the measured quantity as possible, place the hand firmly over the top of the main tube and extend the fork leg. Do this several times to speed up oil drainage into the slider. When the measured quantity has been added, and with the instrument case held in position, connect the damper rod to the chrome bolt as in *Fig.* G7. Using a socket wrench on the chrome bolts, tighten to 40 lbs/ft (5.83 kg/m).

11 **Disc Brake Models.** Secure the master cylinder to the right switch cluster with the four long screws.

12 **Disc Brake Models.** Bolt the caliper assembly to the right fork slider using two bolts and washers tightened to a torque setting of 25 ft/lbs (3.45 kg/m). Fit the hydraulic hose bracket over the studs on the right slider.

13 Fit the front fender, securing with four plain washers and nuts at the bridge stay and one bolt and plain washer at the fork end of each stay.

14 Refit the front wheel as in Section H6 or H8.

15 **Disc Brake Models.** Clip the hydraulic hose to the right fork top cover (two spring clips), feed the front brake stop switch leads through the stop switch cover one at a time and connect the Lucas terminals at the stop switch.

On disc brake models, it is vital to "pump" the front brake lever several times after the wheel has been removed to restore brake pressure before the brake is used.

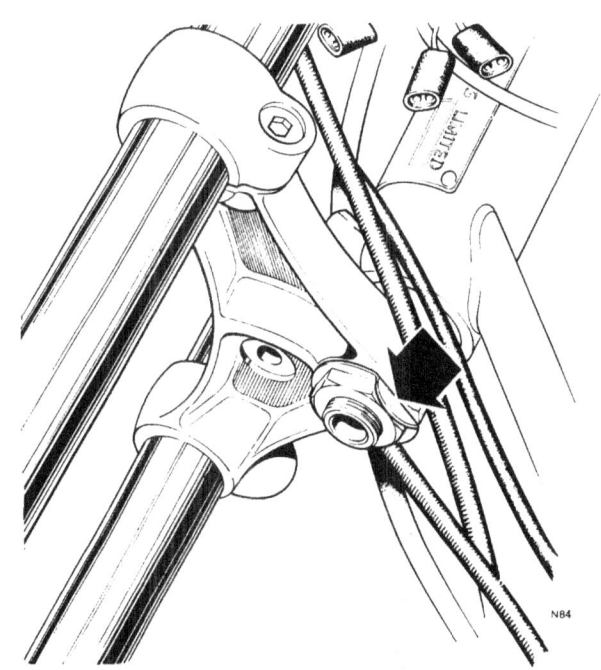

Fig. G9   *Showing stem nut tab washer locked to nut*

NOTES

Brakes, Wheels and Tires H

Brakes Wheels and Tires

Brakes, Wheels and Tires H

SECTION H1

REMOVING REAR WHEEL

(Without disturbing the brake and sprocket).

Two types of rear wheel have been used, the one used prior to 1971 having the rear wheel brake drum and sprocket bolted up to the hub and the 1971 and later type having polyurethane shock absorber segments let into the hub and steel paddles fitted to the rear brake drum engaging in the polyurethane segments. This arrangement permits the wheel and brake drum to be separated merely by removal of the rear axle.

To remove either type of wheel, the motorcycle must be supported with the rear wheel clear of the ground.

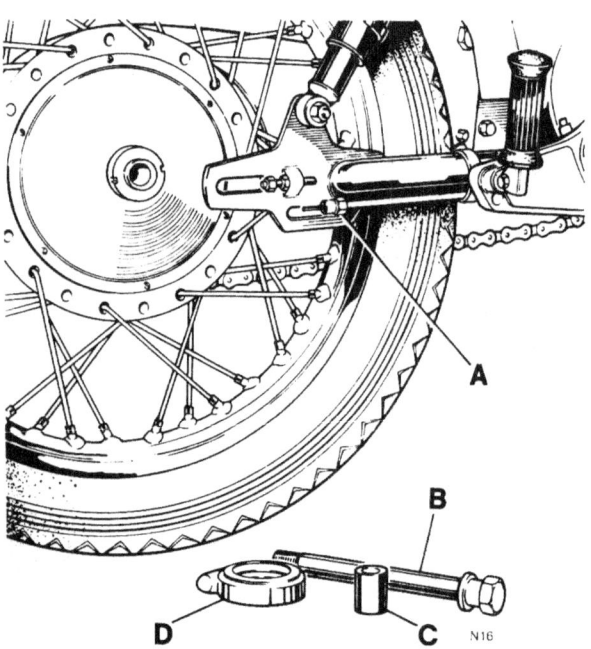

Fig. H1   Rear wheel removal post—1971

1971 and later models – See *Fig.* H1.

1. Unscrew the wheel axle "B" at the right hand side and withdraw.

2. Remove the spacer "C" and speedometer drive gearbox "D" which are loose after the axle is withdrawn.

3. Separate the wheel from the brake drum. If the wheel is difficult to remove, use a lever between the wheel and brake drums to separate the three paddles from the shock absorber segments in the hub.

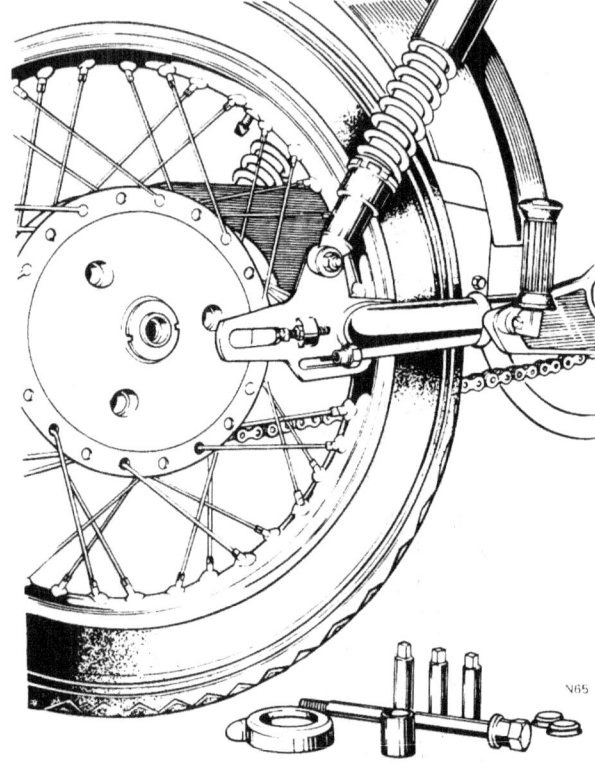

Fig. H2   Rear wheel removal pre-1971

Pre 1971 models – See *Fig.* H2.

1. Disconnect the speedometer drive cable.

2. Remove the rubber plugs which give access to the rear wheel sleeve nuts.

3. Remove the rear wheel sleeve nuts.

4. Withdraw the wheel spindle from the right hand side.

5. Collect the spacer and speedometer drive gearbox which are released as the axle is withdrawn. If the wheel is difficult to remove, use a lever between the wheel hub and brake drum.

Brakes, Wheels and Tires H

SECTION H2

REFITTING OF REAR WHEEL

1971 and later models

Re-assembly is virtually a reversal of the removal procedure, but the following observations are made:

1. Fit the wheel to the paddles, engaging the paddles between the drive and rebound segments in the hub.

2. Fit the speedometer gearbox, exercising care to engage the two drive dogs with the slots in the hub bearing locking ring.

3. Position the dull plated spacer, then slide the wheel axle complete with washer into position and tighten fully.

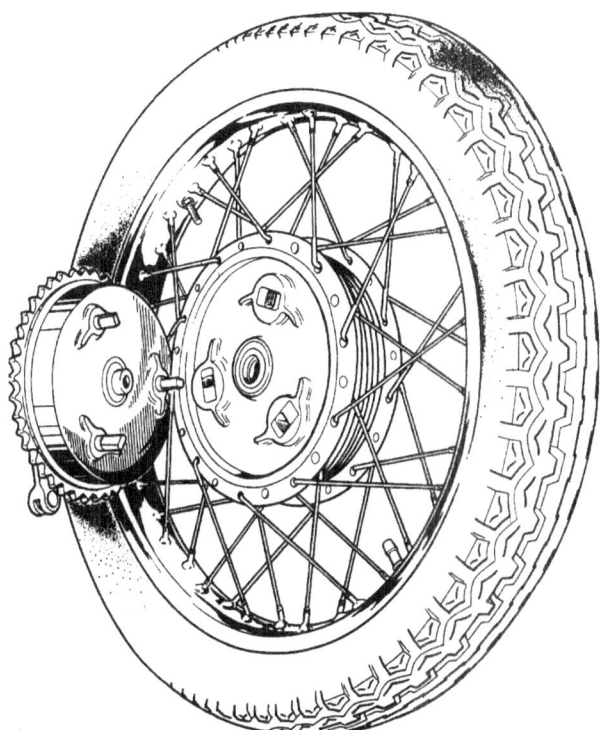

Fig. H3   Paddles and shock absorbing pads

Previous models

1. Turn the brake drum so that one of the three studs is approximately in line with the swinging arm tubes and so facilitate passing the bearing boss on the hub past the other two studs.

2. Fit the wheel to the studs.

3. Fit and tighten the sleeve nuts.

4. Replace the rubber plugs.

5. Fit the speedometer drive gearbox, exercise care to engage the two drive dogs with the two slots in the hub bearing locking ring.

6. Position the dull plated spacer then engage the wheel axle complete with washer and tighten fully.

SECTION H3

COMPLETE REAR WHEEL REMOVAL

In order to remove the wheel complete, support the motorcycle on the centre stand and proceed as follows:

1. Disconnect the rear chain at the split link.

2. Disconnect the leads from the stop lamp switch.

3. Disconnect the rear brake cable rod by removing the adjuster nut (see *Fig.* H4) and pulling the rod through the brake expander lever roller.

4. Disconnect the speedometer cable from the drive box.

5. Slacken and remove the main wheel axle from the right side.

6. Remove the right side spacer, washer and speedometer drive box.

7. Remove the left side axle nut.

8. Pull the wheel over to the right side so that the brake plate stop peg and the dummy axle in the brake drum clear the slots in the swinging arm.

9. The wheel can now be lifted clear.

Brakes, Wheels and Tires H

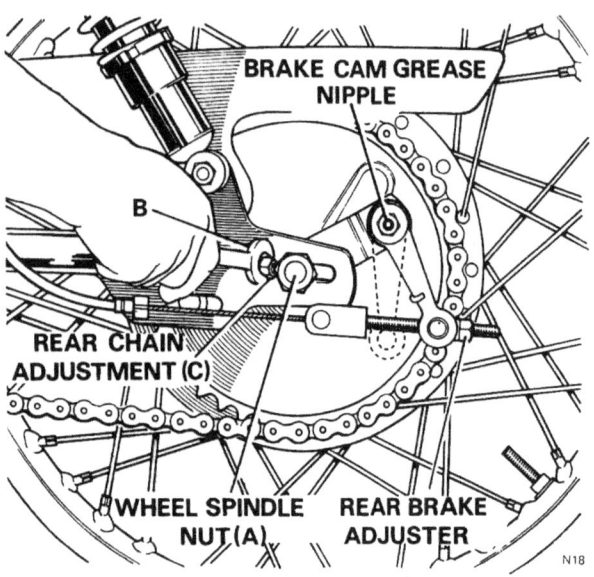

Fig. H4   Rear wheel features

Dismantling

Before dealing with the axle and bearings, separate the brake assembly from the brake drum, then the brake drum from the wheel hub.

1971 and later models utilise shock absorber pads of polyurethane in the hub into which the shock absorber paddles on the brake drum fit. Therefore, on 1971 and later models, the hub can be lifted away from the brake drum without further dismantling.

On pre 1971 models, remove the three blanking plugs from the hub disc and, using a socket wrench, remove the three sleeve nuts securing the hub to the brake drum and separate these items. Lift the brake plate complete with shoes away from the brake drum.

SECTION H4

REAR HUB DISMANTLING

In order to change the wheel bearings, remove the wheel complete as described in Section H3. In the case of pre 1971 rear wheels without shock absorber, the wheel should be parted from the brake drum by removal of three extended nuts from the right hand side. On this type of wheel, illustrated in *Fig.* H5 there is no bearing in the brake drum. The wheel fitted to 1971 and later models should be removed complete as described in Section H3. With the wheel axle removed, separate the brake drum from the wheel hub — the "paddles" on the brake drum are merely a push in fit between the polyurethane shock absorber segments. On the 1971 type, a double row ball journal bearing is fitted to the rear brake drum. The bearing arrangement differs between 1971 and earlier models in the wheels, as will be seen from *Fig.* H6, the later wheel containing an additional double row bearing in the brake drum but a pair of single row bearings in the wheel hub.

Pre 1971 models – See *Fig.* H5.

To dismantle this type of rear hub proceed as follows:

1 At the speedometer drive box side of the wheel unscrew the LEFT HAND THREAD lockring using peg spanner tool, 063965 and remove.

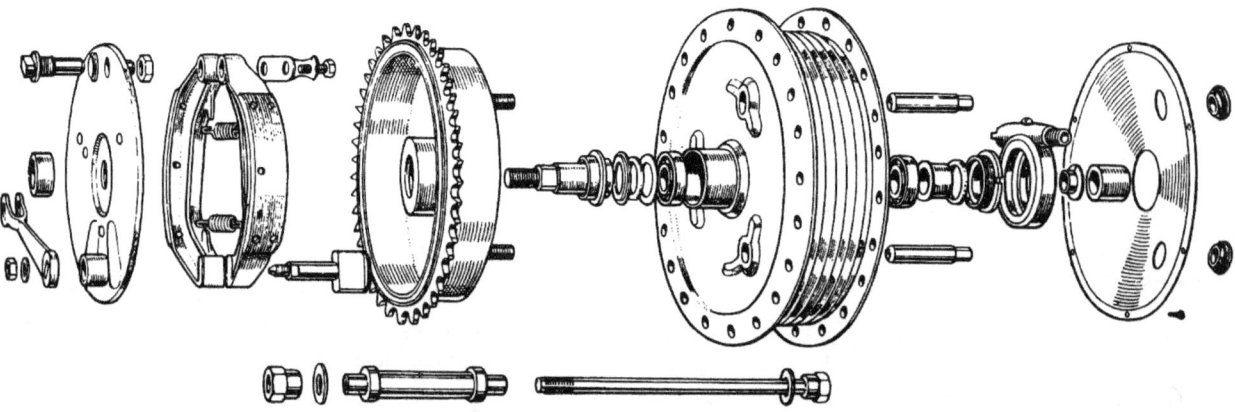

Fig. H5   1970 type rear wheel exploded

Brakes, Wheels and Tires

2 Take out the distance piece and felt washer.

3 Take the rear axle with thick washer and fit over it the large plated spacer which fits between the speedometer drive box and fork end.

4 Insert the axle with washer and spacer through the double row ball journal bearing from the brake drum side of the hub (the brake drum has previously been removed).

5 Using a hide hammer or mallet, drive on the end of the axle until a stop is felt. Driving will have moved the double row bearing further into the hub, moving the bearing spacer tube and in turn, starting to drive the lockring side bearing out of the hub tube. When the stop is felt, the double row bearing has come up against a shoulder in the hub.

6 Remove the rear axle and spacer and insert the front wheel axle, threaded end first from the brake drum side. Hold square and tap gently with a hide

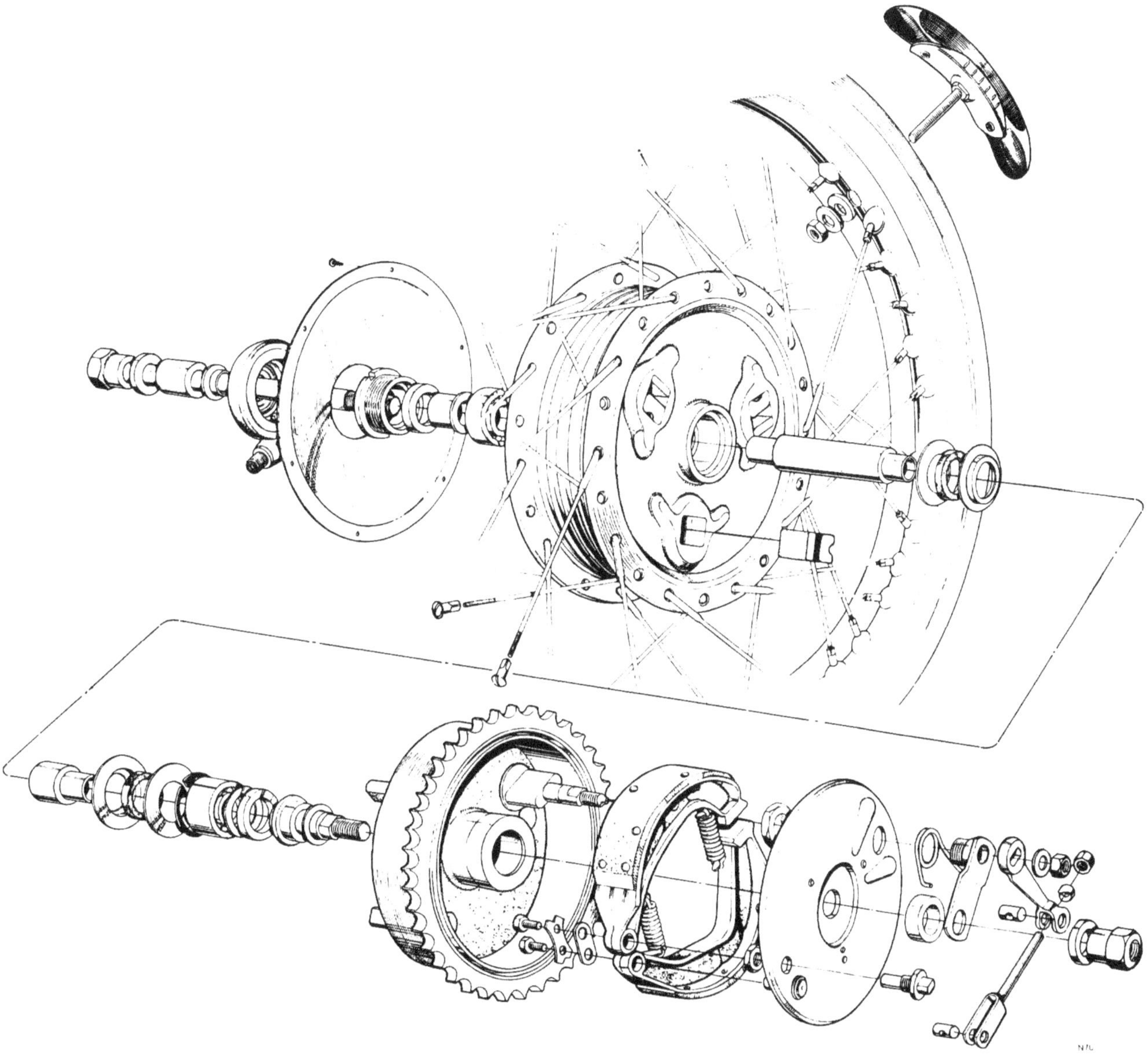

Fig. H6 1971 onwards rear wheel exploded

Brakes, Wheels and Tires

hammer to drive on the bearing spacer and displace the speedometer drive box side bearing and spacer completely from the hub.

7 Remove the front wheel axle and re-insert the rear axle and large plated spacer from the lockring end.

8 Hold central in the brake drum side bearing (the double row bearing) and drive out the bearing complete with felt retaining washer, felt seal and dished washer.

1971 and later models – See *Fig.* H6.

With the exception that the later rear hub has two single row ball journal bearings in the hub, rather than a single row bearing at the lockring (speedometer) side and a double row bearing at the brake drum side, the dismantling and reassembly details are the same as for the previous wheel. Later models incorporate shock absorber segments in the hub and to ensure rigidity of the wheel a double row bearing is incorporated in the brake drum itself. The brake drum bearing is dealt with separately.

SECTION H5

REAR HUB REASSEMBLY

Prior to reasembly, clean and inspect the bearings, felt seal and seal retainers for roughness, wear, damage or corrosion and make replacements as necessary. Proceed as follows:

Pre 1971 models

1 Pack bearings with the recommended grade of grease (see Section K1).

2 Fit the single row bearing into the threaded (lockring) side of the hub, sufficiently to allow the lockring to be fitted.

3 Fit the felt seal and locking ring and tighten. Remember that the lockring is LEFT HAND threaded. Tighten with peg spanner tool 063965. If the peg spanner is not available, take special care not to damage the slots which drive the speedometer drive box.

4 Fit the bearing spacer tube. On pre 1971 models which have a double row bearing at the brake side and a single row bearing at the speedometer drive box side, the bearing spacer has unequal length ends and the long end locates to the single row bearing.

5 Press the brake drum side bearing (on pre 1971 models a double row and on 1971 and later models, a single row bearing) squarely into position in the hub and drive home applying load only to the outer race. Load on the centre race can cause damage.

6 Fit the felt retaining washer, felt seal and dished washer and on pre 1971 models, lightly peen the dished washer into position. 1971 and later models use a push in washer.

The brake drum and sprocket contain the dummy axle and, in the case of 1971 and later models, the double row bearing and sealing felt. The bearing can be removed and refitted to the later brake drum and sprocket as detailed below.

1971 and later models

The later type of rear wheel incorporating a shock absorber is supported by two single row bearings in the hub and a double row bearing in the brake drum. The brake and brake drum are separated from the swinging fork as detailed in Section H3. To remove and replace the double row bearing and seals, proceed as follows:

1 Lift the brake assembly away from the drum.

2 Remove the bearing spacer (the shouldered spacer protruding from the centre of the bearing towards the wheel). This will be a relatively tight fit into the bearing and may need to be gripped in a vice whilst the brake drum is tapped carefully away from it.

3 Prise out the lipped washer covering the felt seal.

Brakes, Wheels and Tires H

4 Collect the felt seal and felt retaining washer.

5 Using circlip pliers, remove the large bearing retaining circlip.

6 Using a hide hammer or mallet, drive the threaded end of the dummy axle. This should pass into the brake drum, displacing the inner felt seal and retainers and driving the double row bearing clear.

7 Clean, inspect and replace as necessary the bearing, seals and retainers. Check that the shock absorber "paddles" are secure in the brake drum.

8 Pack the bearing with the recommended grade of grease (see Section K1).

9 Fit the inner washers to the brake drum, holding in place by inserting the dummy axle, threaded end through towards the brake side.

10 Using a suitable shouldered drift against the edge of the outer race, drive the double row bearing squarely into the brake drum.

11 Fit the bearing retainer circlip, sharp edge outwards, and ensure that it is bedded all the way round the groove. Failure to observe this precaution can permit free lateral movement of the brake drum and sprocket.

12 Fit the inner felt retaining washer and felt seal.

13 Fit the outer lipped felt seal retainer.

The brake drum is now reassembled ready for fitting to the motorcycle.

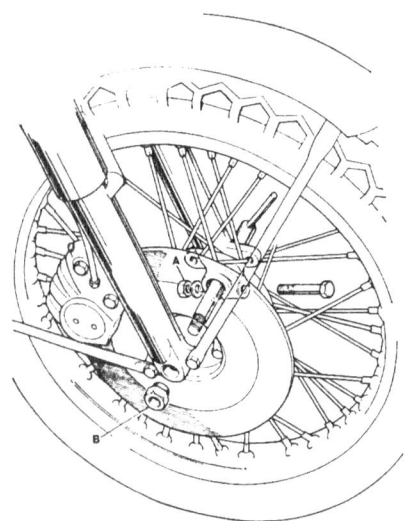

Fig. H7   Disc brake front wheel removal

2 Taking the weight of the front wheel in one hand, withdraw the axle using a tommy bar. It will be found that the wheel can be removed most easily by withdrawing it forwards to disengage the disc from the pads.

3 To prevent the brake pads being ejected by unintentional application of the brake with the wheel removed, place a clean $\frac{1}{4}$ in. (6·7 mm) spacer of wood, metal or plastic between the pads.

4 Collect the wheel bearing dust covers to prevent loss. (See *Fig.* H8).

SECTION H6

REMOVING AND REFITTING FRONT WHEEL (Disc Type)

Removal

Support the motorcycle with the front wheel clear of the ground. The brake assembly remains undisturbed since only the disc is removed with the wheel. Proceed as follows:

1 Slacken the fork end clamping nut. (See *Fig.* H7).

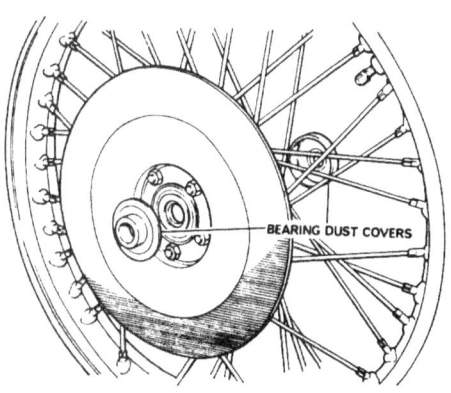

Fig. H8   Disc brake wheel

Brakes, Wheels and Tires H

Refitting

5   Offer the wheel with both dust covers in position and, with care, guide the disc between the brake pads. See *Fig.* H9.

6   Grease and engage the wheel axle from the left side.

7   Before tightening the fork end clamping nut, compress the forks a few times to centralise the fork leg on the axle.

8   Tighten the pinch nut at the bottom of the left hand fork slider to clamp it on to the axle. Do not over-tighten the nut as there is a danger of fracturing the lug.

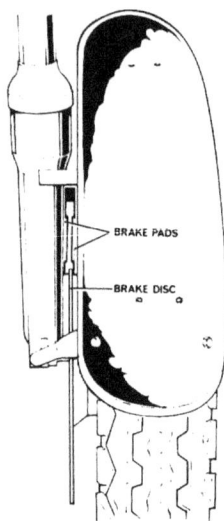

Fig. H9   Guiding brake disc between brake pads

9   If the fork action is stiff, slacken the axle nut and the fork end clamping nut and move the forks up and down to allow the fork tubes to take up alignment on the axle. Re-tighten the nuts.
   If stiffness still remains, release fender stay bolts and move forks up and down, finally retightening the stay bolts.

No adjustment to the brake operating mechanism is required. Apply the brake several times to refill the caliper and restore brake pressure.

SECTION H7

DISMANTLING FRONT HUB, DISC TYPE

To gain access to the front wheel axle and bearings, remove the wheel as described in Section H6. It is not necessary to remove the brake disc. Proceed as follows:

1   Unscrew the bearing locking ring (left hand thread) from the left side of the hub using peg spanner 063965 or, if not available, a pin punch and hammer. If the ring is an extremely tight fit, try tapping from different holes and heat the hub with a gentle flame.

2   Lift away the seal and spacer.

3   Heat the alloy wheel hub with hot water *only* to a temperature of 100°C.

*4   Insert a bar into the bearing spacer tube and force the spacer over fractionally. This will provide just sufficient room to allow a drift to abut on the inner race of the bearing to be removed.

5   Using a suitable drift to the bearing inner race start to drive the single row bearing out. Force the spacer tube over to the other side of the hub and tap on the inner race at the new point. Continue this operation until the bearing is driven out.

*At a later stage an expanding drift will become available which can be placed into the bearing inner race and expanded by the centre bolt to grip the inner race. The tool and bearing together can then be driven out together from the other side of the hub.

6   Lift out the bearing spacer tube. If this has been damaged and cannot be corrected, a new spacer should be obtained for reassembly.

7   Using a suitable sized drift through the hub towards the remaining bearing, drive the double row bearing out of the hub, taking with it the washers and felt seal.

Reassembly of the disc brake front hub is a similar procedure to that detailed fully for the drum brake wheel (Section *H6*).

Brakes, Wheels and Tires H

SECTION H8

REMOVING AND REFITTING FRONT WHEEL
(Drum Type Brake)

To remove the front wheel, support the motorcycle securely on the centre stand so that the front wheel is clear of the ground.

1. Disconnect the front brake cable at the brake cam lever by taking out the clevis pin after removal of the spring clip.

2. Unscrew the brake cable adjuster.

3. Release the axle pinchbolt at the bottom of the left fork leg.

4. Remove the axle nut at the right hand end.

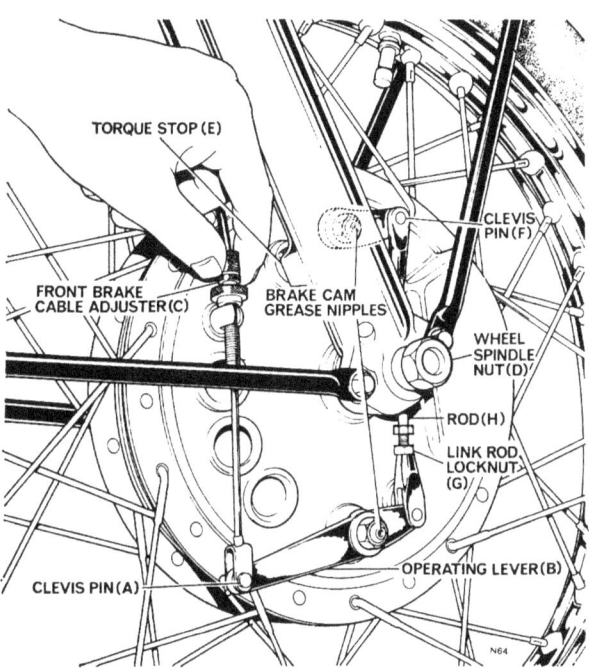

Fig. H10   Drum front brake external features

5. Support the wheel to prevent it dropping and remove the axle using a tommy bar through the cross hole at the left hand end, turning and pulling the axle clear.

6. The wheel is now free to be removed, but it is recommended that the bearings should be protected from dirt ingress, particularly if the tyre is to be changed.

7. Collect the left side bearing dust cover.

Refitting

8. Remove any rust formed on the wheel axle and grease lightly.

9. Offer the wheel to the forks and support the wheel in position with the torque stop engaged with the slot in the right fork slider.

10. Ensure that the dust cover is in position at the left side of the front hub and push the axle home.

11. Fit and tighten the axle nut.

12. Connect and adjust the brake cable.

13. Take the motorcycle off the stand, apply the front brake and depress the front forks two or three times so that the fork legs align themselves correctly on the axle.

14. Lock up the pinch bolt at the bottom of the left fork slider.

Note: On early models, the brake backplate centre hole is oversize. It is thus important on these models to centralise the brake by spinning the wheel and applying the brake fully, holding the brake on whilst tightening the right-hand axle nut.

Brakes, Wheels and Tires   H

SECTION H9

FRONT WHEEL BEARING OVERHAUL

(Drum Brake)

To gain access to the front wheel axle and bearings, remove the wheel as described in Section H8. Remove the front brake plate with shoes and proceed as follows:

1. Unscrew the bearing lock ring (right hand thread) from the left side of the hub, using Peg Spanner 063965 Tool, or, if not available a pin punch and hammer. If the ring is an extremely tight fit, try tapping from different holes and heat the hub with a gentle flame.

2. Lift out the felt seal and distance piece.

3. Insert the front wheel axle from the brake side and drive with a hide mallet. This will drive the double row bearing further into the hub and at the same time drive the single row bearing out.

   CAUTION: Drive carefully until this bearing *just* drops clear, or otherwise the fabricated spacer will be damaged.

4. Withdraw the axle and reverse to enter it through the spacer tube still in the hub.

5. Holding the axle central, drive the double row bearing out, together with the felt retaining washer, felt seal and outer washer.

To re-assemble, first pack the bearings with grease — then proceed as follows:

6. Press the single row bearing into position at the left side of the hub.

7. Fit the distance washer, plain side to the bearing.

8. Fit the felt seal and locking ring which should be tightened fully with Peg Spanner 063965 tool.

9. Insert the bearing spacer from the right, small end first into the hub, ensuring that it is fully home against the single row bearing. Pack the space between the bearing spacer and hub with grease.

10. Enter the double row bearing squarely into the hub, passing the front axle through until it enters the opposite bearing. Drive the end of the spindle until the double row bearing comes up against the distance tube and stops.

11. Fit the smaller felt retainer washer, the felt seal and large steel washer and lightly peen the latter into position at four points. Later models have a push-in washer.

To complete the wheel ready for refitting, refit the brake plate then refit the wheel to the forks as in Section H8.

SECTION H10

FRONT BRAKE ADJUSTMENT

(Drum Brake)

Routine brake adjustment is carried out by means of the cable adjuster (C). See *Fig.* H10. Correct adjustment will allow the wheel to spin freely with the minimum movement at the control lever.

Fig. H10 & H11 show the external features of the drum type twin leading shoe brake. Adjustment by this means is sufficient until such times as the brake shoes or linings are replaced. After replacement of such parts, the lining contact with the drum must be reset by means of the link rod adjustment.

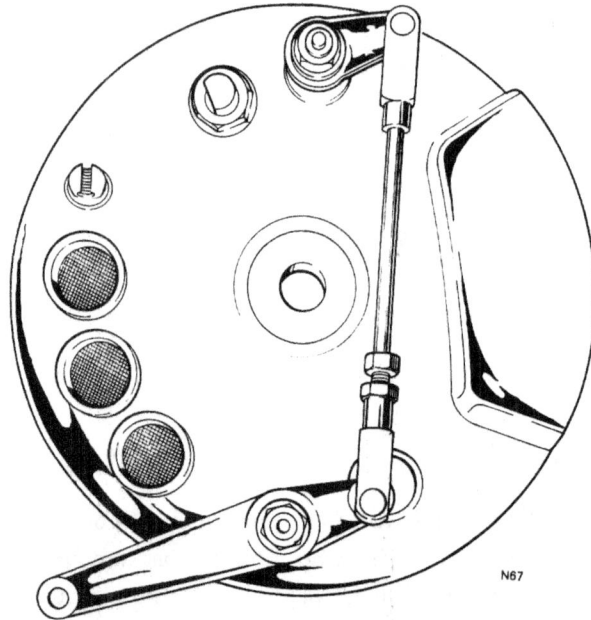

Fig. H11 Twin leading shoe brake plate showing link rod

Brakes, Wheels and Tires   H

Setting the Link Rod

1. Take out the top clevis pin (F). See *Fig.* H10.

2. With the help of a second operator apply both the top and bottom operating levers (B) fully, and adjust the length of the link rod by slackening the link rod locknut (G) and screwing the link rod (H) in or out until with the linings still in contact with the drum the clevis pin can be refitted.

3. Secure the link rod locknut.

4. If necessary, carry out final adjustment on the cable adjuster.

5. NOTE: Should the adjustment run out at the handlebar and cable adjusters, providing the brake linings are examined to ensure that the rivets are not flush with the lining friction surface, the operating cam levers can be reversed to regain adjustment.

FRONT BRAKE (Disc Type)

The disc brake functions by the pressure of friction pads against the disc attached to the front wheel hub. As the brake handlebar lever is applied, brake fluid from the master cylinder reservoir is forced through the brake line to the caliper to force the friction pads against the disc.

The brake requires no adjustment since wear on the pads is compensated for by extra brake fluid passing from the master cylinder reservoir into the system.

SECTION H11

REAR BRAKE ADJUSTMENT

The rear brake is a single leading shoe unit and apart from centralising the shoes in the brake drum when the wheel has been disturbed, adjustment is carried out purely on the cable. Refer to *Fig.* H4.

The rear brake is adjusted by means of the cable adjuster at the operating lever. When the brake is fully applied the operating lever should be approximately in the position shown in broken lines in the illustration. If excessive brake lining wear brings the lever past this position and there is no adjustment left, the brakes should be relined.

After adjustment the wheels should rotate freely. Any tendency to bind will dissipate power and generate heat which will adversely affect the efficiency of the brakes.

To centralise the brake shoes in the drum and thus achieve maximum braking efficiency, slacken wheel spindle nut (A) apply the rear brake fully and hold on whilst the spindle nut is retightened.   Refer to *Fig.* H4

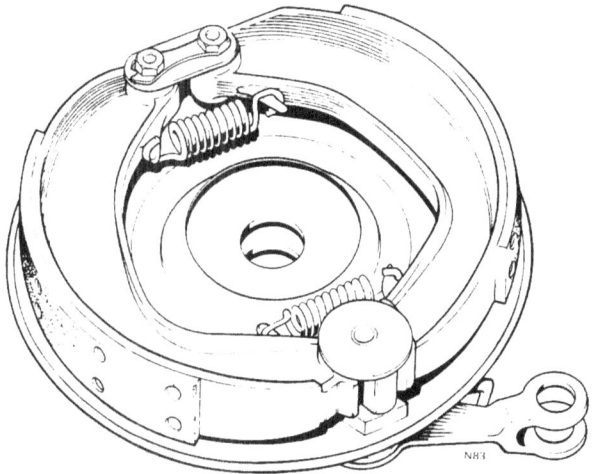

Fig. H12   Rear brake plate with brake shoes assembled

Note that the stoplamp switch must be adjusted as in Section J18.

The rear brake cable is fitted instead of a brake rod to cope with the flexibility of the engine cradle and swinging arm relative to the main frame on which the rear brake pedal is mounted. For this reason under no circumstances must a rod be substituted for the rear brake cable.

SECTION 12

OVERHAULING DRUM BRAKES

The rear brake of all Commando models is of the single leading shoe variety whereas the front brake (on models without the disc brake option) is of the double leading shoe type. The routine for changing brake shoes is detailed separately below for the rear brake, twin leading shoe front brake and twin leading shoe type with available high performance support plate. When sufficient wear has taken place on the brake linings, the shoes complete with linings or the linings only must be renewed. Linings separate from the brake shoes are not

Brakes, Wheels and Tires   H

supplied as spares requirements by the Factory. This is a matter of policy brought about by the fact that the brake linings require linishing after fitting to the shoes and this operation must be carried out with Factory accuracy if the brake is to be restored to full efficiency.

Rear Brake Dismantling – See *Fig.* H12

1. Remove the rear wheel as in Section H3.

2. Lift out the brake plate complete from the brake drum.

3. Remove the springs from the shoes. This can be done either with grip pliers or by levering carefully with a suitable screwdriver. Take care not to damage the spring retaining hooks on the brake shoes. There may be a tendency for the springs to fly when one end is released thus care should be exercised to avoid loss.

4. Flatten back the tab washer and remove the two hexagon headed screws securing the brake shoes to the brake plate bosses.

5. Collect the tab washer and tie plate and lift away the shoes.

6. Remove the nut securing the lever to the expander and lift off the lever.

7. Withdraw the expander cam. If this is too tight to pass through the bush in the brake plate, the area of the expander cam inboard of the thread may have been damaged by overtightening of the nut. In these circumstances, this area of the expander should be eased down such as with emery tape so that it will pass through the bush.

Rear Brake Reassembly

1. Clean the brake plate thoroughly and grease lightly the expander cam boss, pivot pins and bearing area of the expander cam.

2. Fit the expander cam to the plate but do not secure yet from the other side.

3. Assemble the brake shoes to the pivot pins and expander cam. If the brake shoes are of the late type with detachable thrust pads, ensure that the pads are in position between the shoe ends and expander cam.

4. Fit the tie plate, tab washer (using a new one if necessary) and set screws which should be secured fully.

5. Tap over the ends of the tab washer to the set screw heads.

6. Fit the brake shoe springs – these are very strong and in consequence difficult to engage with the brake shoe hooks. Attach one end of each spring, tie a length of stout twine round the hook at the other end and stretch the spring by pulling hard on the twine. As the spring is held approximately in position, guide the end home on to the brake shoe hook using a screwdriver blade.

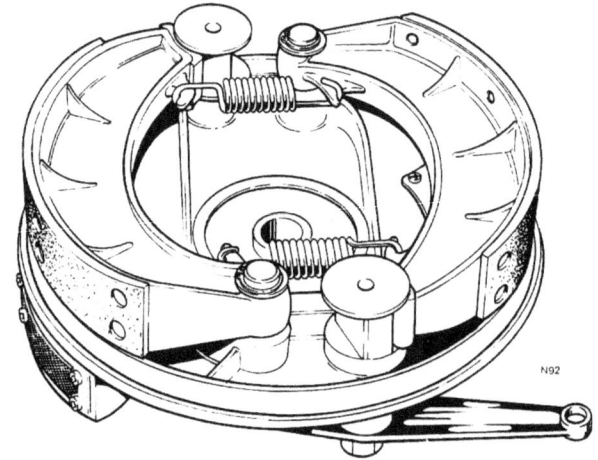

Fig. H13   Twin leading shoe brake

Front Brake – See *Fig.* H13

1. Remove the front wheel as in Section H8.

2. Lift out the brake plate complete from the drum.

3. Clamp the brake plate in a vice at the brake torque stop peg.

4. Remove the circlips from both pivot pins and collect the washers.

Brakes, Wheels and Tires H

5. Either by careful levering or by the use of grip pliers, release one end of each brake shoe spring. Take care not to lose the springs if they should fly when released. Also, take great care not to damage the spring retaining hooks on the brake shoes.

6. Lift both brake shoes clear.

7. The brake cover plate can be dismantled further by detaching both ends of the expander lever tie rod, removing the nut and washer from each expander and lifting clear both expander levers. The expander can then be removed for cleaning and greasing and if necessary the gauze covers can also be removed.

8. Reassembly of this brake is a straight reversal of the dismantling procedure. The brake shoes are identical. When reassembling the brake, lightly grease the expanders and expander bosses in the cover plate and also the pivot pins and working areas at the ends of each brake shoe. Take care to ensure that the brake shoe springs are properly fitted at both ends, and that the circlips are correctly located to the pivot pins.

Front Brake with High Performance Modification – See *Fig.* H14

1. Remove the front wheel as in Section H8.

2. Lift out the brake plate complete from the drum.

3. Clamp the brake plate in a vice at the brake torque stop peg.

4. Flatten back the tab washers at the pivot pin set screws and remove both set screws.

5. Remove the brake support plate. This may prove tight to remove from the pivot pins and expander cams in which case careful leverage may be applied beneath the plate providing the support plate is not distorted at all.

6. Either by careful levering or by the use of grip pliers, release one end of each brake spring. Take care not to lose the springs if they should fly when released. Also take great care not to damage the spring retaining hooks on the brake shoes.

7. Lift both brake shoes clear.

8. The brake cover plate can be dismantled further by detaching both ends of the expander lever tie rod, removing the nut and washer from each expander and lifting clear both expander levers. The expanders can then be removed for cleaning and greasing and if necessary the gauze covers can also be removed.

9. Reassembly of this brake is a straight reversal of the dismantling procedure. The brake shoes are identical. When reassembling the brake, lightly grease the expanders and expander bosses in the cover plate, the pivot pins, working areas at the end of each brake shoe and expander cam end spigots. The latter is imperative and molybdenum disulphide grease is recommended at this point. Take care to ensure that the brake shoe springs are properly fitted at both ends before the brake support plate is offered into position. If a new support plate is being fitted, *do not* open the pivot or expander cam holes at all to ease fitting, or the whole purpose of the modification to tie the pivots and expanders in a fixed relationship will be lost. After fitting the plate securing screws and tab washers, tap the tab washers into position as in *Fig.* H14.

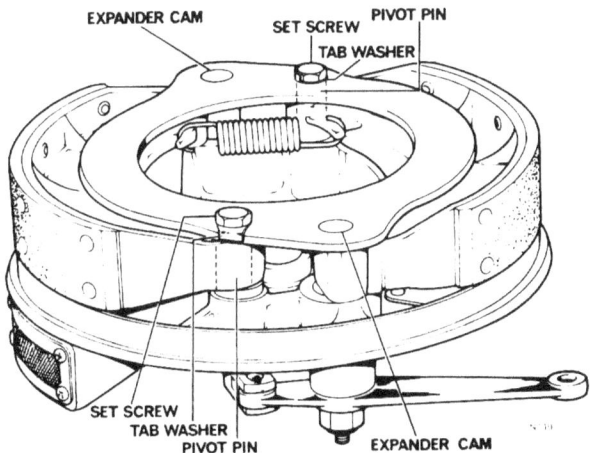

Fig. H14 Twin leading shoe brake with high performance modification

Brakes, Wheels and Tires H

SECTION H13

NORTON LOCKHEED HYDRAULICALLY OPERATED DISC BRAKE

This brake is a very powerful and progressive unit offered from 1972 as an alternative to the drum type brake. The servicing routine is straightforward but it is absolutely essential for the components of the hydraulic system to be handled with particular care, avoiding any possible marking of the bores and pistons of the master cylinder and of the caliper since these are machined to unusually fine limits. Similarly it is vital to exclude even the finest particles of dirt and foreign matter from the hydraulic system and to avoid the use of any fluid or cleaning agent which could cause even the smallest degree of deterioration on the rubber seals. Throughout the following instructions, reference is made to the use of Lockheed Series 329 Hydraulic Fluid for Disc Brakes. This is the fluid used by the factory and recommended for use in the Commando disc brake hydraulic system in subsequent service, the fluid complying with the requirements of USA/Canada Safety Standard 116. The hydraulic system is sealed and the master cylinder and caliper with hose and pipe connected can be removed as an assembly if required without the loss of fluid and without the need for bleeding on reassembly. Providing the bellows seal is in situ in the master cylinder there will be no loss of fluid even from the breather hole in the cap.

It is not necessary to remove the caliper assembly from the fork leg during renewal of the friction pads as described below:

Caliper Friction Pad Renewal

1. Remove the front wheel (see Section H6).

2. Rotate the friction pads slightly and remove.

3. Inspect the friction pads for excessive wear, uneven wear or scoring. If there is any doubt whatsoever on the condition of the pads, obtain new pads. It is important to replace the pads as a pair: never attempt to replace one pad only.

4. Clean the friction pad recesses and exposed ends of the pistons using only a small soft brush. **DO NOT** utilise any solvent or wire brush for the removal of dust, dirt or scale.

5. Smear lightly the piston faces and brake pad recesses with Disc Brake Lubricant.

6. Remove the master cylinder cap and bellows seal to observe the level which will rise during the next operation.

7. Press the pistons back into the caliper, observing the fluid level in the master cylinder to prevent overflowing. If necessary, excess fluid can be siphoned off.

If at this stage it is found that the pistons are locked or seized in position and not free to move, the caliper must be removed, drained and overhauled as described later in this section.

8. On motorcycles using the cast iron disc, a rust build-up may have occurred which prevents entry of the disc between the new friction pads. Remove any such rusting by the careful use of a fine flat file.

9. Ensure that the new friction pads are of the correct friction type to suit the cast iron disc. It is important to consult the replacement parts catalogue and thus obtain the correct pads. Frictional and noise problems will arise if incorrect combinations of disc and pads are used. Any roughness or manufacturing flashes must be trimmed from the edges of the metal backing plate.

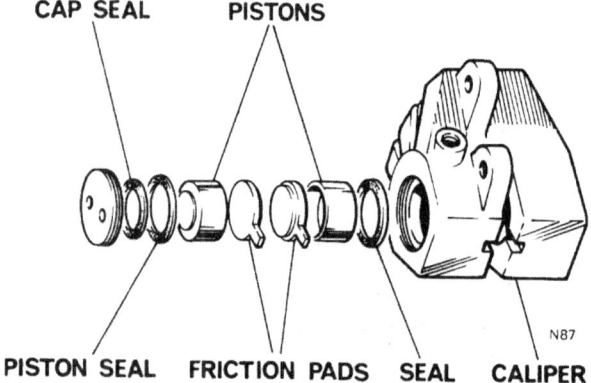

Fig. H15 Exploded view of caliper group

10. Avoiding the friction material, smear the edges of the pad backing plates with Disc Brake Lubricant and press fully home against the pistons.

Brakes, Wheels and Tires H

11 Replace the front wheel as in Section H6, support the motorcycle so that the front wheel spins freely and apply the front brake lever at the handlebar several times to restore the fluid in the caliper and locate the pads correctly.

12 Restore the master cylinder level as in *Fig. K8* using Lockheed Series 329 fluid and replace the bellows seal and cap.

CAUTION: It is dangerous to ride the motorcycle after pad and hydraulic system attention without first applying the brake a number of times to restore pressure and locate the pads to the disc. To avoid glazing of the friction surfaces, the brake must be applied gently if possible over the first 50 miles of use.

Caliper Overhaul

It is unnecessary to remove the front wheel but the hose support bracket must be released from the central fork mudguard bridge mounting studs and the hose to bracket clamp nut slackened to facilitate separation of the hose and pipe from the fork leg. Proceed as follows:

1 Prior to releasing the caliper from the fork leg, ease the fit of the caliper end plug which will be very tight. This will require the use of peg spanner tool 063965. *Do not* yet remove the plug.

2 Remove the two caliper bolts and washers and swing the caliper clear of the fork leg, taking the weight to avoid straining the brake hose.

3 Lift the two friction pads from the caliper.

4 Brush clean the exposed ends of the pistons and the outer surfaces of the caliper body, using methyl alcohol (methylated spirit) if required.

5 Lubricate the exposed ends of the pistons to ease their passage through the seals.

6 Place a clean receptacle below the caliper to receive displaced brake fluid and remove the inner piston. The outboard piston can be removed easily at a later stage if necessary. For this reason we recommend the use of a clamp to restrain the outboard piston. Apply the handlebar brake lever and the inner piston will be ejected into the friction pad cavity, and fluid released. Do not use any tool or airline to remove the piston nor use excessive pressure at the handlebar if the piston is seized.

NOTE THAT THE ONLY SATISFACTORY REMEDY FOR A SEIZED PISTON IS RENEWAL OF THE COMPLETE CALIPER ASSEMBLY.

7 Remove the clamp restraining the outer piston.

8 Slacken the lower brake pipe union nut and separate the pipe from the caliper.

9 Remove the caliper end plug, drain the remaining fluid into the receptacle.

10 Remove the piston from the caliper. If there is any difficulty, push the piston towards the centre of the caliper and clean carefully the outer working surfaces of the piston, removing any traces of dirt, dust or scale with methyl alcohol and/or metal polish before pressing the piston back into the caliper body and withdrawing through the end plug aperature.

11 Using a blunt nosed tool and taking the greatest possible care not to damage the seal grooves in any way whatsoever, remove the pressure seal from the outer bore.

12 Remove the inner piston through the outer cylinder bore then with the same care remove the pressure seal from the groove in the inner bore.

13 Pencil mark "Inner" and "Outer" on the friction material of the pads as applicable for future reference.

Caliper Component Inspection

Clean the pistons, caliper bores and seal grooves with ethyl alcohol or clean brake fluid.

Brakes, Wheels and Tires

1. Examine the pistons and renew if there are any signs of wear, damage or corrosion. No attempt must be made to rectify damage wear or "out of square" thrust faces by machining, filing or polishing. It is permissible only to restore pistons by the ultimate use of a fine metal polish.

2. Examine the caliper bores for abrasion, scratches and corrosion, or damage to the seal grooves. The caliper bores are not normally subject to premature failure or wear but irreparable damage can be caused during removal of damaged or corroded pistons or careless removal of seals with a sharp instrument.

After examination clean all the parts thoroughly in methyl alcohol or clean brake fluid.

Caliper Re-Assembly

1. Coat the new pressure seals with Lockheed Series 329 Hydraulic Fluid and ease the first pressure seal into the groove in the inner bore with the fingers, taking care to bed it correctly. It will be noted that the diameter of the seal is larger than that of the seal groove, in order to provide an interference fit. In addition, the seal groove and seal are different in section so that when bedded, the seal feels proud to the touch at the edge furthest from the bore. This is normal.

2. Coat the inner piston (the pistons are identical) with Lockheed Series 329 Fluid, insert it squarely right through the outer cylinder into the bore of the inner cylinder, closed end into the bore. Leave the piston protruding approximately $\frac{5}{16}$ in. (8 mm) from the mouth of the inner bore.

3. Fit a new pressure seal to the caliper outer bore groove, again bedding it correctly.

4. Coat the second piston with Lockheed Series 329 fluid and insert it open end first into the bore with the fingers. Avoid tilting the piston and continue inserting it gently through the bore until approximately $\frac{5}{16}$ in. (8 mm) of the open end protrudes from the inner mouth of the bore.

5. Replace the end plug using a new 'O' ring seal and tighten into position. For final tightening, the caliper must be secured to the fork leg.

6. Wipe the caliper clean, removing excess fluid which may subsequently contaminate the brake friction pads, taking care not to allow any rag particles to pass anywhere near the brake pipe feed union.

7. Fit the two friction pads and ensure that they seat correctly.

8. Assemble the caliper assembly over the wheel disc and offer the caliper to the fork leg, securing with two bolts and washers.

9. Tighten the caliper end plug using peg spanner tool to 26 lb./ft. torque.

10. Refit the fluid feed hose bracket to the mudguard bridge stud.

IMPORTANT

Before connecting the lower end of the brake pipe to the caliper, note that the pipe olive is specially formed to provide an effective high pressure oil seal against the caliper union seating. The olive is very susceptible to overtightening and if it is severely distorted by overtightening it may be impossible to remove thus rendering the caliper scrap.

11. Examine the union olive of the metal brake pipe for symptoms of previous overtightening such as distortion, damage and cracks and if necessary renew the pipe.

12. Offer the olive of the brake pipe to the caliper, hold the pipe in the required position and run the union screw fully down the thread until the pipe is just "nipped" on to its seating. Tighten the union nut with a spanner *one flat only*, i.e. 60°.

13. Slacken the bleed nipple one full turn and connect with a suitable bleed tube to a clean container (see *Fig. H17*).

14. Fill the master cylinder reservoir with Lockheed Series 329 brake fluid.

Brakes, Wheels and Tires H

15 Operate the brake lever until fluid begins to flow through the bleed tube. During this operation, guard against the master cylinder fluid level becoming too low, otherwise air will be drawn into the system. The master cylinder bellows seal must be removed to observe the fluid level.

If replenishment is necessary during this operation, hold the lever to the handlebar whilst the reservoir is topped up. Similarly, when fluid free of bubbles flows from the bleed pipe, tighten the caliper bleed nipple, whilst the brake lever is held against the handlebar.

16 With the bleed nipple tightened up, remove the bleed hose, apply the brake lever a number of times to check for sponginess (indicating air still in the system and a need for further bleeding) and examine the system for leaks.

17 Finally recheck the fluid level in the master cylinder reservoir, topping up as necessary, then road test the motorcycle.

Master Cylinder Overhaul

Prior to commencing work on the master cylinder it is desirable to obtain a supply of new Lockheed Series 329 Fluid in a sealed container. Where supplies are unobtainable and the fluid may have to be re-used, it is suggested that fluid is collected in a clean jar or receptacle by means of a short length of clean rubber tubing from the bleed screw to the collecting jar. Release the caliper bleed screw one full turn and operate the hand brake

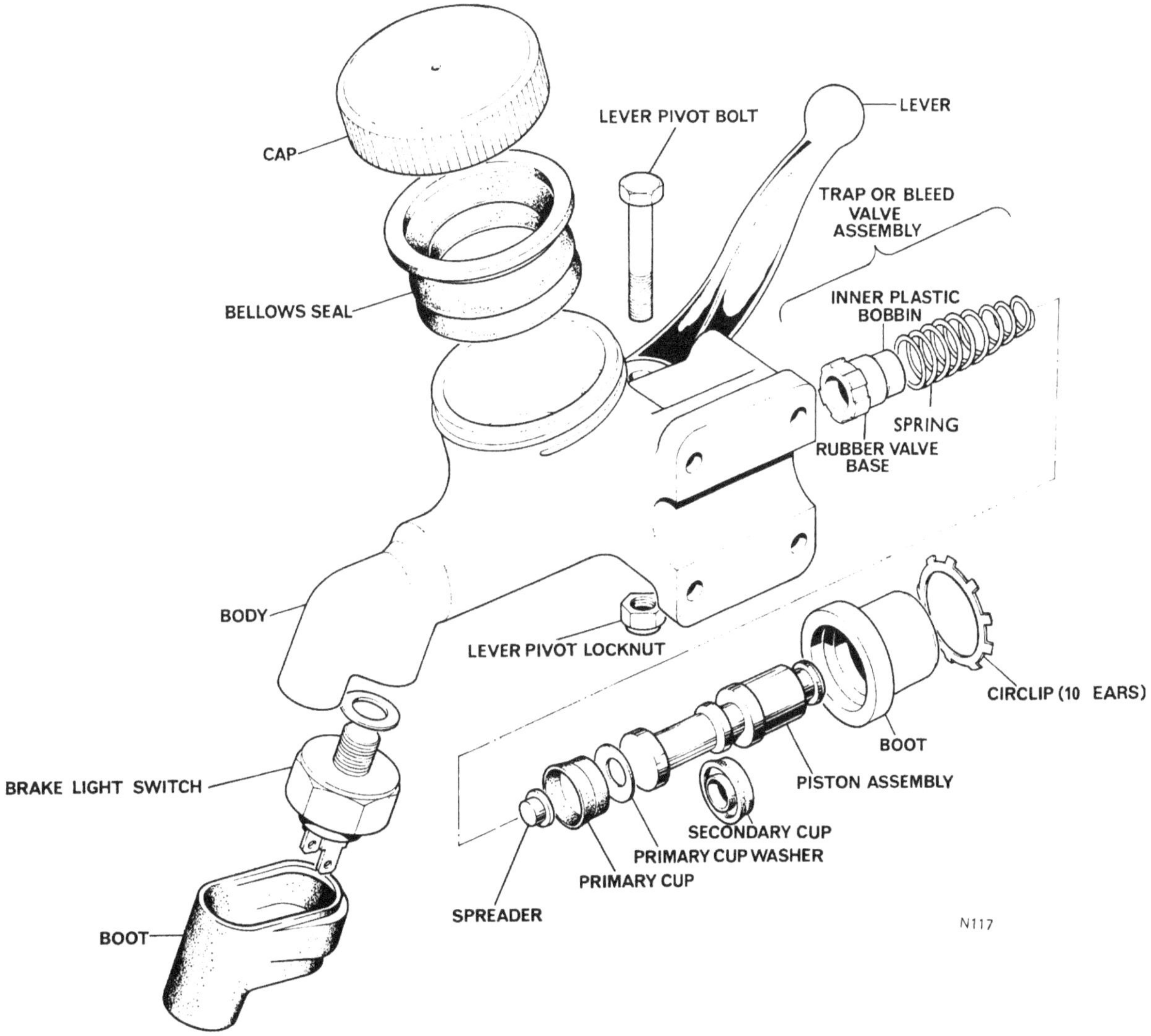

Fig. H16 Master Cylinder—Exploded view

Brakes, Wheels and Tires

lever a number of times until the master cylinder reservoir is empty. Close the bleed screw and detach the drain tube. Store the collecting jar safely and cover carefully to prevent dirt ingress.

Master Cylinder Removal

1 Disconnect the brake stop light pressure switch spade terminals and lift away the plastic switch cover exposing the hose union into the master cylinder.

2 Detach the hose from the master cylinder.

3 Remove the four switch casting screws and lift away the master cylinder complete.

Master Cylinder Dismantling – See *Fig.* H16

1 Remove the reservoir cap and bellows seal.

2 Remove the brake light pressure switch.

3 Remove the pivot bolt locknut and withdraw the pivot bolt and lever.

4 Carefully prise the boot circlip from the lower end of the master cylinder. This can be achieved if care is taken to lift three or four adjacent segments progressively, a little at a time until the circlip is tipped sufficiently to clear the mouth of the cylinder bore.

5 The boot is located into the piston and is best removed with the piston. Lift the piston out complete with boot and secondary cup.

6 Remove the primary cup washer, primary cup spreader, spring and bleed (or trap) valve assembly. To dislodge these items it may be necessary either to bump the casting on a block of clean soft wood to dislodge them or alternatively to apply *gentle* air pressure at the hose union bore and blow the parts free.

Inspection of Master Cylinder and Components

Discard the primary and secondary cups, the trap valve and boot. Clean the master cylinder and piston in brake fluid or methyl alcohol – do not use abrasive materials or solvent fluids.

Inspect the master cylinder body for wear in the piston bore. Normally, if the seals have been operating satisfactorily no wear need be expected, but if seal failure has occurred, the piston may have destroyed the bore finish. If there is any doubt whatsoever, the cylinder must be replaced.

If the cylinder is found to be fit for further service, ensure the two cylinder ports into the reservoir chamber are perfectly clear and clean. Inspect the hose union and switch threads for clean and satisfactory condition, and the lever pivot bolt bore for wear or cracks, or fractures. Replace the master cylinder if any doubt exists.

Check the brake lever for pivot bore wear and possible wear on the piston thrust face. Replace the lever if necessary. Next examine the piston for signs of scuffing on the ground outer diameters, and any wear on the lever thrust face.

Do not attempt to polish or grind the piston in any way, using abrasive compounds, as the slightest residual trace of such materials, even after intensive cleansing will damage master cylinder and caliper working parts beyond repair, and can result in premature brake failure.

Inspect the brake hose for cuts, signs of leakage or deterioration. Replace if the slightest doubt exists.

Master Cylinder Reassembly

After inspecting and cleaning the master cylinder, clean the piston, spring, spreader and cup washer in clean hydraulic fluid, and place in order of assembly on a perfectly clean working surface, in a dust free room or workshop.

DO NOT USE A FLUFFY RAG TO WIPE THE COMPONENTS. ALLOW TO DRAIN.

Soak the new primary and secondary cups in hydraulic fluid for fifteen minutes, kneading occasionally to encourage the special rubber cups to gain their maximum supple state prior to assembly. Ensure the three relief holes in the "crown" of the piston are clear and clean.

1 Take the "hollow" secondary cup and place it non lipped side against the ground "crown" diameter of the piston. Work the cup over the "crown" by hand, then down the piston body, over the

Brakes, Wheels and Tires

shoulder into its groove adjacent to the main body ground diameter.

CAUTION – Do not use any form of tool to ease assembly of the cup to the piston for fear of damage to the lip.

2. Fit the boot over the piston open end towards the piston crown and ensure the upper end is fitted squarely and snugly in the piston groove. The piston is now ready for assembly.

3. Assemble the trap valve to the spring, ensuring the inner plastic bobbin is accurately seated in the rubber valve base, and that the small diameter bleed hole in the bobbin base is clear and free. Ensure the plastic spreader is securely and firmly pressed home on the other smaller diameter end of the spring.

4. Offer the spring/trap valve assembly into the master cylinder, valve end first, keeping the master cylinder bore upright. It is permissible to hold the nose of the casting securely in a soft jawed vice, provided it is in no way overtightened.

5. Assemble the primary cup washer into the bore, open end of the cup facing into the bore, followed by the primary cup washer. Ensure only *one* cup washer is employed at this point. Place this dished primary cup washer, "hump" upwards, towards the open end of the cylinder bore. (The effect of the dished cup washer is to close the primary cup during the return stroke, allowing oil to by-pass the cup and replenish the pressure cylinder).

6. Offer the piston crown first into the cylinder. Place the 10 eared boot circlip over the top of the boot, the slight set on the ears facing away from the cylinder. Ensure fluid is smeared onto the secondary cup and into the mouth of the cylinder bore.

The next series of operations, to locate the piston, boot and circlip by means of the brake lever and pivot bolt can be difficult without the aid of special tools, and the assistance of a second operator. However, if care is taken, assembly can be completed without such help, the difficulty being to locate the base of the boot into the cylinder counterbore and finally locate and snug home the circlip whilst holding the piston assembly within the bore of the master cylinder, against the trap valve spring, long enough (and with sufficient piston thrust pad clearance) to be enabled to fit the hand lever and to locate it with the pivot bolt. The method of assembling these parts is detailed below:

7. Take the master cylinder assembly in the left hand (having assembled up to the point as described above) supporting the casting with the first and second fingers under the switch boss (hose and pressure switch threaded bores pointing downwards) and left thumb on the top of the casting close to the piston thrust "pad." Apply a gentle rotary action with the right hand to the piston thrust pad, at the same time maintaining downward thrust pressure against the trap valve spring assembly – ensuring the lip of the secondary cup enters the cylinder bore freely and without damage to the lip. When the piston has entered the bore, move the left thumb over to maintain the piston within the bore, at the same time using a blunt prod to snug the lower boot shoulder into the cylinder counter bore. Once this is seen to be achieved, and still maintaining pressure on the piston thrust pad, work the boot retaining circlip down to locate and restrain the boot in position. Still maintaining pressure on the piston thrust pad with the left thumb, slide the brake lever into position at the fulcrum slot, engaging the thrust pad close to the operator's left thumb. By holding the lever knob against the chest, alignment of the holes can be achieved, and the pivot bolt slid into position, and located with the locknut.

Brakes, Wheels and Tires   H

Master Cylinder Refitting

Refitting the master cylinder is the exact reverse procedure of the dismantling sequence described above. Refit the master cylinder to the handlebar, the oil pressure switch and brake hose. Slide the plastic switch cover over the hose, hold in a convenient location whilst the brake light wires are connected to the brake switch terminals and slide the cover into final location. Enter the lower hose into the fork support bracket, locate in position with the locknut and tighten up the upper brake pipe union nut. Bleed the hydraulic system as described in the following text, after ensuring that the master cylinder is level on the handlebar.

Bleeding the Hydraulic Brake System

1   Remove the reservoir cap and fill the reservoir almost to the top. Remember that brake fluid ruins paintwork and do not allow fluid to spill during filling.

2   Connect a small bore rubber tube from the caliper bleed screw to a clean jar or receptacle.

3   Unscrew the bleed screw one full turn and start to pump slowly the handlebar lever. As fluid is forced to the caliper and through the bleed nipple, the master cylinder level will drop. Take care throughout the operation that the level does not drop sufficiently low to allow further air to be pumped into the system and top up where necessary.

4   Continue pumping the lever until fluid free of air bubbles exits from the bleed tube into the fluid container then hold the brake lever "on" against the handlebar whilst the caliper bleed screw is tightened and the bleed tube removed.

5   Test the brake for "sponginess." If the action feels "spongy," then air remains in the system and further bleeding must be undertaken.

6   Ensure that the master cylinder reservoir is brought to the correct level then refit the bellows seal and cap.

7   Finally check all unions for security and freedom from leaks.

SECTION H14

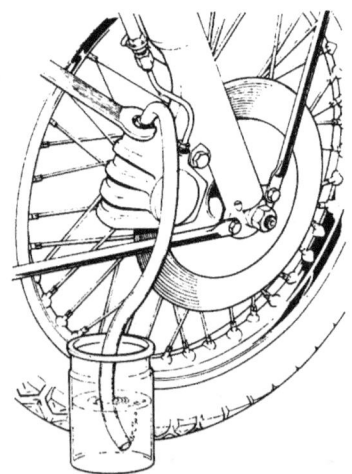

Fig. H17 Bleeding disc brake hydraulic system

TIRES

Tire changing is largely a matter of technique and what to the layman may seem a difficult task is perfectly straightforward when the correct technique is followed. To change either tire, the wheel must be removed. See Sections H6 & 8 for front wheel removal and Section H1 for rear wheel removal. The same basic principles apply for all types of tire – lubricate the beadings such as with soapy water, to allow the beadings to slip easily over the rim, use heel pressure wherever possible in preference to tire levers for easing the tire on to the rim and minimise the risk of damage by "nipping" and ensure that the opposite side of the tire is pressed well into the rim well to provide maximum freedom where the beading is being slid over the wheel rim. *Note:* that the rear tire only has one security bolt to prevent tire "creep" such as under hard acceleration. No security bolt is fitted to the front tire. For this reason separate routines are given for front and rear tires. The full technique is as follows:

Brakes, Wheels and Tires

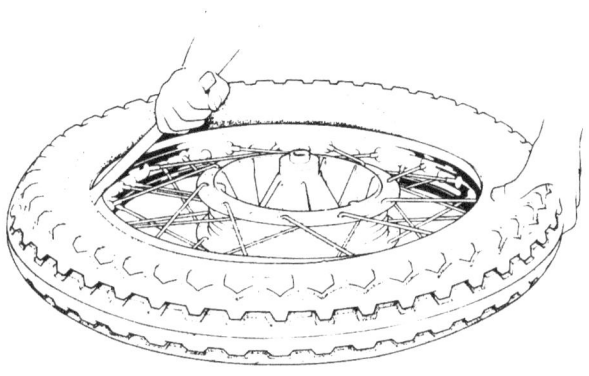

Fig. H18 Levering close to valve whilst pressing opposite bead down into rim

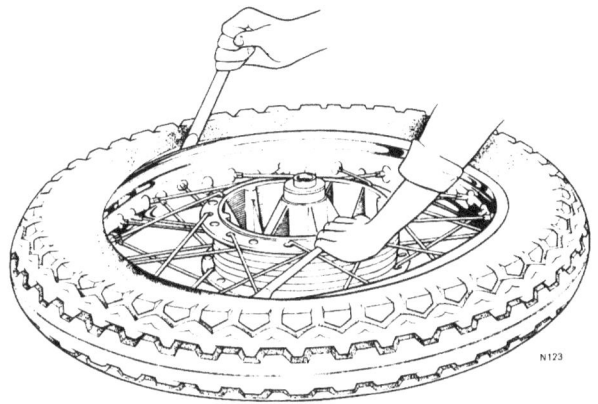

Fig. H19 Two tire levers in use to remove first bead of tire

Removing Front Tire (No security bolt)

1. Remove the dust cap from the valve and using a suitable notched type of cap or removal tool, unscrew the valve core to deflate the tire completely.

2. Remove the knurled ring securing the valve at the rim. Store the cap, core and knurled ring clean for re-use.

3. Lay the wheel down, if possible on a clean surface to avoid scratching and, also to prevent damage to the front axle. In the case of a disc brake wheel, leave the disc uppermost.

4. Tread the tire beading away from the rim — after a great deal of service the tire beading has a tendency to stick.

5. Brush a lubricant such as soapy water onto the tire beading and rim and also dip the tire levers (two short ones are recommended) in the solution before each leverage.

6. Insert the first lever between the tire valve and rim at the valve position, press the opposite side of the tire down into the rim well and apply leverage (see *Fig.* H18).

7. Insert the second lever approximately 4 in. (100 mm) from the first and lever the tire beading over the rim.

8. Remove the first lever and re-insert at the next stage, continuing round the rim a little at a time (see *Fig.* H19) until the beading can be pulled clear of the rim.

9. Push the valve out of the rim and withdraw the inner tube.

10. If it is required to remove the tire from the rim, hold the wheel upright and apply pressure to a lever inserted between the second beading and wheel rim.

Brakes, Wheels and Tires   H

Before fitting note that new Avon tyres have red and Dunlop tyres white paint dots at the lightest point. Note also that the latest Dunlop tyres have directional arrows on the sidewalls.

Refitting Front Tire (No security bolt)

1. If the tire has been removed completely, ensure that the rubber rim tape is fitted properly, rough side towards and central in the spoke nipple area of the rim.

2. Replace the valve core and inflate just sufficiently to "round" the tube and minimise the risk of "nipping" at a later stage. Dust the tube with French chalk and place the tube inside the tire, aligning the paint dots on the tire with the valve stem.

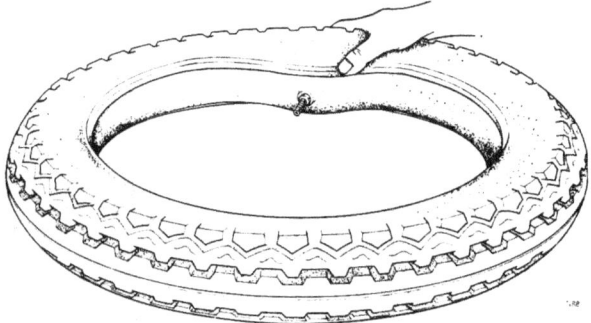

Fig. H20   Tube within cover squeezing cover to hold valve protruding

3. Lay tire and tube over rim ensuring that "front wheel rotation" arrow (if any) points in direction of wheel rotation.

4. Lubricate the beadings with soapy water.

5. Squeeze the beadings together with the hand, permitting the edge of the tube to protrude for approximately 2 in. (50·8 mm) at each side of the valve. Offer the tire and tube to the rim, feeding the valve through the rim tape and rim holes.

6. Pressing this side of the tire into the rim well, and working from the valve, press the first beading over the rim by hand pressure and lever the last few inches into position as in *Fig.* H22. Take special care that the inner tube is not nipped during this operation.

7. Press the second beading into the rim well, starting opposite the valve then use the heel to press the bead into position as far round as possible.

8. As shown in *Fig.* H23, taking care to avoid "nipping", lever the last portion of the beading over the rim, finishing at the valve.

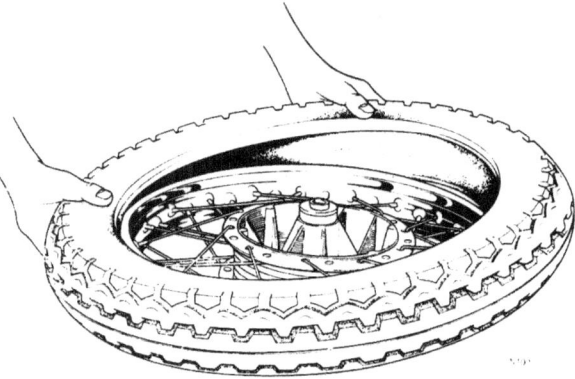

Fig. H21   Refitting tire to wheel with valve engaged in rim hole

9. Push the valve inwards to the rim to ensure that the tube near the valve is not trapped between the beading and rim then pull the valve back and inflate to pressure.

10. To ensure that the tire is true on the rim, check the tire moulded fitting line in relation to the rim. The position can be corrected by "bouncing" the side of the tire on the ground at any point where the fitting line is too near the rim.

11. When the tire is fitted correctly, fit the knurled valve securing rim and replace the valve dust cap.

Removing Rear Tire (Security bolt fitted).

The routine for removing and refitting a tire with security bolt is basically the same as for a tire without security bolt but it is important to deal with this item in the correct sequence. The full procedure is therefore detailed as follows:

1. Remove the dust cap from the valve and using a suitable notched type of cap or removal tool, unscrew the valve core to deflate the tire completely.

Brakes, Wheels and Tires H

2   Remove the knurled ring securing the valve at the rim. Store the cap, core and knurled ring clean for re-use.

3   Unscrew the security bolt nut and push the bolt inside the cover.

4   Lay the wheel down, if possible on a clean surface to avoid scratching.

5   Tread the tire bead away from the rim – after a great deal of service the tire beading has a tendency to stick.

11 Push the valve out of the rim and withdraw the inner tube.

12 If it is required to remove the tire from the rim, hold the wheel upright and apply pressure to a lever inserted between the second bead and wheel rim.

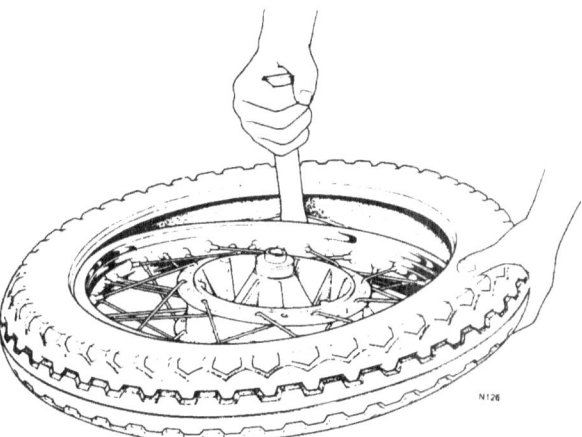

Fig. H22   First bead being levered into the rim

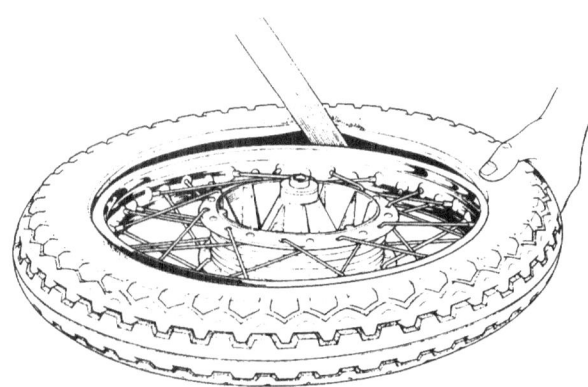

Fig. H23   Careful levering of second bead over wheel rim

6   Brush a lubricant such as soapy water onto the tire bead and rim and also dip the tire levers (two short ones are recommended) in the solution before each leverage.

7   Insert the first lever between the tire valve and rim at the valve position, press the opposite side of the tire down into the rim well and apply leverage (see *Fig. H18*).

8   Insert the second lever approximately 4 in. (100 mm) from the first and lever the tire bead over the rim.

9   Remove the first lever and re-insert at the next stage, continuing round the rim a little at a time (see *Fig. H19*) until the bead can be pulled clear of the rim.

10 Remove the security bolt from the rim.

Refitting Rear Tire (Security bolt fitted)

1   If the tire has been removed completely, ensure that the rubber rim tape is fitted properly, rough side towards and central in the spoke nipple well of the rim.

2   Ensure "rear wheel direction" arrow (if any), is pointing in direction of wheel rotation and fit the first tire beading over the rim without the inner tube, ensuring that the paint dots align with the security bolt hole.

Brakes, Wheels and Tires   H

3. Lift the free side wall as in *Fig. H24* and insert the security bolt less nut. Loosely fit the leather washer and nut.

4. Replace the valve core and inflate just sufficiently to "round" the tube and minimise the risk of "nipping" at a later stage. Dust the tube with French chalk and place the tube inside the tire, feeding the valve through the rim tape and rim holes.

5. Lubricate the bead with soapy water.

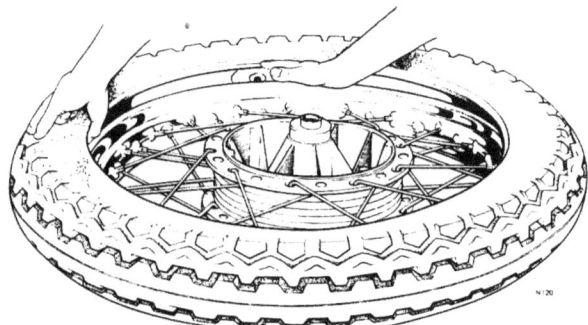

Fig. H24   Lifting cover and engaging security bolt to rim

6. Pressing this side of the tire into the rim well, and working from the valve, press the first bead over the rim by hand pressure and lever the last few inches into position as in *Fig. H22*. Take special care that the inner tube is not nipped during this operation.

7. Press the second bead into the rim well whils keeping the security bolt pressed back into the tire as in *Fig. H25* starting opposite the valve then use the heel to press the bead as far round as possible into position.

8. As shown in *Fig. H25*, taking care to avoid "nipping", lever the last portion of the bead over the rim, finishing at the valve.

9. Push the valve inwards to the rim to ensure that the tube near the valve is not trapped between the bead and rim then pull the valve back and inflate to pressure.

10. To ensure that the tire is true on the rim, check the tire moulded fitting line in relation to the rim. The position can be corrected by "bouncing" the side of the tire on the ground at any point where the fitting line is too near the rim.

11. Bounce the tire several times in the centre of the bead where the security bolt is fitted then tighten the securing nut. Recheck that the fitting line is still equidistant to the rim.

12. When the tire is fitted correctly, fit the knurled valve securing nut and replace the valve dust cap.

Fig. H25   Pressing security bolt back through rim whilst levering second bead into position

Electrical J

Electrical

Electrical   J

SECTION J1

DESCRIPTION

The Commando electrical system is grouped into four areas for the purpose of this manual. The areas are:

Sections J2 to J8:	Those parts connected with the charging system.
Sections J9 to J14:	Those parts connected with the ignition system.
Sections J15 to J19:	Those parts connected with the lighting system.
Sections J20 to J28:	Other electrical equipment.

IMPORTANT

Before starting any electrical test procedures, on 1971 and later models, isolate the 3 AW warning light assimilator by disconnecting the green/yellow lead to the assimilator at the alternator green/yellow lead double snap connector.

The Commando electrical system is positive earth (ground).

SECTION J2

CHARGING SYSTEM

The charging system comprises an alternator with the 6 charging coils connected permanently, (fitted in the primary chaincase and driven by the engine crankshaft). This supplies alternating (A.C.) current to the rectifier where it is converted to direct (D.C.) current. The D.C. current is fed to the lead/acid battery in parallel to the Zener diode which is mounted on the right support plate for the silencer and footrests.

The function of the Zener diode is to regulate the flow of D.C. current and thus prevent overcharging of the battery. Surplus current is directed to the heatsink (in this case, the light alloy support plate for the right hand silencer and footrests) where it is dissipated as heat.

Below are detailed the components of the charging system with applicable test procedures:

SECTION J3

ALTERNATOR – LUCAS TYPE RM21

The alternator produces an alternating current (A.C.) by means of a six-pole permanent-magnet rotor which rotates within a stationary six-pole laminated-iron stator assembly.

The rotor is attached to the engine crankshaft, which revolves at engine speed. The stator sub-assembly, comprising the windings and laminations, is attached to the primary chaincase.

Maintenance

The alternator and associated equipment requires no maintenance except for an occasional check to ensure that all the external cable connections are clean and tight. The rectifier securing nut should make good electrical contact. If it should be necessary to remove the alternator rotor from the engine crankshaft, the use of magnetic keepers is not necessary, but keep the rotor away from magnetically-attracted metal foreign matter.

Testing the alternator in situ

(a) Disconnect the alternator leads at the snap connectors.

(b) Connect an A.C. voltmeter (with 1 ohm resistor in parallel) as detailed in the table below. See Section J25 for instructions on making a 1 ohm resistor.

(c) Start engine and run at approx. 3,000 rev./min. noting voltmeter readings.

VOLTMETER AND RESISTOR ACROSS	MINIMUM VOLTAGE READINGS
	Stator: Two lead
	Type: RM21
White/Green. Green/Yellow	9
Any one lead and stator earth (ground)	NO READING

CONCLUSIONS:

If the reading is low, check the rotor by substitution.
Zero reading indicates open-circuited coil(s).

Electrical   J

Testing the D.C. input to battery

(a) Connect a D.C. ammeter in main battery lead (between battery negative terminal and battery cable), red lead to cable, black lead to battery terminal.

(b) Ensure Zener Diode is disconnected.

(c) Start engine and run at approx. 3,000 rev./min.

The following reading will be obtained if the battery and charging systems are in good condition.

Switch Positions	Minimum Current Reading
Ignition Only	4·5 Amp
Ignition and Lights (Main Beam)	1·0 Amp

CONCLUSIONS:

If the readings obtained are higher than the figures quoted, the system is satisfactory. If the readings are lower, proceed to test the alternator itself as in the preceding text.

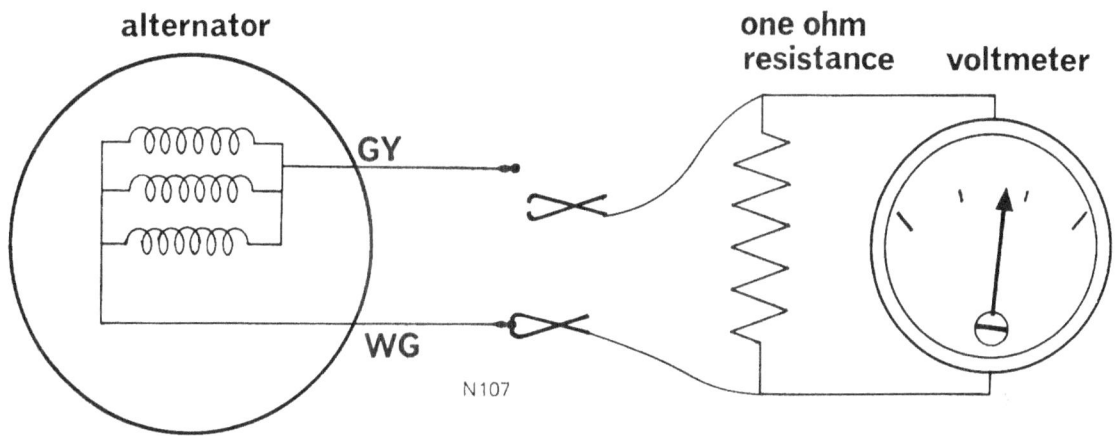

Fig. J1   Alternator test

SECTION J4

RECTIFIER TYPE 2DS 506

The rectifier, which is of the silicon crystal bridge-connected full wave type, requires no maintenance beyond a periodic check on the cleanliness and security of the terminals. If for any reason the rectifier is removed, DO NOT twist the plates in relation to one another since this will break internal connections and render the rectifier unfit for further service. The centre bolt must be held with a spanner whilst the fixing nut is turned.

VOLTMETER AND RESISTOR ACROSS	MINIMUM VOLTAGE READING
Rectifier (Centre Terminal and Earth (frame)	7·5

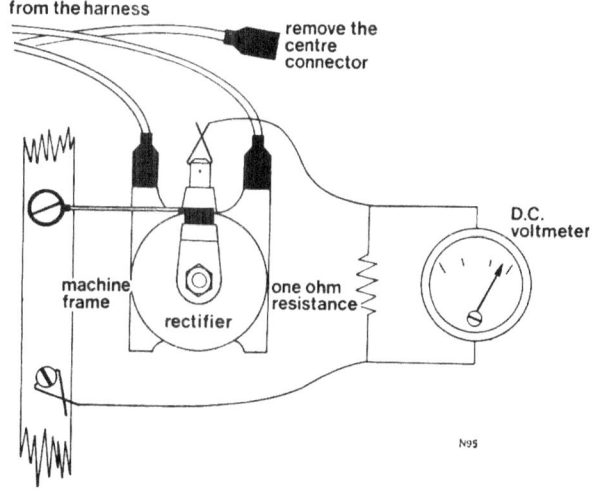

Fig. J2   Rectifier test connections

Electrical J

Testing the rectifier

With alternator leads connected correctly to main harness:

(a) Disconnect lead from centre terminal at rectifier.

(b) Connect D.C. voltmeter (with 1 ohm resistor in parallel). Red lead to earth (frame), black lead to rectifier centre terminal (see *Fig. J2*).

(c) Start engine and run at approx. 3,000 rev./min.

CONCLUSIONS:

If meter reading is equal to, or higher than the value stated, the rectifier is satisfactory. A low reading indicates a faulty rectifier. Remove and bench test.

Bench testing the rectifier

Connect a 12 volt, 45–50 watt bulb and 12 volt battery across terminals 2 and 1 (for a period not exceeding 30 seconds). See *Fig. J3*.

Repeat test with reversed battery polarity.

Carry out similar tests on terminals: Bolt and 1, Bolt and 3, 2 and 3.

The test lamp should illuminate fully in one direction only for each of the connections made.

CONCLUSIONS:

Rectifier must be replaced if:

(a) Bulb shows sign of illumination in both direction
(b) Bulb shows no sign of illumination in either direction

  } for each connection made.

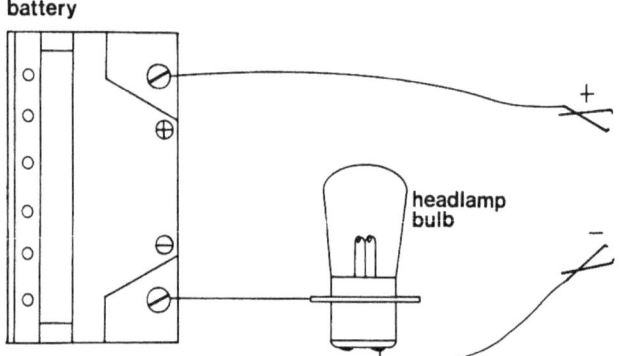
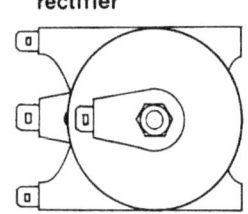
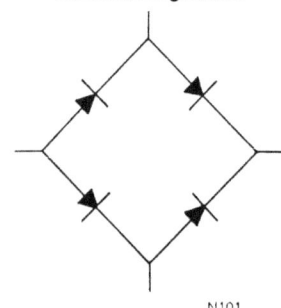

FIRST TESTS

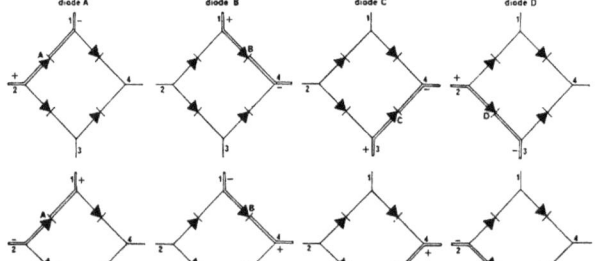

REVERSE DIRECTION TESTS

Fig. J3   Bench testing rectifier

Electrical   J

SECTION J5

Zener Diode

The Zener Diode is a semi-conductor device that becomes conductive in the reverse direction at a critical but predetermined voltage.

Assuming the battery is in a low state of charge, its terminal voltage (the same voltage is across the diode) will also be low, therefore the maximum charging current will flow into the battery from the alternator. At first none of the current is by-passed by the diode, the latter being non-conductive due to the low battery terminal volts. However, as the battery voltage is restored, the system voltage rises until, at approximately 14 volts, the Zener diode becomes partially conductive, thereby providing an alternative path for a small part of the charging current. Small increases in battery voltage result in large increases in Zener conductivity until, at approximately 15 volts, about 5 amperes of the alternator output is by-passing the battery. The battery will continue to receive only a portion of the alternator output as long as the system voltage is relatively high.

Depression of the system voltage, due to the use of headlamp or other lighting equipment, causes the Zener diode current to decrease and the balance to be diverted and consumed by the component in use. If the electrical loading is sufficient to cause the system voltage to fall below approx. 14 volts, the Zener diode will revert to its high resistance state of virtual non-conductivity and the full generated output will go to meet the demands of the system.

When refitting a Zener diode, the contact between the diode and the heatsink must be clean and free from corrosion. The tightening torque for the retaining nut is 24–28 lb./ins. (3·32–3·87 kg/m).

Testing the Zener Diode

(a) Connect D.C. ammeter between Zener Diode Lucar Blade and feed cable (Red lead to Zener, Black lead to cable).

(b) Connect D.C. voltmeter between the Lucar terminal of the Zener Diode and earth (Red lead to earth, Black lead to Zener Lucar Blade).

(c) Ensure all lights are switched off and any accessories unplugged.

(d) Start engine, slowly increase speed and check meter reading.

Special Note: THE BATTERY MUST BE IN A FULLY CHARGED STATE. If the battery condition is poor it should be temporarily replaced by a known good battery.

CURRENT	DIODE VOLTS
Nil	Up to 12·75
2 Amp	13·5 to 15·5

CONCLUSIONS:

Zener Diode must be replaced if:

(a) Current flow commences before 12·75v is reached.

(b) Voltmeter registers more than 15·5v before 2 amps is shown on the ammeter.

SECTION J6

BATTERY

Lead acid batteries are used on all models. On Commando models excepting Interpol, a single Lucas PUZ5A 12 volt battery with translucent case is fitted. Later models use Norton Villiers battery 063244 or Yuasa 12N9·4B. On Interpol, two Lucas type SCZ7E 6 volt batteries are fitted in series. On both battery types, the acid level can be seen through the casing and the electrolyte level is marked clearly on the battery case. A breather vent is used on both types of battery.

Battery Maintenance

Due to continual evaporation and gassing during charging, a weekly inspection must be made on the electrolyte level. Since the level will normally rise whilst the battery is being charged, the level must only be checked during off-charge periods. Any loss of electrolyte should be made good by the addition of distilled water until the level mark is reached. The level should not exceed this mark, for spillage may occur with subsequent damage to surrounding parts.

It is important to keep the battery connections clean and tight. Dirt and moisture must be wiped away from the battery top periodically.

If the motorcycle is stored for a period, the battery should be removed and maintained in a good state of charge every two weeks.

Electrical   J

Checking the state of charge

A hydrometer is required for this check. The specific gravity should be checked for each cell and the results checked with the table below:

	SPECIFIC GRAVITY (Corrected to 15°C (60°F))	
	Climates normally below 25°C (77°F)	Climates normally above 25°C (77°F)
Fully Charged	1·270 – 1·290	1·210 – 1·230
70% Charged	1·230 – 1·250	1·170 – 1·190
Discharged	1·110 – 1·130	1·050 – 1·070

Electrolyte temperature correction:

For every 10°C (18°F) below 15°C (60°F) subtract 0·007.

For every 10°C (18°F) above 15°C (60°F) add 0·007.

A variation of more than 40 points (0·040) between any cells indicates that the battery is suspect and should be thoroughly checked by the battery manufacturer's agent.

High rate discharge check

(Battery must be at least 70% charged).

Connect voltmeter and high rate discharge resistance (0·5 ohm) across battery terminals for 15 seconds.

Directly after 15 seconds the reading should remain steady.

A lower or rapidly falling voltage indicates the battery requires charging or has a faulty cell.

BATTERY VOLTAGE	VOLTMETER READING
12	9·4
6	4·8

SECTION J7

FUSE

A 35 amp fuse is fitted into the battery live (negative) lead close to the battery terminal. The fuse is of the cartridge type, in a nylon holder.

Access to the fuse is gained by pushing the fuseholder body halves together and twisting. At no time must the value of 35 amps be exceeded.

SECTION J8

WARNING LIGHT ASSIMILATOR

Lucas Type 3AW (1971 and later models)
This is an electro-mechanical device for ignition warning light control.

With the ignition switched on, the warning light is supplied with battery current; when the engine is started and the alternator output reaches 6 volts approximately, the contacts inside the unit open and break the warning light circuit, switching off the warning light.

Should the warning light fail to light when the ignition is switched on and with the engine stationary, disconnect the White/Brown lead from the "W L" terminal of the control unit and temporarily reconnect to the "E" terminal; if the bulb lights, this indicates that the control unit is faulty, but should the light still fail, then the bulb, connections, and associated wiring should be checked.

SECTION J9

IGNITION SWITCH (Pre 1971)

The ignition switch is mounted at the front of the left-hand accessory cover. This switch is of the on/off type governing only the ignition circuit. Clockwise rotation turns the ignition "on" and anti-clockwise "off."

SECTION J10

MASTER SWITCH (1971 and later models)

The key operated switch is located to the front of the left hand accessory cover. The switch controls ignition and also energises the lighting system. The switch is a sealed unit requiring no attention other than a routine check on connections. The four switch positions are shown below in *Fig. J4*.
The Switch Positions are:

1. **Parking Lights Only**

   The key may be removed in this position enabling the machine to be parked safely at night.

2. **Off Position**

   Again the key may be removed leaving all circuits isolated.

3. **Ignition Only**

   The key cannot be removed. This position is used during normal daytime running.

Electrical   J

4. **Ignition and Lights**

   Again the key may not be removed. This position is used for night riding.

The lock with keys is captive in the switch body. If for any reason the lock need be replaced, it can be removed from the switch body to which it is held captive by a spring operated plunger. A sharp pointed implement such as a ground-down spoke would be ideal for depressing the plunger through the hole in the side of the switch body. Whilst depressing the plunger the switch body should be shaken and the lock ejected.

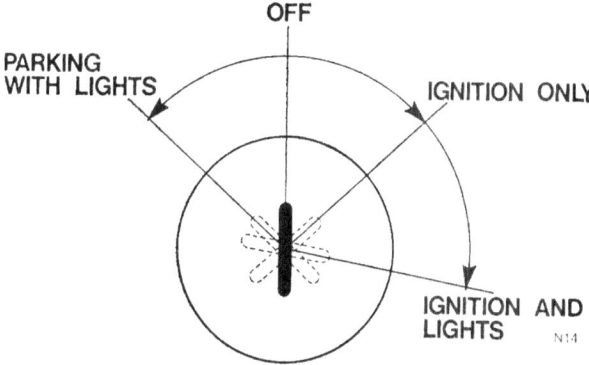

Fig. J4 Master switch positions

SECTION J11

TESTING IGNITION SYSTEM

Testing Sequence for Ignition System

Engine; will not start – difficult to start – misfires.

(a) Check battery.

(b) Check main fuse (if fitted).

(c) Check for spark at both spark plugs.

(d) Ensure timing, contact breaker and spark plug gaps are satisfactory.

(e) Check capacitor by substitution.

(f) Check wiring for loose connections.

(g) Test Zener Diode and ignition system.

(h) Where fitted, check ballast resistor for short circuiting, when hot.

Ignition System Tests

(a) Connect D.C. voltmeter Black lead to C.B. terminal of contact breaker and Red lead to earth.

(b) Ensure contact points are open.

(c) Switch on ignition. Voltmeter should indicate battery volts.

(d) Ignition still on, close contact points. Voltmeter reading should fall to zero.

Note: Repeat the test for each coil with its appropriate contact set.

CONCLUSION:

No reading for test (c) may indicate faulty ignition switch, open circuit primary winding, broken lead, short circuit to earth on C.B. lead, faulty capacitor or blown main fuse.

Low reading indicates high resistance in the primary circuit or across ignition switch contacts. A reading for test (d) indicates voltage drop across the contact points (dirty) or poor distributor earth.

SECTION J12

IGNITION COILS

The ignition coils whether of the 12 volt or 6 volt type consist of primary and secondary windings wound concentrically about a laminated soft iron core, the secondary windings being next to the core.

The primary winding usually consists of some 300 turns of enamel covered wire and the secondary some 17,000 – 26,000 turns of much finer wire – also enamel covered. Each layer is paper insulated from the next in both primary and secondary windings.

When the contact breaker opens, causing a sudden cut-off of current flow in the primary windings, H.T. current is induced in the secondary windings and a spark occurs at the spark plug.

Note: The coils are of the oil filled type and must be protected from mechanical damage which will cause leakage.

Electrical   J

IGNITION COILS LUCAS TYPE 17M6 (6VLOT)
1971 and later Models

Six volt ignition coils are used in conjunction with a ballast resistor to allow their use in an otherwise 12 volt electrical system. This system has been adopted since an adequate spark is available with the battery in a heavily discharged state. The ignition coils are sealed units, requiring only a periodic check on connections.

IGNITION COILS LUCAS TYPE 17M12
(12 Volt) – Certain 1972 Models

Twelve volt ignition coils, again of the oil filled, sealed type, are used on some models and require no ballast resistor.

TESTING AN IGNITION COIL
(17M6 and 17M12 Types)

An electrical test set is necessary for full testing of the ignition coil and though a similar set-up can be produced as shown in *Fig.* J5 provision will have to be made for a contact breaker which can be motored at 100 r.p.m. Use a 6 volt battery for this test.

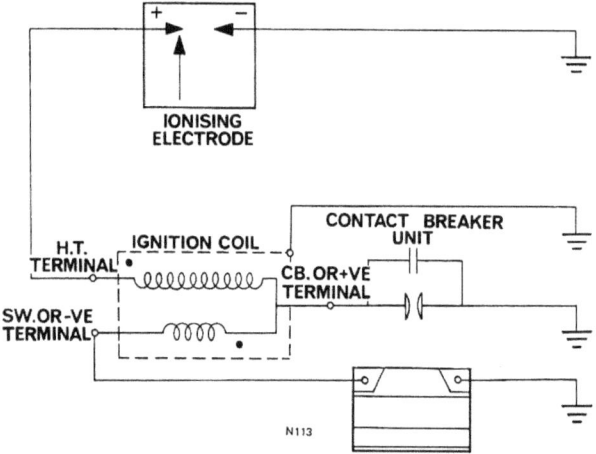

Fig. J5   Ignition coil testing arrangements incorporating 3 point test

Before commencing the main test, check the condition of the primary windings. This is done by connecting an ohmeter across the low tension terminals. At 20°C the minimum resistance should be 1·7 ohms and maximum resistance, 1·9 ohms for 17M6 (6 volt) coils and 3·3 ohms minimum and 3·8 ohms maximum resistance for 17M12 (12 volt) coils.

Set the adjustable gap to 8 mm for the 6 volt coil or 9 mm for the 12 volt coil and connect up as in *Fig.* J5. If the coil is in good condition, sparking should occur regularly with no more than 5% missing per 15 seconds.

BALLAST RESISTOR
(With 6 volts coil, 1971 and later Models)

This permits the use of 6 volt coils in an otherwise 12 volt system. The two coils are wired in parallel with the resistor in series. When the battery voltage has dropped

due to heavy current taken such as by the use of an electric starter, the ignition coils are fed direct, by-passing the resistor and thus enabling the coils to work at their approximate potential. The ballast resistor can only be tested against its resistance value of 1·8–2 ohms.

CONTACT BREAKER ASSEMBLY – LUCAS
TYPE 6CA

The contact breaker and auto advance mechanism are covered fully in Section C39 & C40 adjacent to engine ignition timing details.

SECTION J13
CAPACITOR PACK TESTING

The capacitors can be tested in situ. To test, turn on the ignition and take voltage readings across each set of contacts when open. If no reading is gained, the capacitor is unserviceable due to a breakdown of the internal insulation. If a reading is gained but the capacitor has reduced capacity, evidenced by excessive arcing and severe burning of the contact points, a new capacitor should be substituted on the affected cylinder.

CHANGING A CAPACITOR
(1971 and later Models)

Remove the complete coil cluster (see Section C1). Release the capacitor pack (2 screws and nuts). Remove the rubber cover: the individual capacitors are retained to the base plate by single nuts.

Electrical J

Reassembly is a direct reversal of the foregoing. Take care to reconnect the wiring correctly. If necessary consult the wiring diagram at the end of this section.

CHANGING A CAPACITOR (1970 Models)

The capacitors are screwed individually to the coil clips and are accessible from beneath without disturbing the coils.

SECTION J14

SPARK PLUGS – CHAMPION N7Y

Protruding nose self-cleaning spark plugs are fitted. It is most important to use the correct heat grade since a spark plug of too low heat grade can cause pre-ignition and subsequent damage to the engine.

To avoid damage to the insulator, use the plug spanner provided in the tool kit to remove and refit the spark plugs. The spark plugs should be tightened firmly (not excessively) to ensure a gas tight joint.

When adjusting the gap to the recommended setting of ·028 in. (·59/·72 mm), only the side contact must be adjusted. Under no circumstances attempt to bend the centre electrode to adjust the gap.

SECTION J15

LIGHTING SYSTEM (1971 and later Models)

The lighting system operates on direct current drawn from the battery (or from the rectifier where the 2MC capacitor replaces the battery) and controlled by the 4 position master switch (described in Section J10). As the master switch is turned to the "lights on" position, the tail lamp, instrument lights and pilot lamp illuminate. Selection of headlamp illumination is controlled by the switch in the top of the headlamp shell. Headlamp high beam or dip beam are selected by the two position switch included in the handlebar right switch cluster. When high beam is selected, a warning light in the headlamp shell illuminates.

LIGHTING SYSTEM (1970 Models)

The lighting system operates on direct current drawn from the battery and controlled by the 3 position toggle switch in the headlamp shell. Left position is "off", centre position is "pilot lights", and right position is main beam.

When high beam is selected, the warning light in the headlamp shell illuminates.

SECTION J16

HEADLAMP
TO CHANGE THE HEADLAMP AND PILOT BULBS

Release the screw on top of the headlamp shell adjacent to the rim. The rim with light unit can then be lifted out from the top first. Press down the main bulbholder towards the reflector and rotate counter clockwise. The holder will lift away and the bulb can be removed.

The pilot bulbholder complete with pilot bulb should be pulled away from the light unit. The bulb is a bayonet fitting into the bulbholder.

Note: Do not touch a quartz halogen bulb envelope with the fingers. Accidental marks can be removed with alcohol.

SECTION J17

TO CHANGE THE TAIL/STOPLAMP BULB

The lens is secured by two bright plated screws Release these and lift away the lens and thin gasket. The bulb is a bayonet fitting into the bulbholder. Note that the bulb will only fit the correct way into the bulbholder on reassembly. Take care not to crack the lens by overtightening the screws.

SECTION J18

STOP SWITCHES

Front Brake Stop Switch (Drum Brake)

This is a sealed compression switch fitted into the front cable which cannot be serviced. Check periodically on the cleanliness and security of the spade terminals.

Electrical J

Front Brake Stop Switch (Disc Brake)

A sealed Lucas compression switch is incorporated in the master cylinder. This unit cannot be serviced though a check should be made periodically on the cleanliness and security of the lead terminals.

Rear Brake Stop Switch – Lucas Type 118SA

The switch is a sealed unit though the rubber should be lifted and filled with grease at intervals to exclude water. It is mounted by screws in slots to allow for position adjustment.

Rear Stop Switch Adjustment

Care must be taken during adjustment since incorrect positioning causes the plastic switch to function as the brake pedal stop, resulting in failure of the switch body. Slacken the nuts and screws holding the switch to the plate with slots on the brake pedal. Set the rear brake pedal to suit the riders preference – this is done by adjustment of the stop bolt and locknut. Adjust the rear brake cable to the desired setting. Move the switch up, a little at a time, until the switch plunger is central to the abutment and until the least depression of the pedal causes the stop light to illuminate. The recommended switch depression is $\frac{1}{32}$ in. (0·0793 mm). Tighten the switch securing screws and allow the pedal to return to rest, ensuring that the switch is not fully compressed before the pedal stop is reached.

SECTION J19

HANDLEBAR SWITCH CLUSTERS

(1971 and later Models)

The switch clusters are accommodated in light alloy castings. Whilst the switches are not sealed units, the method of assembly renders reassembly by an owner or dealer extremely difficult, if not impossible, and we must recommend against attempts at dismantling.

The right switch cluster includes, at the bottom, the kill (or cut-out) button and a spare button at the top. The 3-position flick switch operates the direction indicators which are available as optional extras. The switch functions as below:

1. With the lever in the central position and no buttons being pressed, the only leads connected are the White and White/Yellow. This is because the lower push button operates a normally closed (i.e. push to open) switch.

2. Pressing the lower push button opens the White-White/Yellow leads (Ignition cut-out).

3. Pressing the upper push button connects the White lead to the White/Red lead. This button has no function at the present.

4. Moving the switch lever to the upper position connects the light Green/Brown lead to the Green/Red lead (L.H. indicators where fitted).

5. Moving the switch lever to its lower position connects the light Green/Brown lead to the Green/White lead (R.H. indicators where fitted).

The left hand switch cluster accommodates the horn button (at the bottom), the headlamp flasher at the top and the two position dip switch. The headlamp flasher permits the headlamp to be flashed as an overtaking warning when the lights are not switched on.

The lever on this switch has only two positions, upward and horizontal.

1. With the switch lever in the horizontal position and no buttons being pressed the only 2 cables connected are Blue and Blue/Red (Dip beam).

2. Moving the lever to its upper position connects the Blue lead to the Blue/White lead (Main beam).

3. Pressing the lower button connects the White lead to the Purple/Black lead (Horn).

4. Pressing the upper button connects the White lead to the Blue/White lead (Headlamp flasher).

Note: These clusters may easily be reversed from side to side depending upon owner preference.

SECTION J20

POWER TAKE-OFF SOCKET

(1971 and later Models)

This is located on the front of the airbox or on 1972 models, on the right side of the battery carrier, and provides a power source for any accessory selected by the owner, providing the battery capacity is borne in mind. With the battery in good condition and fully

Electrical   J

charged, the maximum rating of 8 amps at the 10 hour rate is available. We recommend that the engine is run up as soon as possible after the power take-off socket has been used to restore the battery to a good state of charge.

Caution must be exercised not to discharge the battery completely. The same power socket is used for charging the battery from an outside source.

Important

When tightening the stanchion locknut against the body of the flasher lamp, ensure that the torque loading figure of 35–45 lbs./ins. is not exceeded.

Flasher Unit Lucas Type 8FL

The unit is clipped into the mounting bracket and if for any reason the bracket is to be removed, the unit must first be withdrawn from the clip.

SECTION J21

FLASHING DIRECTION INDICATORS
Bulb replacement

To replace the bulb, unfasten the screws retaining the lens and carefully remove the lens. The bulb is then removed by pushing inwards and rotating anti-clockwise. When replacing the lens, ensure that the lens body locates into the sealing gasket, before the retaining screws are tightened.

Checking for faulty operation

If a fault occurs in the system, the following procedure should be adopted.

1. Check that the bulb filaments are not broken.
2. Check that all flasher circuit connections are clean and tight.
3. Switch on ignition and check with a voltmeter that the flasher terminal "B" is at battery voltage.
4. Connect together flasher unit terminals "B" and "L" and operate the indicator switch. If the flasher lamps on the respective side now light without flashing, the flasher unit is faulty and should be replaced with the same type of unit as the original.

If a flasher lamp stalk is replaced

On reassembly, take care not to damage the green lead when passing through the screw thread of the lamp shell. Final adjustment of the lamp position *must* be made by tightening of the locknut and not by straining the flasher unit.

SECTION J22

ALTERNATING HORN SET INTERPOL ONLY TYPE HC3

SPECIAL NOTE: This equipment is not available in U.S.A.

The alternating horn set comprises an alternating horn control, special 9H horns, two 6Ra relays, a switch and suitable connectors. Details of the individual units are as follows:

HC 3 Alternating Horn Control

This is a transistorised multivibrator, designed to pulse two 6Ra continuously rated relays alternately. The frequency of the unit is set during manufacture and cannot readily be altered. Hence the risk of faulty setting due to tampering is eliminated. The unit must be mounted so that its temperature does not exceed 50°C. Connection polarity must be observed. The alternating horn wiring is shown in *Fig.* J6.

Horns

These are type 9H and have been reset after a "running-in" period to ensure maximum life. They must be rigidly mounted on a solid member of the vehicle with no loosely mounted components in the vicinity otherwise the tone will be adversely affected. It is recommended that the horns are mounted facing forward. The flares should be tilted slightly downwards to allow any water entering the horn trumpets to drain out.

Electrical   J

Relays

Standard 6Ra continuously rated relays are used. These should be so positioned that the cables carrying the horn current are as short as possible.

Technical Data

Frequency of Notes	438–495 Hz
Ratio of Notes	8 : 9
Sound Intensity	90 dB at 50 ft. (15·24 m)
Cycle of Signal	1–1·2 Hz
Power Consumption	60 watts

Testing Procedure

If the horns do not sound when the switch is operated, check the voltage at the HC 3 control as follows:

1. Connect a voltmeter, red lead to the cable removed from the +ve terminal, black lead to the cable removed from the —ve terminal. Operate switch, voltmeter should read the nominal voltage of the system.

If the voltage is satisfactory at the control unit proceed to check the individual horns and relays separate from the control unit as follows:

1. Remove leads from one "R" terminal and the +ve terminal on the control unit and join together. Operate switch, the relay should be energised and the associated horn should sound, if satisfactory.

2. Repeat above operation by joining together the leads removed from the other "R" terminal and the +ve terminal.

3. If both horns and relays operate normally, the fault is in the HC 3 control unit. Replace unit.

4. If either horn does not sound, check further by earthing leads connected to "C1" in the relay. If horn now operates satisfactorily, the fault is in the relay. Replace unit.

Other faults, i.e.: continuously sounding horns, incorrect cycle of operation, etc., can be attributed to a faulty control unit, which should be replaced.

Retuning the 9H Alternating Horns

After horns have been in use for a long period there will probably be a deterioration in performance due to normal wear of the contact breaker mechanism. If the rest of the system is in order, proceed to reset the horn contacts as follows:

Contact Adjustment on Motorcycle

1. Connect a voltmeter across the terminals of the horn, to check the voltage as the adjustment is being made.

2. Connect an ammeter (range 0–25A) between terminals "C1" and "C2" of the relay which supplies the horn to be tuned.

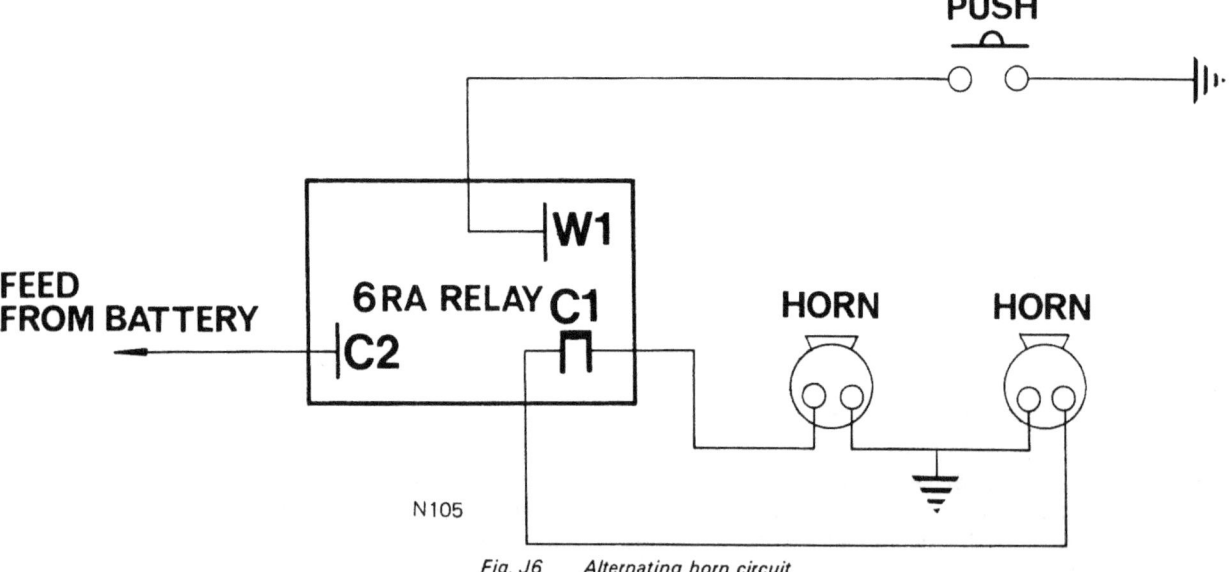

Fig. J6   Alternating horn circuit

Electrical   J

3 The adjustment screw should be tuned while operating the horn until the ammeter indicates the appropriate current consumption (see below). Turn the screw clockwise to reduce the ammeter reading.

NOTE:

1 Do not under any circumstances disturb the centre core slotted screw and locknut.

2 It is essential, when adjusting on the vehicle, that the wiring is not overloaded. This could be caused by attempting to sound the horn, while the contacts are out of adjustment, and hence do not open. If the horn supply is fused, the fuse should be shorted out until adjustment has been completed.

Contacts Setting Data

High Note Horn

	Setting Current	Setting Voltage
12 volt	3·0 – 3·5A	13 volts

Special Low Note Horn

	Setting Current	Setting Voltage
12 volt	3·0 – 4·0A	13 volts

Horns should be checked for a good clear note over the following voltage range.

12 volt	11–12–15 volts

SECTION J23

HORN ADJUSTMENT (SINGLE STANDARD HORN)

The horn is shown in *Fig.* J7 with the adjustment screw arrowed. Adjustment will take up wear on the moving parts which, if not attended to, will cause roughness and a loss of performance.

To adjust the horn, operate the horn button and slowly turn the adjustment screw anti-clockwise until the horn just fails to sound. Release the horn button and turn the adjustment screw clockwise one notch at a time until the original performance is regained. The amount of adjustment may be expected to vary between a quarter and three-quarters of a turn. Note that if original performance is not restored, the horn must receive attention by the electrical manufacturer.

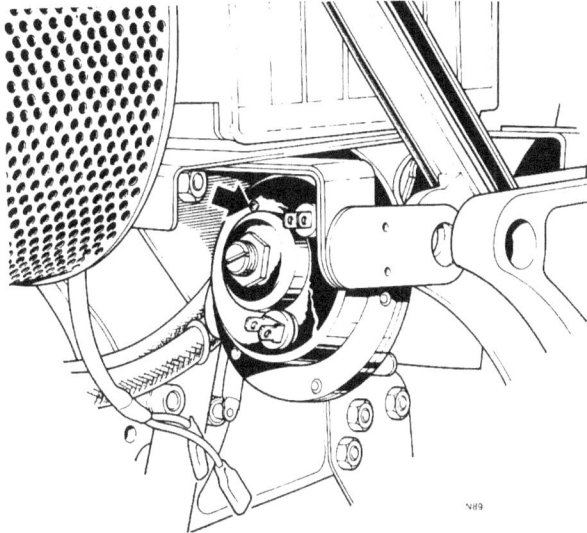

Fig. J7 Horn in position—note cross headed adjuster screw for horn contact breaker (arrowed)

SECTION J24

ELECTROLYTIC CAPACITOR 2MC

The capacitor is an electrolytic polarised type, spring mounted to the rear of the battery. This unit will be damaged beyond repair if it is connected incorrectly. The small ($\frac{3}{16}$ in.) terminal is the Positive ground (earth) terminal with a red spot on the terminal rivet. The double terminal is the Negative connection. The capacitor should only be fitted with the terminals pointing downwards. The battery may be removed altogether or be completely discharged whilst the 2MC capacitor permits normal starting and running. With the capacitor in use, the lights may be used whilst the engine is running though there is no parking facility.

Periodically the capacitor should be tested by disconnecting the battery terminals – the negative terminal should be insulated to prevent a possible short circuit. Start and run the engine – full lighting should be available. If the engine fails to start and run, test as follows:

(a) Disconnect capacitor.

(b) Connect capacitor direct to 12 volt battery for 5 seconds (see polarity note).

(c) Disconnect battery and let charged capacitor stand for 5 minutes.

(d) Connect D.C. voltmeter across the terminals (see polarity note) and note the steady reading* which should not be less than 9v for a serviceable unit.

*Some meters may show immediate needle overswing which should be ignored.

Electrical J

Polarity note: 2MC capacitors are polarity conscious and correct battery connection must be made. The smaller Lucar terminal blade (rivet marked red), is positive and the larger double Lucar connector forms the negative terminal.

Conclusions:

If meter reading is less than 9v, capacitor is leaking (inefficient) and must be replaced.

SECTION J25

HOW TO MAKE UP A ONE OHM RESISTOR

The 1 ohm resistor must be accurate otherwise correct voltage (or current) values will not be obtained.

A suitable resistor can be made from 4 yards 18 S.W.G. (·048 in. dia.) NICHROME wire together with two flexible leads and suitable crocodile clips, see *Fig.* J8.

To Calibrate

Bend the wire into two equal parts.

(a) Fix a heavy gauge flexible lead to centre bend of the wire, and connect this lead to the positive terminal of a 6-volt battery.

(b) Connect a voltmeter across the battery terminals.

(c) Connect an ammeter to the battery negative post.

(d) Take a lead from the other terminal of the ammeter, connect a crocodile clip to it, and connect to the free ends of the wire (which should be twisted together).

(e) Move the clip along the wire, making contact with both wires until the discharge reading on the ammeter exactly equals the number of volts shown on the voltmeter. The resistance is then 1 ohm.

(f) Cut the wire at this point, twist the two ends together and fix a second heavy gauge flexible lead.

(g) Wind the wire on to a hollow asbestos former 2 in. dia. (approximately).

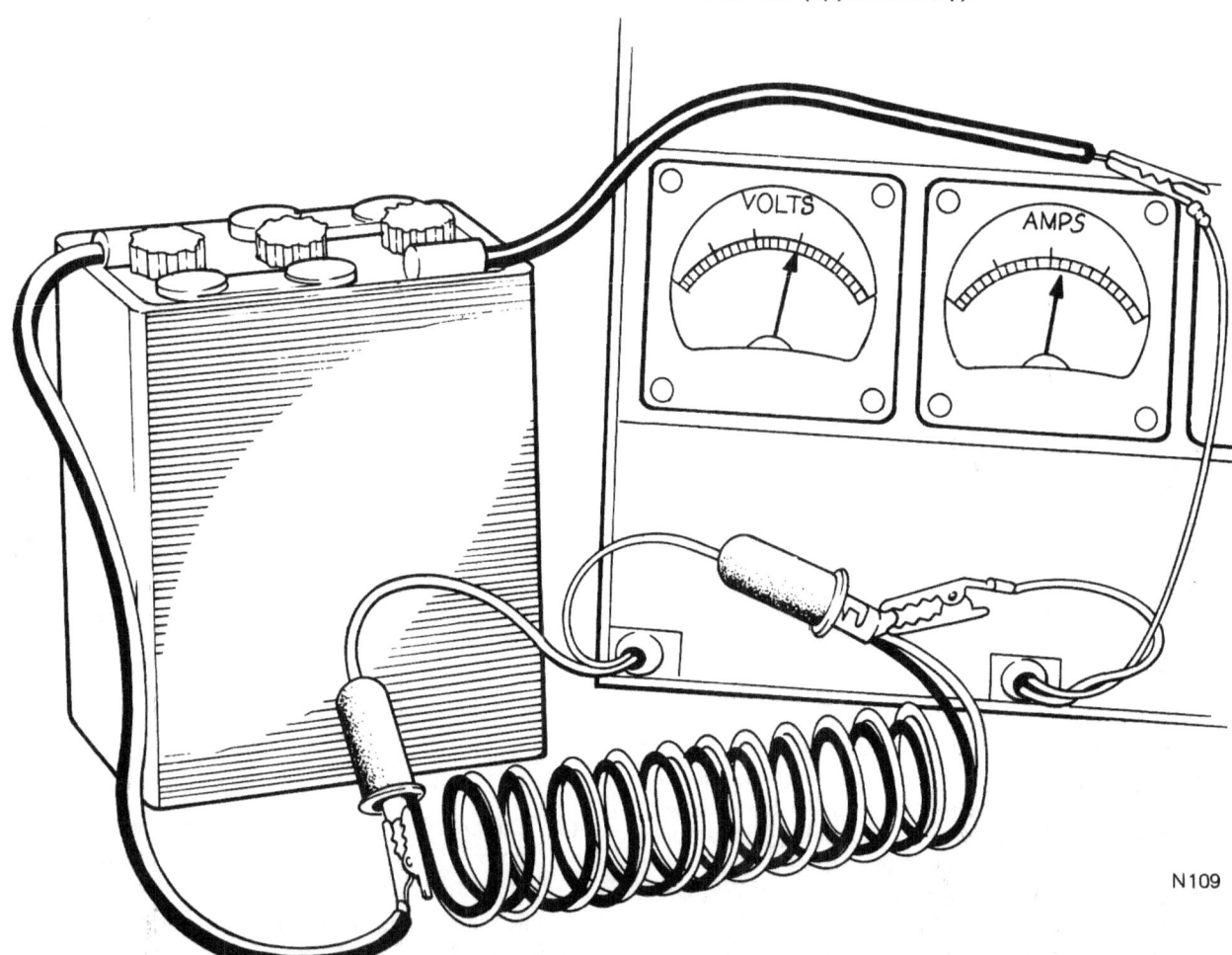

N109

Electrical   J

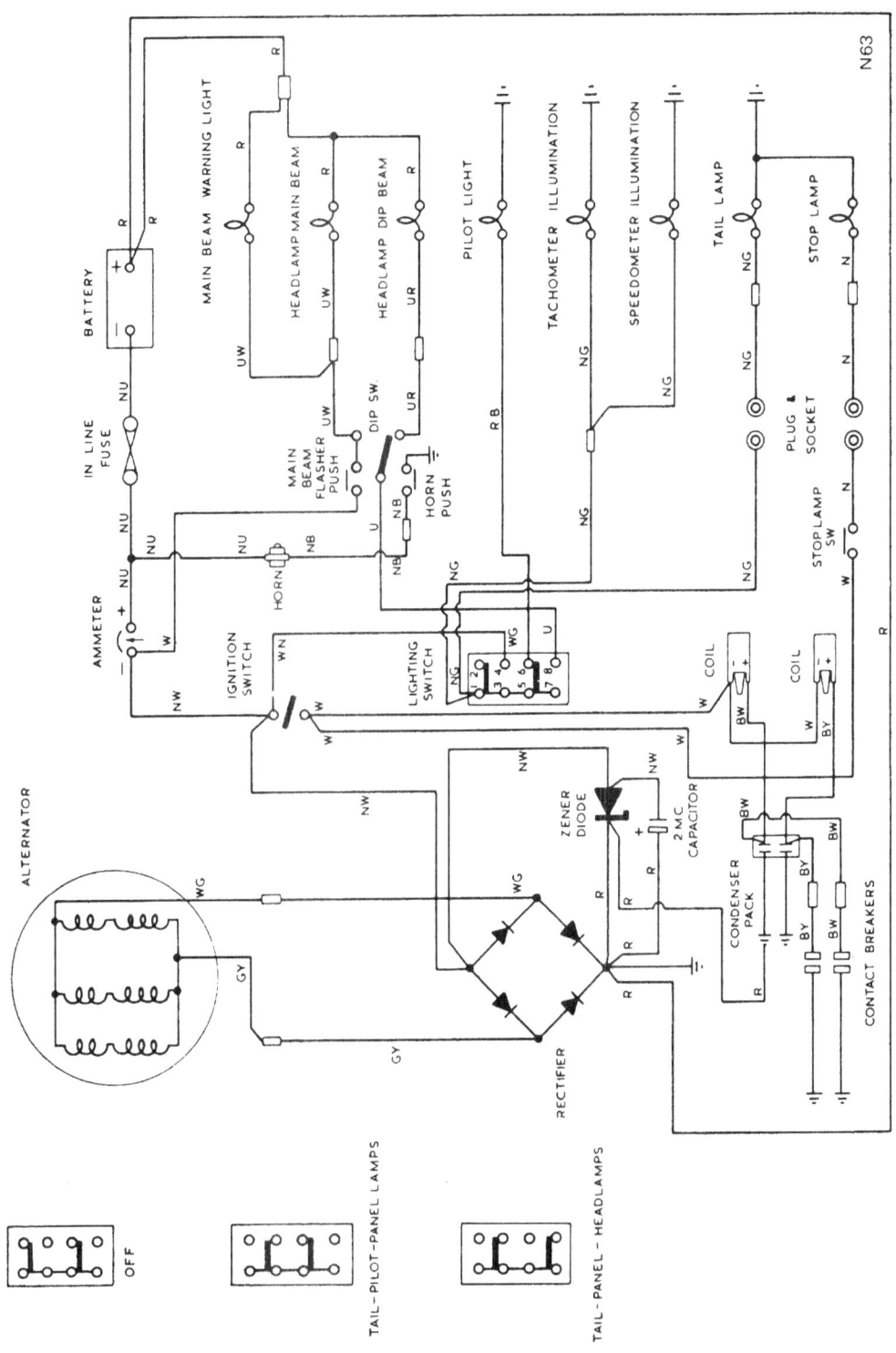

Fig. J9   Pre-1971 wiring diagram. All models

Electrical J

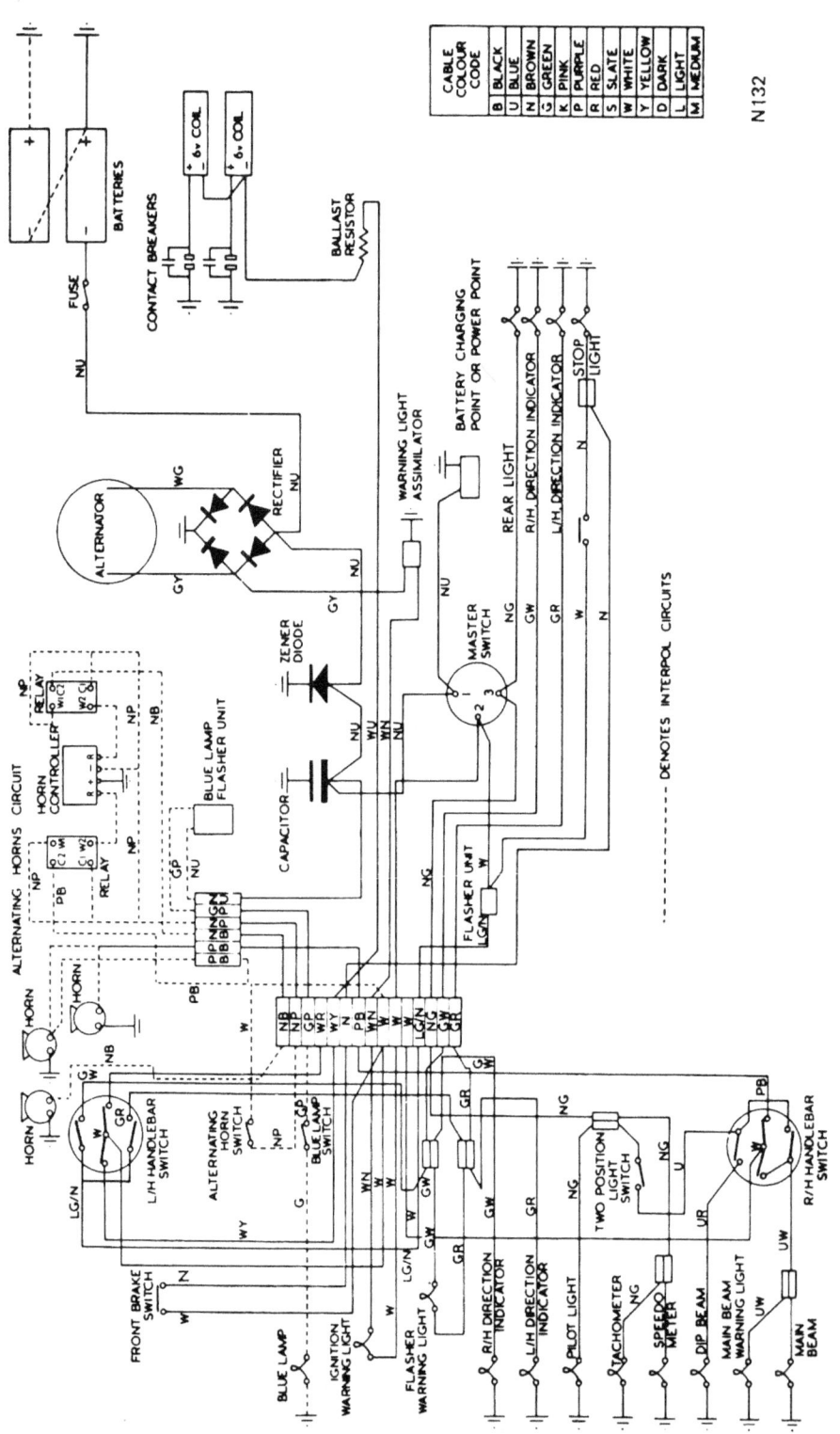

Fig. J10 1971 wiring diagram. All models

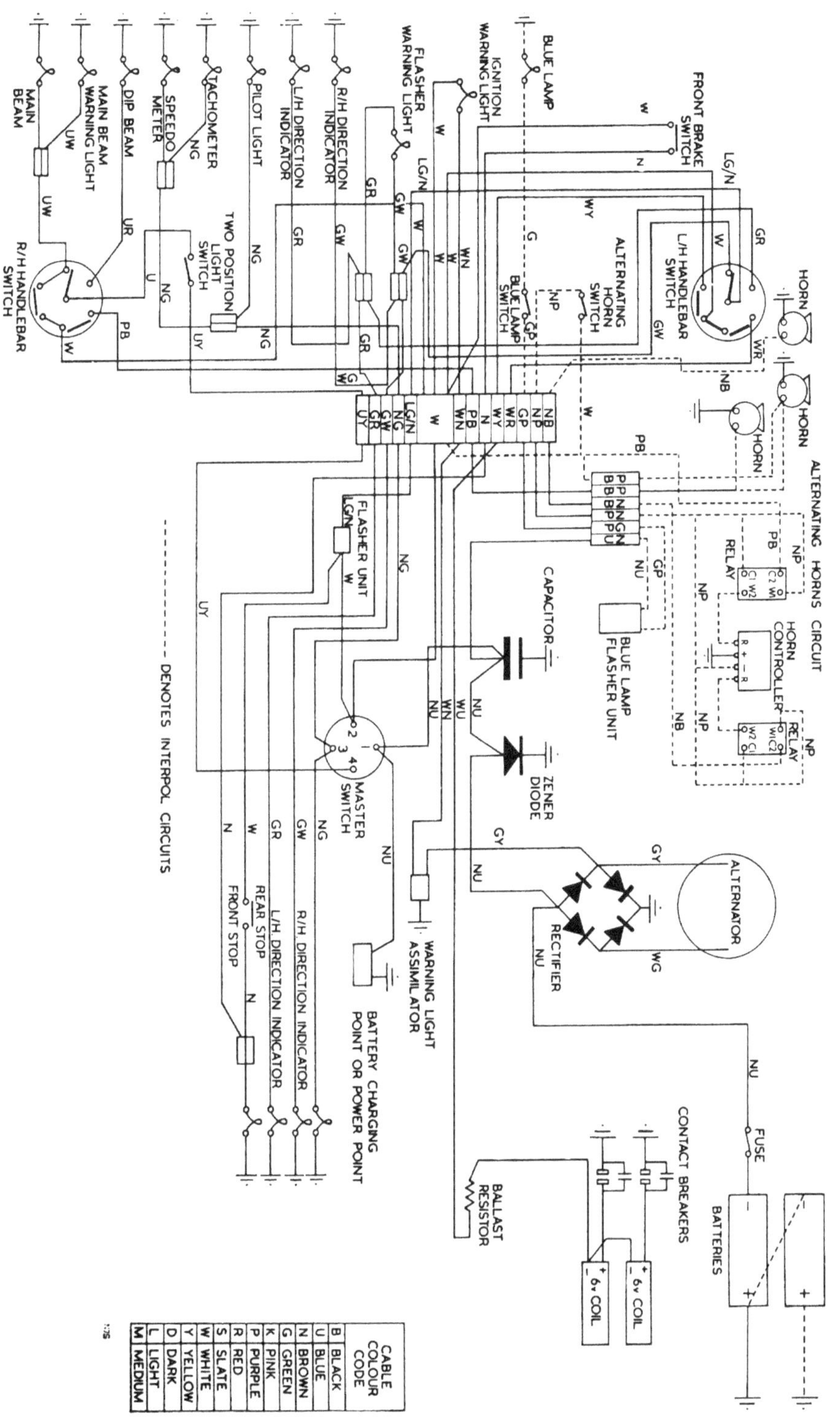

Electrical J

Fig. J11 1972 and 1973 wiring diagram. All models

NOTES

Routine Maintenance K

Routine Maintenance

Routine Maintenance K

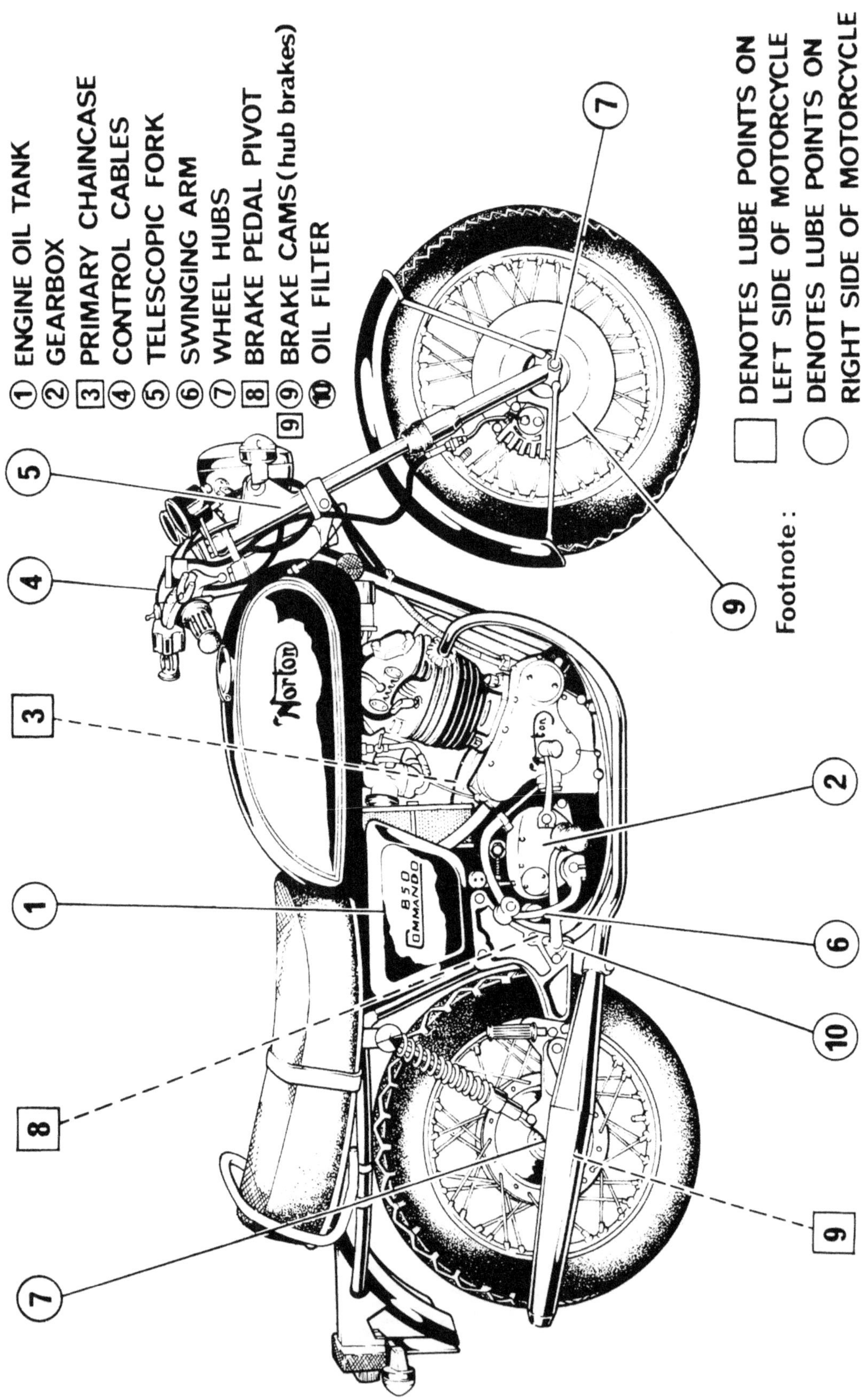
① ENGINE OIL TANK
② GEARBOX
3 PRIMARY CHAINCASE
④ CONTROL CABLES
⑤ TELESCOPIC FORK
⑥ SWINGING ARM
⑦ WHEEL HUBS
8 BRAKE PEDAL PIVOT
9 ⑨ BRAKE CAMS (hub brakes)
⑩ OIL FILTER
Footnote :
□ DENOTES LUBE POINTS ON LEFT SIDE OF MOTORCYCLE
○ DENOTES LUBE POINTS ON RIGHT SIDE OF MOTORCYCLE
1
2
3
4
5
6
7
8
9
10
Norton
850 COMMANDO

Routine Maintenance

SECTION K1

BREAKING IN

In the process of manufacture the best possible materials are used and all machined parts are finished to a very high standard but it is still necessary to allow the moving parts to "bed in" before subjecting the engine to maximum stresses. The future performance and reliability of the engine depends on the care and restraint exercised during its early life.

For the first 500 miles, throttle openings should be limited to about one-third of twist grip movement and the cruising speed should be varied as much as possible within this limit. Provided the engine is not allowed to labour, the actual road speed is relatively unimportant but throttle control should be smooth and the gearbox used to the full to enable the engine to cope with the prevailing conditions without undue stress. This will also assist in "break-in" of the gearbox components. At all times avoid violent acceleration.

After the 500 miles service the amount of throttle opening can be increased progressively but the cruisins speed should still be varied. Full throttle should not be used until the machine has covered at least 1,000 miles and even then only for short bursts until 1,500 miles has been covered, whereupon maximum performance may be sought whenever desired.

During the "break-in" period, a certain amount of adjustment will be necessary as the components bed in. Attention should be given to valve rocker adjustment, chain tension, contact breaker points gap and brakes, all of which tend to settle down.

Do not allow the oil tank level to fall too low as with the reduced amount in circulation the oil will become unduly hot.

On motorcycles equipped with the disc brake, it is most essential to avoid glazing of the friction surfaces during the first few miles of use. During the first 50 miles only it is necessary to apply the disc brake gently to mate the friction surfaces. After 50 miles of use, the brake will be fully bedded down and ready for maximum application.

SECTION K2

ROUTINE MAINTENANCE INTRODUCTION

This section tables the maintenance periods for various operations, co-relates these operations to other sections of this manual and details those operations not falling within the normal scope of the overhaul sections.

Routine Maintenance K

Efficient lubrication is of vital importance and it is false economy to use cheap grades of oil. When buying oils or grease it is advisable to specify the brand as well as the grade and, as an additional precaution, to buy from sealed containers.

UNIT	ENGINE	PRIMARY CHAINCASE	GEARBOX	SWINGING ARM BUSHES	HUBS AND FRAME PARTS	FRONT FORKS	REAR CHAIN	EASING RUSTED PARTS
Castrol	Castrol HD40 or Castrol GTX	Castrol GTX	Castrol Hypoy	Castrol Hi-Press	Castrol LM Grease	Castrolite 10W/30	Castrol Graphited Grease	Castrol Penetrating Oil
Mobil	Mobiloil 40 or Mobiloil Super Mobiloil 20W/50	Mobiloil Super or Mobiloil 20W/50	Mobilube HD90	Mobilube HD140 or C140	Mobilgrease MP or Mobilgrease Super	Mobiloil Super	Mobilgrease MP or Mobilgrease Super	Mobil Spring Oil or Mobil Handy Oil
Esso	Uniflo or Esso Extra Motor Oil 20W/50	Esso Uniflo	Esso Gear Oil GX90/140	Esso Gear Oil GX90/140	Esso Multipurpose Grease H	Esso Uniflo	Esso MP Grease Moly	Esso Penetrating Oil
Texaco	Havoline SAE40 or Havoline 20W/50	Havoline Motor Oil 20W/50	Multigear Lubricant EP90	Multigear Lubricant EP140	Marfak All-Purpose Grease	Havoline Motor Oil 10 w / 30	Marfak All-Purpose Grease	Graphited Penetrating Oil
Duckhams	Flectol HDX40 or Duckhams Q20/50	Duckhams Q20/50	Duckhams Hypoid 90	Duckhams Hypoid 140	Duckhams LB10 Grease	Duckhams Q5500	Duckhams "Chainguard"	Duckhams Adpenol Penetrating Oil
Sun Oil	Sunlube 2800-C SAE50 or Sunoco Special Motor Oil	Sunoco Special Motor Oil	Sunep 1070	Sunep 140	Sunep 1130	Sunoco Special Motor Oil 20W/50	Sunoco MD2 Moly	Sunoco Penetrating Oil
Filtrate	Filtrate Racing 40 or Filtrate Super 20W/50	Filtrate Super 20W/50	Filtrate EP90	Filtrate Gear 140	Filtrate Super Lithium Grease	Filtrate AT Fluid F	Filtrate Linklyfe	Filtrate PDQ
Gulf	Gulf Formula G40 or Gulf Multi-G 20W/50	Gulf Multi-G 20W/50	Gulf Multi-purpose Gear Lubricant 90	Gulf Multi-purpose Gear Lubricant 140	Gulfcrown Grease No. 2 or Gulflex A	Gulf Multi-G 10W/30	Gulflex Moly	Gulf Penetrating Oil
BP	*BP Super Visco-Static 20W/50	BP Super Visco-Static 20W/50	BP Gear Oil SAE 90 EP	BP Gear Oil SAE 90 EP	BP Energrease L2	BP Super Visco-Static 10W/40	BP Energrease A0	BP Penetrating Oil
Shell	*Shell Super Motor Oil	Shell Super Motor Oil	Shell Spirax 90 EP	Shell Spirax 90 EP	Shell Retinax A or CD	Shell Super Motor Oil	Shell Retinax A or CD	Shell Easing Oil

* NO SUITABLE MONOGRADE AVAILABLE

LUBRICANTS RECOMMENDED

The engine lubricants recommended above are suitable for all operating temperatures above 0°C (32°F). For ambient temperatures above 32°C (90°F) HD50 monograde engine oils are recommended.
Approval is given to companies other than those listed, provided they have similar grade characteristics and meet API service SD/SE performance.

Routine Maintenance

SECTION K3
MAINTENANCE TABLE

The following table lists the normal servicing operations, the section numbers affected and the servicing intervals. The service carried out after the motorcycle has completed its first 500 miles is deliberately omitted, being outside the scope of normal routine maintenance and being covered in detail elsewhere.

		Section
Weekly	Check tire pressures and wheel alignment	K15
Every two weeks	Check battery electrolyte level	K13
Every 250 miles (400 Km)	Check engine oil tank level	K4
Every 500 miles (800 Km)	Check and adjust rear chain	C41
Every 1,000 miles (1600 Km)	Check primary chaincase oil level	K8
	Oil all control cables	—
	Adjust both brakes (disc brake is non-adjustable)	H12/13
	Check disc brake fluid level	K12
	Examin disc brake pads for wear	H16
	Examin disc pads for wear	H16
Every 3,000 miles (5000 Km)	Check timing and adjust contact breaker points	C38
	Clean spark plugs and set gaps	K12
	Change primary chaincase oil	K7
	Check clutch adjustment	C35
	Check primary chain adjustment	C41
	Change engine oil and cartridge filter (where fitted)	K3
	Relubricate and adjust rear chain	C41
	Check gearbox oil level	K4
	Grease rear brake pedal pivot	H13
	Check Isolastic mounting for free play	F13/14
	Check and adjust valve rocker clearances	C10
Every 6,000 miles (10000 Km)	Change gearbox oil	K5
	Change oil in forks	K9
	Check and adjust camshaft chain	K16
	Clean contact breaker points	C40
	Lubricate contact breaker cam felt and auto advance unit	C39 & C40
	Grease brake expander lever pivots	H5 & H12
	(one stroke of grease gun) Fit new air filter element	E10
	Check and oil swinging arm bushes Check and oil swinging armbushes	K10
	Check loose or unequal spoke tension — front and rear wheels	
	Check front and rear wheel spindle clamp and nut tightness	
	Check front and rear tire tread and wear pattern.	
	Rebalance wheels where necessary	
Every 12,000 miles (20000 Km)	Re-pack wheel bearings (including the rear wheel sprocket bearing) with grease	H4 & H10
	Dismantle and clean both carburetors and check for wear	E3
	Check rear chain for wear and adjust	C41

See Table of Recommended Lubricants

    Check steering head bearings

    Check head steady and head steady mounting rubbers

    Check and tighten all front mounting and rear engine bolts

    Check swinging arm spindle

Routine Maintenance K

SECTION K4

ENGINE OIL TANK LEVEL

The oil tank content is indicated on a dip stick incorporated in the tank filler cap which is removed by pressing and turning the cap anti-clockwise.

Access to the tank filler cap is made by: releasing the two hand discs retaining the rider's seat, raising the seat slightly rearwards (except the Fastback models) and lifting it clear.

Before filling fresh oil, run the engine for three to four minutes to return excess oil from the crankcase, observing the oil circulating through the oil tank filler orifice.

Allow the oil to settle in the tank, then fill sufficient oil of a recommended grade until the correct oil level is shown on the dipstick. The oil level should not exceed the "H" mark or fall below the "L" on the dipstick. It is most important not to exceed the "H" to prevent oil overflowing into the air filter, causing high oil consumption.

(see *Fig.* K2, item A) or on earlier models by taking out the oil filter union securing the oil pipe (see Fig. K3). This should be carried out when the oil is warm so that it flows more freely from the tank. The crankcase drain plug (see *Fig.* K4, item A) should be removed and the small amount of oil in the sump allowed to drain off.

Clean the filter on 850 and remove and clean the adjacent magnetic plug.

The 850 and earlier 750 type of filter can be dismantled for cleaning as shown in *Fig.* K5.

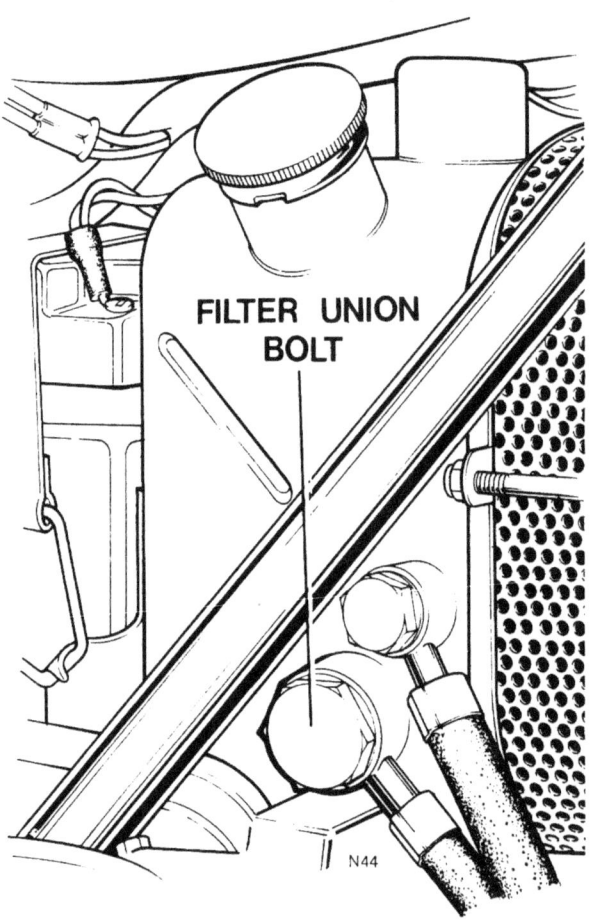

Fig. K3   1970 "S" Roadster oil tank unions

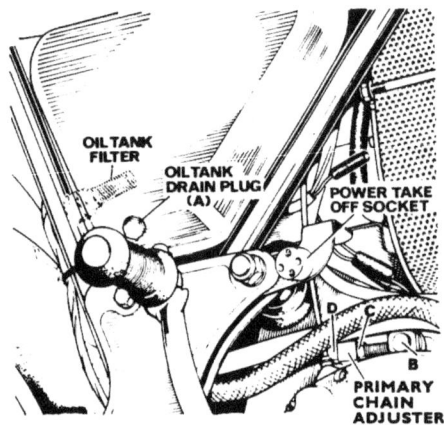

Fig. K2   Oil tank filter and drain plug

SECTION K5

ENGINE OIL CHANGING

Remove the rider's seat, where applicable take out the two right side cover top fixing bolts, and lift the cover clear at the bottom rubber mounting. Drain the oil from the tank by removing the oil tank drain plug, where fitted,

Replace the oil tank and crankcase drain plug or on earlier models the oil filter and oil pipe. Fill the tank to the dip stick level with fresh oil and run the engine at a steady speed to check the oil circulation. The oil level should not exceed the "H" mark or fall below the "L" on the dipstick.

As the oil in the sump has been drained off, a moment or two will elapse before the scavenge side of the pump begins to return the oil to the tank. Run the engine for

Routine Maintenance K

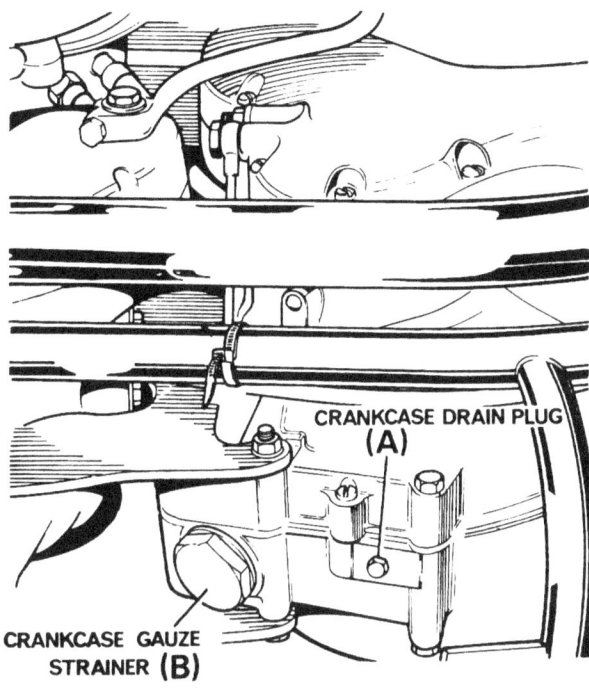

Fig. K4   Crankcase strainer and drain plug.

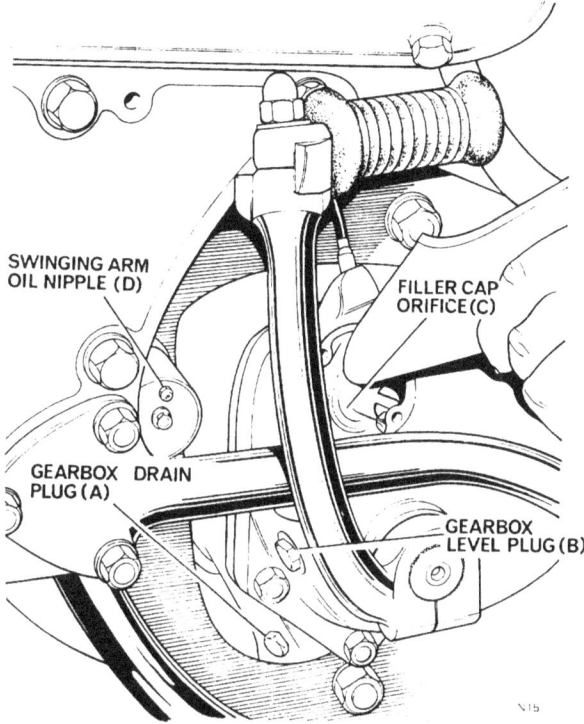

Fg. K6   Gearbox drain and level plugs

three minutes, then stop the engine and allow the oil to settle in the tank for a further two minutes. Recheck the oil level and top up as required. Finally, refit the side panel (where applicable).

A coarse mesh metal filter is incorporated with the oil feed pipe fixing bolt. This should be cleaned at 2,500 miles intervals – and when the oil is changed.

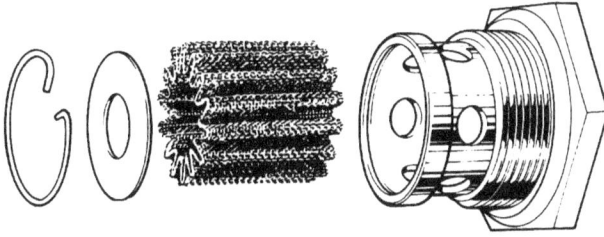

Fig. K5   Crankcase gauze strainer (all models except 1972/73 750 cc)

On late models equipped with the cartridge type oil filter as shown shaded in Fig. K7, the filter must be changed at this stage. It will be seen that the filter is located behind the gearbox between the Isolastic mounting plates. The filter is of the spin on type. It is prevented from rotating loose by a retaining strip and screw clip. To change the filter, remove the screw clip, place an oil drain trip under the filter and unscrew. It is unusual for the element to require much effort to turn it free but

this operation can be aided by the use of a strap wrench. If for any reason the filter remains immovable and since it is in any case scrap, it can be removed by piercing with a large screwdriver or similar implement and using the screwdriver as a lever to turn the filter free. Remove the filter and old sealing ring. Moisten the new sealing ring with oil and install the new filter hand tight only.

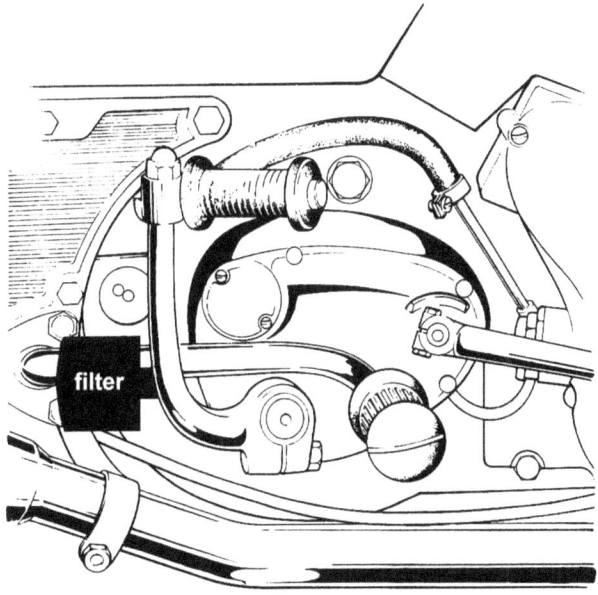

Fig. K7   Cartridge type oil filter location

Routine Maintenance K

Replace and tighten the screw clip sufficiently tightly to prevent the element turning. Do not overtighten since this may crush the filter.

SECTION K6

GEARBOX OIL LEVEL

An oil level plug is fitted in the gearbox cover (see *Fig.* K6).

To check level, remove plug (see *Fig.* K6, item B) whereupon oil should seep gently out if level is correct. If topping up is necessary, remove the filler cap (see *Fig.* K6, item C) and replenish with correct grade of oil until the oil begins to seep from the level plug orifice. Replace the filler cap and the level plug.

SECTION K7

GEARBOX OIL CHANGING

The gearbox oil should be changed after a run so that the warm oil flows more freely (see *Fig.* K6). Remove the filler cap and drain plug (A) and drain the oil into a suitable container. Replace the drain plug and fill the gearbox through the filler cap orifice (C). Allow time for oil to pass through the inner cover into the shell. When the level plug is removed, oil should run from the level plug hole (B). Allow the surplus oil to drain off and replace the level plug and filler cap. If this method is not followed a false level indication will be gained.

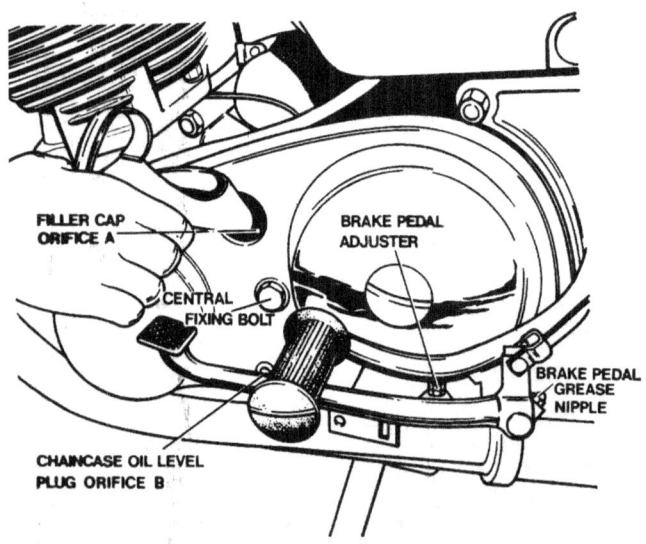

Fig. K8   Primary chaincase plugs

SECTION K8

PRIMARY CHAINCASE LEVEL

An oil level plug is fitted in the primary chaincase outer cover. (See *Fig.* K8). To check level, remove plug (see *Fig.* K8, item B) whereupon oil should seep gently out if correct. If topping up is necessary, remove the filler cap (see *Fig.* K8, item C) and replenish with correct grade of oil until the oil begins to seep from the level plug orifice. Replace the filler cap and the level plug.

Note: under no circumstances allow more than 7fl. oz. (200 cc) of oil in primary case.

SECTION K9

PRIMARY CHAINCASE OIL CHANGING

Remove the footrest and place a metal tray under the chaincase. Unscrew the central fixing bolt (see *Fig.* K8) and break the joint to allow the oil to drain into the tray. Wash out the case with clean kerosene (paraffin). Refit the outer case and remove the filler cap, and level plug (B). Pour fresh oil into the filler cap orifice (C) until it begins to run from the level plug hole. Allow the surplus to drain off and refit the level plug and filter cap. Refit the footrest.

SECTION K10

SWINGING ARM PIVOT LUBRICATION

For lubrication purposes, a grease nipple (D) is used on the plate covering the right side of the swinging arm bush housing.

To maintain the **oil** content, use a grease gun filled with S.A.E. 140 oil and inject oil sufficient to fill the cavity every 5,000 miles, alternatively, remove the oil nipple and fill with an oil gun. It is important to check that the cavity is filled. The only means of checking is to remove the spindle locating bolt (see in *Fig.* F9) and fill until oil runs from the hole. Refit the bolt.

SECTION K11

FRONT FORK OIL CHANGING

Under normal conditions the front forks will require no servicing other than an occasional change of oil. Should the oil level become low it will be indicated by excess movement of the forks, but only after considerable mileage.

Each fork leg is provided with a drain screw (see *Fig.* G5) and each leg should be treated separately. Remove the drain screw, take care not to lose the small fibre sealing washer. Take the machine off the stand, apply the front brake and move the forks up and down to

Routine Maintenance

expel the oil. Allow a few minutes for draining and repeat the operation with the other leg. Whilst draining the right fork leg, the forks should be turned on full right lock, and conversely for draining the left fork leg.

Refit the drain screws, place the machine on the centre stand. Remove handlebars to improve accessibility.

Unscrew the large filler plug at the top of each leg, remove the speedometer and tachometer and lift the front wheel to expose the springs.

Support the wheel with a block of wood to hold the springs clear. Using two spanners, unscrew the filler plugs from the damper rods.

Remove the wooden block and allow the forks to extend fully. Pour in a measured 150 cc (5 fl. oz.) of oil into each leg (see *Fig.* K9). Because of the springs inside the main tubes the oil will be slow to run down. Cover the top of the tube with the hand and "pump" the fork up and down to assist filling.

Expose the springs again and before refitting the filler plugs to the damper rods ensure that their locknuts are screwed down to the bottom end of the thread on the rod. Lock the filler plugs and locknuts together then screw in and tighten the filler plugs.

SECTION K12

CHECKING HYDRAULIC BRAKE FLUID LEVEL (Optional disc brake)

The disc brake is hydraulically operated. Before taking the motorcycle on the road from new or after attention to the disc brake, ensure that the master cylinder reservoir contains the correct amount of fluid.

The master cylinder contains a flexible bellows seal which fits into the reservoir over the fluid. DO NOT FILL THIS. Lift the bellows out (see *Fig.* K10) and lay on the upturned cap so that dirt does not adhere. Check that the fluid is to a level of $\frac{1}{2}$ in. (12·9 mm) from the top of the reservoir and if necessary, correct the level using the recommended hydraulic fluid. Replace the bellows seal closed end downwards then refit the cap tightly.

Hydraulic brake fluid absorbs moisture and it is most important to keep the cap on tight and also to store the fluid only in sealed containers. The breather hole in the cap must be kept clear and no dirt or foreign matter must be allowed to enter the system.

Important: Hydraulic brake fluid must be handled with care as it will attack paintwork and certain types of rubber and plastic.

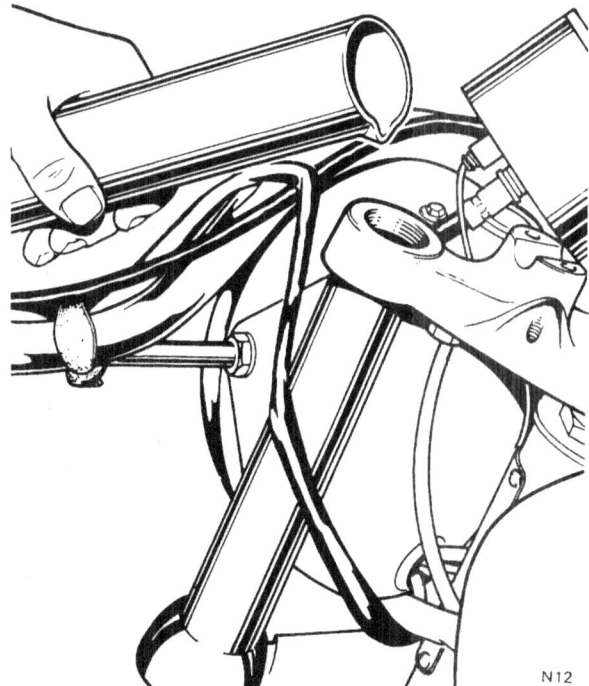

Fig. K9   Refilling fork leg with cap bolt removed

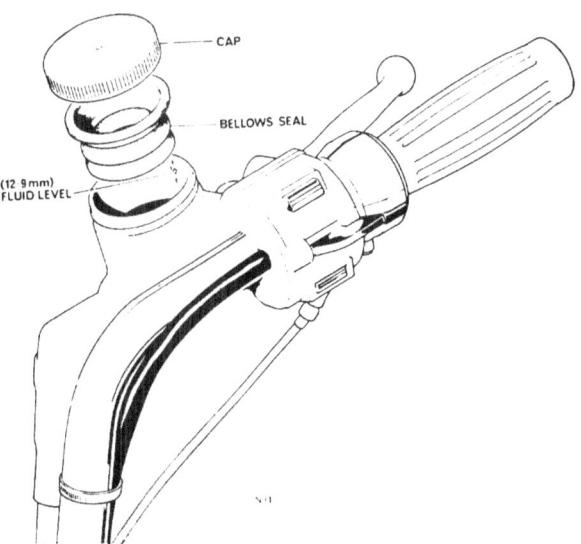

Fig. K10   Checking master cylinder hydraulic fluid level

Routine Maintenance

SECTION K13

CHECKING BATTERY ELECTROLYTE LEVEL

For access to the battery remove the L.H. accessory cover by turning the ring above the ignition switch to remove the Dzus fastener. The cover is then lifted out at the front and clear of the rear pegs. To remove the battery lift the metal loop of the rubber strap clear of the battery retaining bar. Disconnect the red ground lead from terminal "+" and the blue/brown lead from terminal "—" on the battery. Slide the vent pipe clear. Lift the battery clear, taking care not to spill acid. The electrolyte level is embossed on the battery case, visible on the left side of the battery casing (see *Fig.* K11). At two weeks intervals, more frequently in hot climates, the level of the electrolyte should be checked. If necessary, add distilled water to maintain the level indicated on the side of the transparent battery case. Do not use tap water as this may contain impurities harmful to the battery. Never use a naked light when examining the cells. (See *Fig.* K11).

If the machine is to be out of use for a lengthy period, have the battery fully charged and give it a short refreshing charge at 1 ampere about every two weeks. This will suffice to keep the battery in serviceable condition. When the battery is fully charged, the specific gravity of the electrolyte should be 1·270/1·290 at 60°F (16°C).

SECTION K14

SPARK PLUGS

It is most important to use the correct grade of spark plug, as a spark plug with a low heat factor can cause pre-ignition and subsequent damage to the engine.

The Champion N7Y is recommended for both Commando and Combat engines and supersedes the N6Y type previously recommended.

To avoid damage to the insulator, use the plug spanner provided in the tool kit to remove and refit the spark plug, which should be firmly tightened to ensure a gas tight joint.

To adjust or reset the spark plug gap, this is affected by bending the earth, or side wire, which is ductile. Do not attempt to bend the centre electrode. The correct plug gap is 0·023 in. to 0·028 in. (0·59 mm to 0·72 mm).

Before refitting the plugs, see that the sealing washers are sound, and clean the threads of the spark plug body.

A smear of graphite grease applied to the threads of the plug will assist in subsequent removal.

SECTION K15

TIRE PRESSURES

Two different types of tyres, Dunlop K.81 (TT100) and Avon "GP" tyres, are used, in pairs, on Commando models. Although these tyres differ in detail, both require that tyre pressures be varied to cope with changes in the loading of the motorcycle.

The following chart lists approved tyre pressures corresponding to loads.

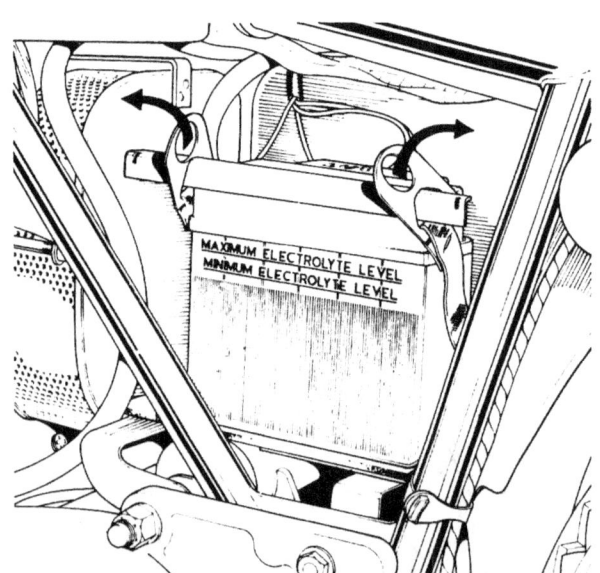

Fig. K11   *Battery electrolyte level mark (illustrated — Lucas battery)*

Routine Maintenance

		lb/sq.in.	Kg/sq.cm.
Commando with one 168 lb.			
(76·2 Kg) rider:	Front	22	1·547
	Rear	24	1·687
Commando with two 168 lb.			
(76·2 Kg) riders:	Front	24	1·687
	Rear	28	1·969
Commando with two 168 lb.			
(76·2 Kg) riders and pannier			
luggage up to 100 lb.			
(45·36 Kg):	Front	28	1·969
	Rear	32	2·250

SECTION K16

ADJUSTING CAM TIMING CHAIN

It is found that slackness of the cam chain can result in snatch, jarring shocks being delivered to the contact breaker and auto advance mechanism. This causes premature wear on these parts. We specify that the chain tension should be checked at 5000 mile intervals but, naturally, any obvious slackness evidenced by noise in this area should be taken up, irrespective of mileage. Adjust the cam chain tension to between $\frac{1}{8}$ in. and $\frac{3}{16}$ in. slack (that is, up to down movement) on the top run of the chain. To do this necessitates removal of the contact breaker and auto advance mechanism (use the withdrawal tool 064298 for the auto advance cam). Next take off the timing cover, and the cam chain and slipper tensioner are exposed. The oilway exposed by removal of the cover must be blocked to prevent the loss of oil. Note that chain tension can only be adjusted correctly if there is no play in the intermediate spindle.

To check the chain tension, remove the sparking plugs so that the engine will turn easily and use a $\frac{9}{16}$ in. Whit. socket or ring spanner on the camshaft sprocket nut and turn slowly anti-clockwise so that the lower run of the chain will be kept tight on the slipper and a true check of the tension can be made on the top run.

In this way the spanner will control the alternating oad of the valve springs on the camshaft and it will be easy to find any tight spot to which the tension should be adjusted as described.

To increase chain tension, slacken the two nuts securing the slipper and lift it a little at a time, checking at each stage after nipping up the nuts whether the tension is correct. When the correct tension is achieved secure the slipper nuts to 180 lb. in (15 lb. ft.).

It is most important when refitting the timing cover to use the camshaft oil seal guide 06-1359 to avoid damage to the seal in the timing cover.

VELOCEPRESS MANUALS - MOTORCYCLE

1930'S BRITISH MOTORCYCLE CARBS & ELEC COMPONENTS (BOOK OF)
1930'S BRITISH MOTORCYCLE ENGINES (OVERHAUL & MAINTENANCE)
1930'S BRITISH MOTORCYCLE GEARBOXES & CLUTCHES (BOOK OF)
AJS 1932-1948 SINGLES & TWINS 250cc THRU 1000cc (BOOK OF)
AJS 1945-1960 SINGLES 350cc & 500cc MODELS 16 & 18 (BOOK OF)
AJS 1955-1965 SINGLES 350cc & 500cc (BOOK OF)
ARIEL UP TO 1932 (BOOK OF)
ARIEL 1932-1939 PREWAR MODELS (BOOK OF)
ARIEL 1933-1951 (WORKSHOP MANUAL)
ARIEL 1939-1960 4 STROKE SINGLES (BOOK OF)
ARIEL 1958-1964 LEADER & ARROW (BOOK OF)
BMW R26 R27 (1956-1967) FACTORY WORKSHOP MANUAL
BMW R50 R50S R60 R69S (1955-1969) FACTORY WORKSHOP MANUAL
BRIDGESTONE 90 SERIES FACTORY WSM & PARTS CATALOGUE
BRIDGESTONE 175 SERIES FACTORY WSM & PARTS CATALOGUE
BRIDGESTONE 350 SERIES FACTORY WSM & PARTS CATALOGUES
BSA BANTAM ALL MODELS FROM 1948 ONWARDS (BOOK OF)
BSA SINGLES & V-TWINS UP TO 1927 (BOOK OF)
BSA SINGLES & V-TWINS UP TO 1930 (BOOK OF)
BSA SINGLES & V-TWINS UP TO 1935 (BOOK OF)
BSA SINGLES & V-TWINS 1936-1939 (BOOK OF)
BSA OHV & SV SINGLES 250-600cc 1945-1959 (BOOK OF)
BSA OHV & SV SINGLES 250cc (ONLY) 1954-1970 (BOOK OF)
BSA OHV SINGLES 350 & 500cc 1955-1967 (BOOK OF)
BSA TWINS 1948-1962 (BOOK OF)
BSA TWINS 1962-1969 (SECOND BOOK OF)
CYCLEMOTOR (BOOK OF)
DOUGLAS 1929-1939 PREWAR ALL MODELS (BOOK OF)
DOUGLAS 1948-1957 POSTWAR ALL MODELS FACTORY SHOP MANUAL
DUCATI 160cc, 250cc & 350cc OHC MODELS FACTORY SHOP MANUAL
HONDA 50 ALL MODELS UP TO 1970 INC MONKEY & TRAIL (BOOK OF)
HONDA 90 ALL MODELS UP TO 1966 (BOOK OF)
HONDA 125-150cc TWINS C/CS/CB/CA FACTORY WORKSHOP MANUAL
HONDA 250-305 TWINS C/CS/CB FACTORY WORKSHOP MANUAL
HONDA 450 CB/CL 1965-1974 K0 TO K7 WORKSHOP MANUAL
HONDA C100 SUPER CUB FACTORY WORKSHOP MANUAL
HONDA C110 SPORT CUB 1962-1969 FACTORY WORKSHOP MANUAL
HONDA TWINS & SINGLES 50cc THRU 305cc 1960-1966 (BOOK OF)
HONDA TWINS ALL MODELS 125cc THRU 450cc UP TO 1968 (BOOK OF)
INDIAN PONYBIKE, BOY RACER & PAPOOSE ILL PARTS LIST & SALES LIT
J.A.P. ENGINES 1927-1952 & MOTORCYCLES 1934-1952 (BOOK OF)
LAMBRETTA 1947-1957 ALL 125 & 150cc MODELS (BOOK OF)
LAMBRETTA 1957-1970 LI & TV MODELS (SECOND BOOK OF)
MATCHLESS 1931-1939 ALL MODELS 250cc THRU 990cc (BOOK OF)
MATCHLESS 1945-1956 350 & 500cc SINGLES (BOOK OF)
MATCHLESS 1955-1966 350 & 500cc SINGLES (BOOK OF)
NEW IMPERIAL ALL SV & OHV FROM 1935 ONWARDS (BOOK OF)
NORTON 1932-1939 PREWAR MODELS (BOOK OF)
NORTON 1932-1947 (BOOK OF)
NORTON 1938-1956 (BOOK OF)
NORTON 1955-1963 MODELS 19, 50 & ES2 (BOOK OF)
NORTON 1955-1965 DOMINATOR TWINS (BOOK OF)
NORTON 1960-1970 TWIN CYLINDER FACTORY WORKSHOP MANUAL
NORTON 1971-1975 COMMANDO FACTORY WORKSHOP MANUAL
NSU PRIMA 1956-1964 ALL MODELS (BOOK OF)
NSU QUICKLY 1953-1963 ALL MODELS (BOOK OF)
PANTHER 1932-1958 LIGHTWEIGHT MODELS 250 & 350cc (BOOK OF)
PANTHER 1938-1966 HEAVYWEIGHT MODELS 600 & 650cc (BOOK OF)
RALEIGH MOPEDS 1960-1969 (BOOK OF)
RALEIGH MOTORCYCLES 1919-1933 (BOOK OF)
ROYAL ENFIELD 1934-1946 SINGLES & V TWINS (BOOK OF)
ROYAL ENFIELD 1937-1953 SINGLES & V TWINS (BOOK OF)
ROYAL ENFIELD 1946-1962 SINGLES (BOOK OF)
ROYAL ENFIELD 1958-1966 250cc & 350cc SINGLES (SECOND BOOK OF)
ROYAL ENFIELD 736cc INTERCEPTOR FACTORY WORKSHOP MANUAL
RUDGE 1933-1939 (BOOK OF)
SUNBEAM 1928-1939 (BOOK OF)
SUNBEAM 1946-1957 S7 & S8 (BOOK OF)
SUZUKI 50cc & 80cc UP TO 1966 (BOOK OF)
SUZUKI T10 1963-1967 FACTORY WORKSHOP MANUAL
SUZUKI T20 & T200 1965-1969 FACTORY WORKSHOP MANUAL
SUZUKI TWINS 1962 ONWARDS 125-500cc WORKSHOP MANUAL
TRIUMPH 1935-1939 PREWAR MODELS (BOOK OF)
TRIUMPH 1935-1949 (BOOK OF)
TRIUMPH 1937-1951 (WORKSHOP MANUAL)
TRIUMPH 1945-1955 FACTORY WORKSHOP MANUAL
TRIUMPH 1945-1958 TWINS (BOOK OF)
TRIUMPH 1956-1969 TWINS (BOOK OF)
VELOCETTE 1925-1970 ALL SINGLES & TWINS (BOOK OF)
VESPA 1951-1961 (BOOK OF)
VESPA 1955-1963 125 & 150cc & GS MODELS (SECOND BOOK OF)
VESPA 1955-1968 GS & SS (BOOK OF)
VESPA 1963-1972 90, 125 & 150cc (THIRD BOOK OF)
VILLIERS ENGINE UP TO 1959 INC. 3 WHEELERS (BOOK OF)
VILLIERS ENGINE UP TO 1969 (BOOK OF)
VINCENT 1935-1955 (WORKSHOP MANUAL)
YAMAHA 1961-1967 YA5 & YA6 (WORKSHOP MANUAL & ILL PARTS LIST)
YAMAHA 1971-1972 JT1& JT2 (WORKSHOP MANUAL & ILL PARTS LIST)

VELOCEPRESS TECHNICAL BOOKS – MOTORCYCLE

CATALOG OF BRITISH MOTORCYCLES (1951 MODELS)
LUCAS ELECTRONICS BRITISH M/CYCLES REPAIR & PARTS (1950-1977)
MOTORCYCLE ENGINEERING (P.E. Irving)
MOTORCYCLE ROAD TESTS 1949-1953 (Motor Cycle Magazine UK)
SPEED AND HOW TO OBTAIN IT (Motor Cycle Magazine UK)
TUNING FOR SPEED (P.E. Irving)

VELOCEPRESS MANUALS - THREE WHEELER'S

BSA THREE WHEELER (BOOK OF)
VINTAGE MORGAN THREE WHEELER (BOOK OF)

VELOCEPRESS MANUALS - AUTOMOBILE

ALFA ROMEO GIULIA WORKSHOP MANUAL 1300 TO 2000cc 1962-1975
ALFA ROMEO GIULIA TECH MANUAL CARBURETED CARS FROM 1962
ALFA ROMEO GIULIA TECH MANUAL FUEL INJECTED CARS FROM 1969
ALFA ROMEO GIULIETTA & GIULIA 750 & 101 SERIES 1955-1965 WSM
AUSTIN-HEALEY SPRITE & MG MIDGET WORKSHOP MANUAL 1958-1971
BMW 600 LIMOUSINE FACTORY WORKSHOP MANUAL
BMW 600 LIMOUSINE OWNERS HAND BOOK & SERVICE MANUAL
BMW 2000 & 2002 1966-1976 WORKSHOP MANUAL
BMW ISETTA FACTORY WORKSHOP MANUAL
CORVAIR 1960-1969 WORKSHOP MANUAL
CORVETTE V8 1955-1962 WORKSHOP MANUAL
FIAT 500 FACTORY WORKSHOP MANUAL 1957-1973
FIAT 600, 600D & MULTIPLA FACTORY WORKSHOP MANUAL 1955-1969
JAGUAR E-TYPE 3.8 & 4.2 SERIES 1 & 2 WORKSHOP MANUAL
JAGUAR MK 7, 8, 9 & XK120, 140, 150 WORKSHOP MANUAL 1948-1961
METROPOLITAN FACTORY WORKSHOP MANUAL
MGA & MGB OWNERS HANDBOOK & WORKSHOP MANUAL
MG MIDGET TC, TD, TF & TF1500 WORKSHOP MANUAL
PORSCHE 356 1948-1965 WORKSHOP MANUAL
PORSCHE 911 2.0, 2.2, 2.4 LITRE 1964-1973 WORKSHOP MANUAL
PORSCHE 911 2.7, 3.0, 3.2 LITRE 1973-1989 WORKSHOP MANUAL
PORSCHE 912 WORKSHOP MANUAL
TRIUMPH TR2, TR3, TR4 1953-1965 WORKSHOP MANUAL
VOLKSWAGEN TRANSPORTER, TRUCKS & WAGONS 1950-1979 WSM
VOLVO 1944-1968 ALL MODELS WORKSHOP MANUAL

VELOCEPRESS TECHNICAL BOOKS - AUTOMOBILE

FERRARI 250/GT SERVICE AND MAINTENANCE
FERRARI GUIDE TO PERFORMANCE
FERRARI OWNER'S HANDBOOK
FERRARI TUNING TIPS & MAINTENANCE TECHNIQUES
HOW TO BUILD A FIBERGLASS CAR
HOW TO BUILD A RACING CAR
HOW TO RESTORE THE MODEL 'A' FORD
MASERATI OWNER'S HANDBOOK
OBERT'S FIAT GUIDE
PERFORMANCE TUNING THE SUNBEAM TIGER
SOUPING THE VOLKSWAGEN
SOLEX CARBURETORS (EMPHASIS ON UK & EU AUTOMOBILES)
SU CARBURETORS (EMPHASIS ON UK AUTOMOBILES)
WEBER CARBURETORS (EMPHASIS ON ALFA & FIAT)

VELOCEPRESS BOOKS & GUIDES - AUTOMOBILE

ABARTH BUYERS GUIDE
COMPLETE CATALOG OF JAPANESE MOTOR VEHICLES
FERRARI 308 SERIES BUYER'S AND OWNER'S GUIDE
FERRARI BERLINETTA LUSSO
FERRARI BROCHURES AND SALES LITERATURE 1946-1967
FERRARI BROCHURES AND SALES LITERATURE 1968-1989
FERRARI OPP, MAINTENANCE & SERVICE H/BOOKS 1948-1963
FERRARI SERIAL NUMBERS PART I - ODD NUMBERS TO 21399
FERRARI SERIAL NUMBERS PART II - EVEN NUMBERS TO 1050
FERRARI SPYDER CALIFORNIA
HENRY'S FABULOUS MODEL "A" FORD
MASERATI BROCHURES AND SALES LITERATURE

VELOCEPRESS BOOKS – RACING

CARRERA PANAMERICANA - MEXICAN ROAD RACE (BOOK OF)
DIALED IN - THE JAN OPPERMAN STORY
IF HEMINGWAY HAD WRITTEN A RACING NOVEL
VEDA ORR'S NEW REVISED HOT ROD PICTORIAL

AUTOBOOKS WORKSHOP MANUALS & BROOKLANDS ROAD TEST PORTFOLIOS

FOR A COMPLETE LISTING OF THE AUTOBOOKS & BROOKLANDS TITLES THAT WE CURRENTLY HAVE AVAILABLE, PLEASE VISIT OUR WEBSITE.

www.VelocePress.com